MAKING AMERICANS

QUENTIN ANDERSON

BOOKS PREVIOUSLY PUBLISHED

The Imperial Self:
An Essay in American Literary and Cultural History

The American Henry James

EDITED WITH INTRODUCTION
Henry James: Selected Short Stories

EDITED WITH JOSEPH A. MAZZEO
The Proper Study:
Essays on Western Classics

EDITED WITH STEPHEN DONADIO AND STEVEN MARCUS
Art, Politics and Will:
Essays in Honor of Lionel Trilling

Making Americans

An Essay on Individualism and Money

Quentin Anderson

Harcourt Brace Jovanovich, Publishers

New York *San Diego* *London*

Library of Congress Cataloging-in-Publication Data
Anderson, Quentin, 1912–
Making Americans: an essay on individualism and money/by Quentin Anderson.
p. cm.
ISBN 0-15-155941-4
1. American literature—History and criticism. 2. National characteristics, American, in literature. 3. Individualism in literature. 4. United States—Civilization. 5. Economics in literature. 6. Money in literature. I. Title.
PS169.N35A5 1992
810.9—dc20 92-8693

Designed by Lydia D'moch
Printed in the United States of America

First edition

A B C D E

Contents

Acknowledgments

I wish to thank William Jovanovich who had the temerity to ask for this book and the patience to wait for it and those whose conversation animated the scene for me during the years it took shape—both my friends and the Fellows of the New York Institute for the Humanities at New York University. I am also grateful for the support of the National Humanities Center, where I began work on this project in 1979–80. Permission to reprint extracts from my previously published work has been graciously granted by *Daedalus: Journal of the American Academy of Arts and Sciences*, by *Prospects: The Annual of American Cultural Studies*, and by Columbia University Press, publishers of *The Columbia Literary History of the United States*. Thanks also go to the *New Yorker*, whose editors granted special permission to quote from "Notes and Comment," as well as the *New Republic*, for a quotation from a review, and to Diana Trilling for quotations from her *Claremont Essays*.

"Quand on n'a pas
de caractère il faut bien
se donner une méthode."
—Albert Camus

CHAPTER 1

Builders of Their Own Worlds

Democracy proposes that everybody count for one and that the choice of the majority is to prevail. But in nineteenth-century America three writers we have come to regard as representative of our distinctive character, Ralph Waldo Emerson, Henry David Thoreau, and Walt Whitman, gave no weight to the numerical addition of existing voices. Nor did the idea of the collective majesty of the people, which informed the French Revolution, exist for them. What they proposed instead was an alteration of individual consciousness: everybody was to aspire to be the One, to become capable of a dazzlingly complete imaginative grasp of the world. They acknowledged that the access to godlike power was so far apparent to few, and to those few only at times, but they urged their contemporaries to look within, to clear their vision of the obscuring smudges of family and daily business, so that they might see that the whole of things was glorious and as open to their perception of it as if they had made it for themselves. What society and organized religion could not do for you, you could do for yourself, and only through yourself; each could possess all in vision.

This astounding extrapolation of individual powers, which I described in *The Imperial Self* (1971), puts most of the facts of one's life in the background; they become barriers to a personal expansion. Since we cannot actually escape a human condition which involves birth, growth, and death or the ties of parenthood and life in a community, this claim for individual powers may be thought of as simply aberrant—as it often was at the time—or as a response to the character of the surrounding culture. My thesis in this book is that it clearly was an inclusive attempt to counter the prevailing cultural ethos and that similarly inclusive efforts at cultural transformation persist and inform American literature and thought from the Jacksonian period to the present day. In short, our culture repeatedly produces opponents who demand something impossible and in itself contradictory: a revolution in individual attitudes toward the country we inhabit. Why do Americans continue to make such apocalyptic demands on each other, demands whose very generality works to further a diminution in their capacity to grant each other a full measure of existence—as if others could be granted reality only after transforming themselves?

The answer is so familiar as to be almost inapprehensible. The experience of American individuals was, to a far greater extent than in Europe, framed by expectations of personal gain and loss; it followed that those who attempted to escape this aspect of the cultural climate were impelled to make claims for the individual which greatly exaggerated his power to disembed himself from his milieu. Europeans, for whom the rising ascendancy of commerce was a far more visible spectacle—since it appeared against the background of established classes, institutions, and traditions—contributed brilliant analyses of a phenomenon they faced more directly. Americans, however, produced no Balzac or Zola, and proponents of revolutionary social change were few and occupied peripheral positions. This failure attests to an immersion in commerce so complete as to make it difficult indeed to imagine a comprehensive change in the social structure; the idea of an escape seemed open only to individuals.

The "commercial republic" James Madison had described in *The Federalist Papers* had come into being and was in many respects an unparalleled success, but what loomed largest for our three writers, in the time of Andrew Jackson and Martin Van Buren, was not the republic but a commercial society in which individuals pursued private ends. We may put it as Alexis de Tocqueville did: the individual American in pursuit of identity and a settled sense of things had to turn to material acquisition for the only assurance the society offered.[1]

The United States, which gave so many a high degree of personal freedom, lacked many of the socially defined goals present in societies in which family, tradition, and institutional complexity defined the individual's choices. It is also clear that the new nation afforded fewer defenses against the ascendancy of the most impersonal forms of social relationship: those created by monetary distinctions and by acquisition and exchange in general. Neither a shared sense of the national interest nor organized religion proved able, except in wartime, to stand up to the pervasive influence of values based on money. What Emerson, Thoreau, and Whitman offered was a form of individualism which firmly subordinated all activities involving others to the exercise of the visionary powers of the self. Whatever called for the participation of others diminished those powers; the reciprocity demanded in everyday life, in joint endeavor, in sexual and verbal and monetary exchange, fatally obscured the primacy of vision by pinning you to a multiplicity of roles. Nothing less than an epistemological overturn could rescue the self from fragmentation. To know the scene of existence was to have an undivided consciousness of it.

In effect these three men were making what most historians have judged a premature assertion: the announced ends of the republic had been seriously undermined by the institution the Revolution had not touched, the whole nexus of relations associated with money and property. This trio ignored all the possibilities of change in the society and proclaimed that the road to a community of equals lay solely in a transformation of individuals—a wholesale secular conversion. It was this singular proposal to which their admirers responded; it is to be found in Emerson's early work, in the first two editions of *Leaves of Grass* (1855, 1856), and in Thoreau before he subscribed to the activities of John Brown.

What remained after one had seen through every aspect of associated life—eating, making love, getting a living, caring for the children, making a name for oneself in the society? These things had to be seen through, had to become transparent, so that one might perceive that great order which was our preeminent object, the only object adequate to the selfhood which was or might become ours. The name they often gave that object, "nature," begged the whole question of the civilization to which these men belonged; theirs was an effort, necessarily incomplete, to articulate a fresh set of ties between our individual existence and its complement, being in general, to see ourselves not in the light of the vexed history of the species but in that of a total conception of the scheme of things.

The version of selfhood this implies is striking not simply in its extravagance but in its divergence from earlier western parallels. Gnostics, late medieval free spirits, certain English revolutionaries studied by Christopher Hill, the English romantics had all made wide claims for the self, but they regularly acknowledged that they were actively contending with a going order, divine or social. All three of these Americans would have refused to admit that they were externally threatened by the character of their society, in a fashion later described as alienated. They sought to subordinate ties to others, ties which threatened their capacity to possess the world entire, but society was too ephemeral to be an opponent. They denied, that is, that they were expending their energies on denial because the spectacle they sought and sometimes glimpsed was too august to be compared to the mere dailiness of associated lives. They recognized individuals who displayed extraordinary powers not because these individuals had an importance as historical agents but because they were splendid instances of our generic possibilities. It was not society which furnished the motives which animated Emerson, Thoreau, and Whitman; it was, as they saw it, their very nature as human beings which led them to focus on that larger object which those immersed in society were blind to.

Yet the very fact that their common aspiration was patently impossible to realize suggests that it was adopted in the face of a threat to what they most cherished in themselves, that it was both radical and enforced by what was, in their theory, unable to overset them. Theirs was, after all, an attempt to extricate themselves.

As I have indicated, the leading clue to the nature of what provoked such assertions of the powers of the self is to be found in that aspect of their culture whose effect on them they denied, the only pressure which had an equal generality: the fact that the citizens of the United States were more alone with money—had, that is, fewer defenses against the imaginative domination of acquisition, possession, the reduction of all questions to those of exchange values—than any western people who had heretofore existed.

How else, one might ask, could the task of taking possession of a thinly populated continent have been undertaken, except, that is, by a citizenry impelled by economic motives? Our boasted newness, the fact that our civic order conferred rights which few others enjoyed, was necessarily complemented by an unprecedented vulnerability to the relatively impersonal dominion of standards derived from the hope of personal gain.

In the three decades preceding the Civil War the depth of the nation's immersion in the impersonal processes of exchange became apparent to a few people as something more fundamental than the momentary ascendancy of a set of greedy "speculators"—the most common view of the cause of the panic of 1837. It seems clear that a revulsion against the "Monster Bank" had the character of a popular feeling, although historians have shown that conflicting hopes of financial gain had much to do with the opposition to a national bank. What counted most heavily for the three writers discussed here was an erosion of the possible bases of a sense of the nature and powers of the individual. To repeat: democracy and egalitarianism offered individuals an almost unprecedented degree of individual freedom, yet the commercial character of the new republic sharply limited the variety of recognized ways in which that freedom could be employed.

To fasten our attention on the implications of an attempt to find a calling in this period—as did Henry Nash Smith in writing on "Emerson's Problem of Vocation"—is to begin to explore a dilemma which was common to all the young men of the time who sought to enlarge their horizons beyond money-making.[2] The vocations chosen or created by our three writers seemed to isolate them but were in effect proposals to all their peers. Emerson became preacher to all those who felt isolated because they felt enclosed by the limiting character of the commercial nation; Whitman adopted a role closer to that of a shaman than that of a (socially defined) "poet." He meant to call forth a reality for others which his own "interior republic" of awareness embraced,[3] while Thoreau proposed the making or remaking of selves capable of the ample perceptions he enjoyed in his daily walks. What was common to the chosen vocations of these three men was an awareness—premature in the eyes of historians—of a desiccating sameness in the preoccupations of those about them to which the natural order in even its least exalted manifestations provided an inspiriting contrast; woods, fields, and waters appeared to have so much more to say about the possibilities of human existence than the domesticated life of the village, town, or even nation. Such a sameness, later attributed to industrial civilization, was perceptible in Concord and demanded a thoroughgoing refocusing of attention on the part of its inhabitants if they were ever to glimpse the fullness of human realization.

Such a sameness, a determined shrinkage in the field of vision, could not be combated piecemeal or by persuasion; it called for Whitman's "new man," for people with a new and far wider perceptual field.[4] It is clear that these three felt isolated and appealed to others on that ground long before the population at large began to manifest such feelings—and then, we might put it, only if they could afford to—but the trio does furnish a striking forecast of what was to come.

Their inclusive assertion of the powers of the self departs from the opportunities to seek one's own salvation that Protestantism had made available and leans initially on the widely diffused notion of the "moral sense."[5] When Emerson supplemented the latter with the assurance of access to the noumenal realm provided by Kant's successors, when, that is, he was able to speak of the "Reason" as offering a secure grasp on reality to individuals, his armory was complete. He had intellectual justification for starting from his own perception of the world rather than from what the society offered as a governing view of it. How to express a religious passion which no longer found communal expression? He cultivated it at home and offered an example to others who found themselves equally estranged from congregational worship.

What Emerson was doing when he spoke or wrote with hearers or readers in mind (his distinction between speech and print was far less marked than ours) is misapprehended if one regards it as the activity of someone preaching a doctrine labeled "transcendentalism." The term made Emerson uneasy simply because there was no such doctrine. I rehearse here what must be more fully explained—I am tempted to say experienced—in later chapters. Putting the social fact before the Emersonian assertion, we must imagine an Emerson who had reached adolescence among those, including his aunt, Mary Moody Emerson, whom he saw as sharing a faith. His belief in her faith was sustained, but he saw it was not his and that others had a faith which, increasingly, seemed empty to him, seemed so distracted by the world's business as to be hollow. He could not believe that the means publicly available to him would summon anyone to the exalted sense of things he experienced. He was alone, yet they too were alone and did not realize it. His own delighted sense of things was intermittent, yet he could not doubt its centrality, nor the possibility of exhibiting it in such a way as to jog others into enjoying what they could only enjoy by entering into themselves as he had.[6]

Hearing or reading Emerson offered his admirers an often

intoxicating spiritual enfranchisement which those who disliked or ridiculed him saw as an attack on morality and civil order as well as established churches. Francis Bowen, reviewing Emerson's *Nature* of 1836, remarked acidly, "A hermitage is no school of morals."[7]

It has always been easy to understand why the young, confronted by a world constricted, shaped, blocked, *owned* by their elders who had already defined themselves, discover a tonic presence in Emerson. Far from confining them to a hermitage, he aroused a sense of infinite possibilities which were tacitly denied by the very being of a settled and defined adult world. But this account of Emerson as food for the young works to blur and obscure his subversive power, which was a solvent of the humdrum character, the taken-for-granted flatness, of a commercial society for adults as well. What was condemned as moonshine, a vague religiosity, answered a felt need for a place in a world no longer informed by a set of divine sanctions. Emerson didn't simply fill a void where religion had once been; he premised the need for an interior struggle to right one's perspective on an existing world. His was no spiritual nostrum but a supple, shrewd, and inclusive assault on things as they were, an assault directed not at the things made but at the processes through which people, individuals, were defining their very lives.

If Emerson deprecated any doctrine, any set of governing ideas, and simply carried on the activity of being or becoming "Emerson"—a preacher to everyone's potential, interior self—why do we find him impersonal? A married man with children, a devoted attendant at the meetings of a Concord circle of merchants and farmers, even on occasion a rather grumpy churchgoer, who saw to it that his daughters attended regularly, a writer capable of lively sketches of character such as "Ezra Ripley, D.D." or "The Chardon Street Convention," the composer, at the time of his second marriage, of a historical address on Concord, and so on, Emerson was far from appearing a "come-outer," as he called the reformers of Chardon Street's gathering. Yet his appeal to his fellows was indeed impersonal, and was necessarily so, since he was combating a widespread set of mind among those around him which he was far too practical to believe he could dissolve with his rhetoric. Only his example might serve, and his speeches and his writings were chiefly aimed at an exemplary end for which he had many names, such as "a union ideal in actual individualism." Mothers, fathers, and children and those immersed in village life might properly have asked: where is the continuity in our lives in all this? Can illuminated moments have consequences for tomorrow, or are they not hopelessly enclosed experiences for most of us?

The harsh answer which Emerson himself gave in "Experience" is that the root meaning of our lives is indeed found among the "bleak rocks" of our own musings.[8] The correspondence of this answer to the spectacle of a nation gripped by the impersonal, atemporal world of money is what needs exploration. If money had indeed worked to reduce the variety and intensity of felt human bonds in the society as a whole, the process would, in the degree that it affected large numbers of people, surely be hard to discern. Most of those who found themselves distanced from others, and taking a view in which monetary relationships occupied more of their sense of others than was the case abroad, would hardly have been able to make Emerson's response. They would instead obey King Lear's injunction to find out their enemies now, as they in fact did during the panic of 1837. Emerson's response was not to denounce a discrete group of others (the speculators) as greedy and irresponsible but to condemn a widespread blindness to the true nature of mankind's relation to the experienced world. The fault was not that of a nameable set of rascals but of all those who had denied their own true nature and mistakenly blamed their fellows as the wrong-doing others.

Emerson had withdrawn to a ministry addressed to individuals in their singleness, not in their affiliated social state. Committed to invoking their visionary powers, he undertook to shock them into awareness of what they might come to see. He was not a reformer but the herald of an epistemological overturn which could only take place in individuals. Few were prepared to see how radical his demand was or how it had been provoked by the contemporary scene, but those who did were incited as he was by the solitariness they felt and were delighted to find that it could be seen as a fulfilling—even glorious—way of grasping things. Genius has the uncomfortable habit of perceiving what has not been actualized or given form by others. From the point of view of those who find society inescapable Emerson's was a desperate step, but the very conviction that society is indeed inescapable leads us to see that it was in fact a reaction to the times in which he lived, as it also was for Thoreau and Whitman.

It is the very differences between these two and Emerson and the no less striking differences between Thoreau and Whitman which make the coincidence of their views of the cultural matrix they tried to transform significant. Regarding them from a distance in time, it is evident that they addressed a common concern, shouldered a common burden, realized the job of creating an American identity within a discernible set of limiting conditions. Emerson's realization of those conditions fired up the energies of both the younger men, yet it exhibits both the power and the inadequacy of what we once blithely called "influence," since their voices remained so distinct. It was not a common set of ideas or a common emotional endowment which allied them but a common awareness of the scene on which they found themselves.

Emerson's realization of the character of his time cannot be ours, since it was an original discovery, yet it continues to amaze us, especially of course since we can now take a fuller measure of it than did his contemporaries, by reading his journals and letters. The stance he took before his world, the claim for the self I have emphasized and spoken of as a response to a situation he found urgent and even desperate, is the one he offered the public, and the one which has sunk into American consciousness because it appears to have emerged from it. Our theme is not that of the biographer who tries to do justice to every facet of a life but is an attempt to discover what being Emerson had to do with being an American of his time and of ours.

In Emerson, Thoreau, and Whitman the public stance took the form of a proclamation that they enjoyed a mode of possessing the world which only "poets" or "makers" could share. In Emerson the "poet" is possessor of land and sea in a world in which others who have not come to share his vision are but "tenants and boarders."[9] He is one who is willing, as Emerson puts it in "Experience," to pay "the costly price of sons and lovers" for "reality." The term "poet" is nowadays open to misapprehension; it is in our use too limited to carry the full range of implications here. All three of these writers offered what they hoped would prove an inviting example of the result of paying that price: possession of a view of the whole of things which was as yet fragmented by their daily lives. Everybody was to become the maker of his world. The masculine pronoun is appropriate; women were thought hopelessly bound by the interlaced reciprocal offices of their lives which fatally limited their visionary capacity.

What has oftenest obscured our estimation of the part these three played among us is the subsequent creation of a realm of art conceived as distinct from direct address to the American people. By tucking Emerson, Thoreau, and Whitman into niches reserved for artists we long elided and softened their demand for a revolution in each American, and our use of them as somehow representative of our culture remains superficial because it fails to acknowledge their persistent subversive force.

They did not think of themselves as speaking for the special concerns of art, and they had no way of anticipating the disappearance of the belief that the associated lives of Americans ought to represent an integrated body of practice and value. It was the character of our associated life which led them to offer an alternative, and radically different, sense of things.

No matter how illusory their hope was, they thought they could get others to see that a single overriding context was available to their hearers and readers, a context in which occupations, ties to others, and material interests were set aside in favor of a generic view of the human situation. The fact that they tacitly, and sometimes overtly, excluded slaves and women limits but does not cancel the force of their address to a society given over to commerce. What we must, I think, acknowledge is that Emerson, Thoreau, and Whitman were not fighting a straw man; they were encountering an actuality they had reason to regard as devastating to their sense of themselves. A solitary, total, and guiltless possession of the world was the only alternative they could conceive, and it is one over which we may boggle.

Was the society indeed so loosely textured? Did what was called "transcendentalism" amount to a "revivalism of the intellectuals," as Richard Hofstadter called it?[10] Were single persons in fact the only conceivable sources of illumination for these three geniuses? Studies of the Jacksonian period may not have made enough of the likeness between two movements which emphasized moments of experience: the one an announcement of utter subjection at the mourner's bench, which took place at revivals; the other a moment of triumphant realization of the union of self and its object, as in Emerson's passage on becoming a "transparent eyeball."[11] Organized religion had played a part: Emerson's view of things emerges from the Unitarianism of William Ellery Channing. The doyen of American Unitarianism had asserted that we were godlike insofar as we brought God's attributes to bear in our life and conduct. Chief among them was the gift of reason, "God's vicegerent" in us all.[12] Channing also insisted, in writing against an excessive concern with associations for benevolent purposes, that our individual exercise of reason must not be clouded by such piecemeal efforts at reform,[13] anticipating Emerson's denunciation of all merely social efforts to do good, which amounted to a species of apostasy, a delegation of bits of what should remain integral and inviolate, one's inner monitions. Only these inner promptings attested our access to universal truth.

"Individualism," the term Tocqueville made his own, has often been employed too broadly by cultural historians, as if it had been in each case a conscious choice to act for oneself in a society which was so constituted as to offer a maximum number of permitted variations in behavior. What we fail to acknowledge is the way and the degree to which individualism was enforced by social conditions. Channing and Emerson were recoiling from a traffic in good intentions each with its booth, slogans, and merit badges. Yet they could hardly escape the medium in which they moved. Theirs was a society in which freedom had been reduced to the freedom to make a claim in one's own behalf.

That claim might be realized through the acquisition of property or status—the former was increasingly found in association with the latter—or it might be a claim to spiritual possessions—more precisely, to a capacity for imaginative dominion or even to a capacity to create what was apprehended, which is discussed in the following chapter. Channing clung to the church, operating on the social scene as a source of authority; Emerson conferred all authority—moral, imaginative, and spiritual—on an ideal selfhood he strove to realize in himself and exemplify for others. He was persuaded that such a claim to an inclusive imaginative dominion could be distinguished from all that was debasing in a claim to possessions of one's own. The only sort of drama he permitted himself, since his was not an effort to act on others directly, was the quasi-dramatic tension he set up by appropriating the language of political economy for spiritual uses, a rhetorical gambit which Thoreau employed as well, particularly in the initial section of *Walden*, "Economy."

Perhaps the most significant of the rejections made by these imperial selves was a rejection of faith in the republic in which they lived. Ready as they were to celebrate examples of heroic civic virtue in the past, their notion of its theoretic link to a community prepared to recognize it as the very basis of a republic was dim or altogether absent. The citizen capable of acknowledging the qualities of those fit to rule in a secular world threatened by force without and corruption within, the ideal described by J. G. A. Pocock in *The Machiavellian Moment*, had no place in their thought. Their effectual detachment from the founders' conception of the society took place before the Civil War. For them "market man," as Pocock calls him, had already made any approximation of the ancient republican ideal illusory. Indeed their individualism precluded the recognition of the skills of the statesman as *social*.

Michael Walzer's treatment of the debates in the revolutionary convention in France which centered on the question of the transfer of sovereignty from the crown to the people suggests how fundamental was Tocqueville's error when he spoke of the American state as a power which loomed over those who had created it.[14] No such imaginative weight attended the individual American's view of the newly created republic. Both fact and hope nurtured a sense of inclusion in a vast and promising human venture for the millions of nineteenth-century America, but the sense of nationhood played a much smaller part than it did elsewhere in the West. Yehoshua Arieli's term "state-nation" makes the needed emphasis;[15] we were, as Perry Miller repeatedly reminded us, a "made" nation, founded on a compact we had written down at a datable moment, and the nation could not draw on a funded reverence, biological or traditional, for adherence to a belief in its overriding importance. All this is familiar; what has not been sufficiently emphasized is the radical consequence for individual minds and sensibilities. We have recognized the precision of Michel de Crèvecoeur's framing of the question of American identity, asking what the American is rather than what sort of nation the Americans have created. The question was asked by others, as Emory Elliott's *Revolutionary Writers* informs us. Writers of the immediately post-Revolutionary period invented hermit sages, woodland Solons, who were implored for answers. The answers forthcoming from Emerson, Thoreau, and Whitman were in large measure definitive, but we have simply failed to see what they imply. What they chiefly imply is that the only alternative to a career of acquisition is the effort to achieve a total imaginative possession of one's world.

Who among Europeans was, or could have been, led to apprehend this breathtaking shortcut? For Marx an end to history as he conceived it was indeed similar; a fully realized humanity would no longer need such institutional props as the state. But the path which led to this consummation was one of prolonged conflict. We may surely accuse Marx of extrapolating his hopes for a transformation of society far beyond what has proved practicable or theoretically viable. But Emerson extrapolated a hope for individuals where he stood, canceled the presumption that the past was compelling, and announced that the realization of our humanity was in sight. Was this possible because he did not live among nations enduring conflict without and within?

Conor Cruise O'Brien's assertion that the inhabitants of western nations have made a commitment to nationalism matching in intensity their former attachment to religion is hardly borne out by the United States, which claimed that it had been founded on principles applicable to mankind in general.[16] To be superior with respect to principle implies that others should adopt your basic character. The principles are held to be universal rather than national. Chief among them are the rights accorded individuals. All this is familiar, but its effect on the situation of the particular citizen has a more immediate bearing on the work of Emerson, Thoreau, and Whitman than we have yet acknowledged.

Yet what I have described as an adventurous shortcut on the part of three writers when contrasted with the imaginative situation of European writers and thinkers may well have seemed less so in the Jacksonian period and the presidency of Martin Van Buren. The nation was new, had been founded within the memory of men still living, and was nonetheless held to be based on universal principles, now for the first time held universally applicable. Did Emerson, Thoreau, and Whitman not walk through an open door? Had not the contention that this country's new civic order was a kind of capstone of western man's long search for a just form of government inspired a further conclusion: that individuals are in themselves capable of becoming originating sources of moral and spiritual authority?

We may be altogether sure that this apparently plausible connection doesn't hold; it is far easier to see this extraordinary trio as making a distinctive use of religious impulses than as concerned with political institutions. In his first two editions of *Leaves of Grass* (1855, 1856) Whitman celebrates American institutions but always with the assumption that they will take on the supreme virtue they now lack when we have become exemplars of his "new man," the mortal divinities he glimpses in the eighth section of "Crossing Brooklyn Ferry."

Emerson was not seeking a symmetry between the announced design of the new nation and the selfhood he wished to achieve. Rather he saw the nation's sole justification as its provision of circumstances that would enable him to make that selfhood, to compass the widest possible view of existence; this was the goal of our species as he conceived it. Institutions were useful in the measure that they left you free to pursue your inclusive goal.

To share in collective hopes or fears, to become a partisan or enter into conflict, to play any limiting role, was to forfeit your precious chance to grasp the whole. Unavoidable ties to family, friends, townsmen were, in your halcyon moments, felt as intrusive, as motes in your vision of things. This passion for isolation had its reward in a sense that existence was indeed a sufficient object; that you had powers of perception congruent with its ordered multifariousness. Viewing this impulse to visionary possession from our cultural distance, it seems plain that its power to dissipate the disruptions and pressures of daily life was not the least of its attractions.

Emerson and the two younger men whom he helped to launch on paths parallel to his own had assumed a curious and anomalous stance toward the society in which they lived. Renouncing any action with or upon their fellows, they set about offering a fresh mode of construing experience which, while avoiding any explicit acknowledgment of religious faith, strongly resembles the office of Jesus as Unitarians—who did not grant him divinity—conceived it. To be akin to Jesus was simply to aspire to a similar exhibition of fully realized human possibilities; to show, as William Ellery Channing put it in a sermon delivered in 1828, a "likeness to God." Or, recalling Whitman's line in "Song of Myself," to become one of the millions of Christs streaming forth from the tomb.[17] This meant denying that you sought to impose your belief on others; it meant, in short, exemplifying a realized humanity, a performance of showing and telling on a grand scale. This performance was addressed not to any constituted public but to the latent divinity of single persons who might conceivably respond to the spectacle of an exemplary self by awaking to their own inward possibilities.

To be thus awakened was to glimpse your chances to see the world as an object made for your grasp, to see it *en bloc.* The faces of those around you, the issues that preoccupied them, the fragmentation of your consciousness vanished. Your access to the universal reduces your fellow citizens to conditions rather than fully present others; you are for the moment seer and judge of the whole. Others are, in the degree that you assume the right to define existence on the basis of your own authority, necessarily viewed impersonally, as means, or parts of your design, or threats, but never as players on a dramatic scene. Others who share similar aspirations, those who figure in the chilling discussions of friendship in Emerson and Thoreau, may facilitate your access to the universal but must not claim recognition as characters in the lesser world of daily affairs. These three undertook the job of nudging others into an awareness of their potential sovereignty. To assure others that they could, by turning to their hidden inward resources, make it alone required extraordinary rhetorical and poetic skills. Our three writers employed all their practical sagacity about the world of daily experience to make the isolation they knew others felt into the very ground of their earthly salvation.

To understand the felt needs which led to making these wide claims for the powers of the self, to describe the consequences of making such claims for those who adopted them, and to explore the significance of these attitudes as indices of the character of the culture at the time, I rely on an examination of individual works by figures we have treated as central. Since my topic has to do with self-definition and its consequences, this is the available evidence. I am here employing the emphasis on the self we find in Emerson and am maintaining that individualism's resort to universal claims is a response to the character of the culture he saw about him. If so, we must grant that this sentence from a lecture of 1842 is not an instance of the extravagance of a peripheral "transcendentalist" but is central to our understanding of the times. The sentence runs: "That which is best in nature, the highest prize of life is the perception in the private heart of access to the Universal."[18] What might be considered a devastating pronouncement if one nourished hopes for the human community has here become the most positive of aspirations.

Viewed in this way, the surrounding community is pervaded by a suffusing unreality; what counted was an apprehension of "nature," was found, that is, within a context wider and more permanent than any the existing society could offer.

Before I turn to further instances, in these and other writers, of the claim that the self had a natural capacity to embrace reality, two other consequences of this claim should be premised. The first is its compatibility with a sense of the physical properties of things and with our techniques for making them serve us, with nature in its most immediate sense as a scene of work and sensual gratification. There are, of course, interesting complexities here, which are treated in the following chapter; Emerson and Thoreau tended to give primacy to literal vision, which they thought of as somehow uniting flowers, leaves, and vistas with an order which shone through all existence. In Whitman, touch plays a role along with vision, and the step he took in taking public possession of his body is very nearly unique. Yet it is a familiar fact that these three writers, who scanted the middle ground of human intercourse, paid a high tribute to the natural scene and the ways in which it delighted us and fell into accord with our humblest needs and most exalted purposes.

The second point, of which much has been made, but perhaps not enough, follows from the common presumption in all three that they could somehow abrogate the constraints of the temporal in human affairs. If one could take possession of the whole scene of existence, if only at moments, one's personal history, and history in general, could be caught up in a moment of vision. This "eternizing impulse," as we may call it, is vividly suggested in this quotation from Thoreau's journal.

> One moment of life costs many hours, hours not of business but of preparation and invitation. Yet the man

> who does not betake himself at once and desperately to sawing is called a loafer, though he may be knocking at the doors of heaven all the while, which shall surely be opened to him. That aim in life is highest which requires the highest and finest discipline. How much, what infinite, leisure it requires, as of a lifetime, to appreciate a single phenomenon! You must camp down beside it as for life, having reached your land of promise, and give yourself wholly to it. It must stand for the whole world to you, symbolical of all things. The least partialness is your own defect of sight and cheapens the experience fatally. Unless the humming of a gnat is as the music of the spheres, and the music of the spheres is as the humming of a gnat, they are naught to me. It is not communications to serve for a history,—which are science,—but the great story itself, that cheers and satisfies us.[19]

In this passage it is not the language of political economy but that of theology which has been appropriated for the uses of the imperial self. "Preparation," readiness for the reception of grace, has lost the somewhat equivocal character it had for theologians, since it bordered on the heresy that grace might be earned, and the divine injunction to labor is dismissed as well. Thoreau's playful proposal, in his address as a graduating senior at Harvard, that the seventh day should be devoted to toil and the other six allotted as a "sabbath of the affections and the soul, in which to range this widespread garden, and drink in the soft influences and sublime revelations of Nature," is now earnestly proposed. The promised land may be reached in a stride if we but give ourselves wholly to a "story," which becomes wholly ours, as we become whole in beholding it. Six thousand years after the creation,

Christian providence may be compassed in a flash, and heaven is all around us now. "Science," it appears, is but the anatomy of what may be had with a corporeal fullness if we achieve the required correspondence to being at large. To give a full and undistracted attention to but one phenomenon is to see it flower into a "symbolical" presentment of the whole.

Thoreau's use of the term "story" in this passage has a central significance in any description of the claims for the imperial self I am describing. This story has neither characters nor events, nor does it involve temporal succession. The moment of illumination spreads before and after, becomes a moment in eternity in which self and its object are merged. Such closures with being are recorded in Emerson and Whitman as well. They abolish "partialness"; we are no longer bound to our origins, do not encounter other minds, have no past to burden us or future to hope for or dread. An identity validated in this way presents itself with its own certification of a full-fledged human existence: the power to entertain its universal object attests its own being. But this beholder of all is also beheld by human others and must acknowledge that scene as well, no matter how much unreality he ascribes to it.

The gulf between this effort at self-definition and that of Nathaniel Hawthorne is a wide one and offers a revealing contrast, not simply because as a writer of fiction Hawthorne offers simulacra of the fragmented selves Emerson, Thoreau, and Whitman saw as hopelessly confined to social roles, but because Hawthorne happens to have been wholly dedicated to the conviction that our lives are to be understood and valued solely through the character and quality of our relations to other people.

Hawthorne's fictions represent us as occupying a position in a web of human ties, as do George Eliot's, although his registration of those ties depends far more on the reader's presumed awareness of moral principles. He called on what he assumed to be most widely diffused among his readers: the imperatives of conscience. George Eliot shared Hawthorne's concern with moral issues, but she could draw on the resources afforded by a much denser social scene, addressing readers aware of settled social expectations and traditionally defined obligations. Hawthorne's tumultuous and shifting society afforded few instances of a taken-for-granted way of life against which change could be sketched. He had to invent the world of seventeenth-century Boston, create a Salem of his own, and build a plausible Brook Farm. His work is necessarily more abstract, yet his abiding interest lies in the interplay between individuals and the community they inhabit. An escapee from solitude himself, he was forever imagining situations in which a passion or a quirk of character led to isolation, broken ties with others, irreconcilable divisions. He was no less conscious of the cost of communal rigidities which precluded recognition of individual claims, and in the early story "My Kinsman Major Molineux" and in *The Scarlet Letter* these rifts between self and society and their effect on our most intimate bonds are intertwined to produce masterpieces. The clashing demands of the individual's passions or convictions and those of community are at the heart of Hawthorne's work. As John A. Thompson long ago remarked, *The Scarlet Letter* deals with irreconcilable conflict in a fashion we recognize as akin to Freud's *Civilization and Its Discontents.*[20]

Hawthorne sees a world in which the effort to discover a basis for one's identity in nature without reference to our inescapable ties to others is not simply injurious to the individual but is bound to issue in a distortion as grave as that which overtakes the searcher for the unpardonable sin in

Hawthorne's "Ethan Brand." By embarking on a search for a universal rule applicable to mankind at large the inquirer commits himself to an insensate fanaticism: his fellows are no longer his fellows but objects for his research, and he is fatally cut off from them. In the same fashion the elders of Boston find themselves possessed of a universal rule applicable to all adulterers, and Young Goodman Brown, following his attendance at the witches' sabbath, believes himself empowered to make a universal judgment of the sinfulness of his townsmen. Clearly, the worst thing we can do in Hawthorne's eyes is to deny the full humanity of those around us. Such an effort is found among those who proclaim that they mean to do us good as well as those who try to harm us. The malign Westervelt of Hawthorne's *Blithedale Romance* is an overt exploiter of others, but in the event he proves less capable of harm than the insular reformer, Hollingsworth, whose passion for prison reform makes him utterly ruthless.

For Hawthorne the movement from estrangement and isolation to a selfhood sanctioned by reciprocal relations with others was liberating and enlivening. The youngster whose mother's meals were set down before her closed door may almost be said to have found an identity in Sophia's arms, and if he did in fact shed tears when he read *The Scarlet Letter* to her it was because he knew the cost of bearing existence as a solitary man. The difference between the way in which he conceived of his place in the world and that which Herman Melville exhibits in *Moby Dick* offers yet another instance of the effort to conceive an American identity in the face of a society which provided few established paths to its fulfillment.

Melville begins his masterpiece with the sentence "Call me Ishmael." He is at once referring to a character who was driven out of his community and providing his narrator with the stance of detachment which qualifies him as a universal spectator, one for whom the total scene is matter for solitary appraisal. The human condition has become Ishmael's object, and the fact is logically associated with what he speaks of as an alternative, "pistol and ball," since suicide is an expression of an inclusive judgment: continued existence is unbearable.

On the opening page of "The Custom House," which introduces *The Scarlet Letter*, Hawthorne refers to his "inmost Me" in terms which make it clear that it is not our business, that—in the familiar phrase from the story which follows—the worst thing one can do is "violate the sanctity of a human heart." Hawthorne assumes that he may find a number of understanding and sympathetic readers, friends to his work, who, we may add, could communicate their pleasure to each other. Writing, then, is a social act which will engage some, be ignored by others. Those who respond accept another voice in the great mixed chorus which sounds for them all. The axes of these opening emphases on personal identity are distinct. Hawthorne's axis runs from the mystery of his identity to its veiled manifestation for others, others who have a virtual presence for the writer; together they help to constitute, through the words he has chosen, a public space of discourse bounded on every side by the "inmost Me" of those who, in their turn, discover a measure of common response to the world as they imagine it.

Melville, who writes in the person of a narrator, does not appear to be speaking for himself, but since he creates no such public space in what he writes we know that he must be. He addresses us through an Ishmael who faces a single and intractable world in which, as we know when we have finished his book, no other voice can make an effectual difference. The public space Hawthorne hopes to create has vanished. Ishmael's focus becomes ours, no presumption that we are somehow present to Melville as hoped-for sharers of a social world remains; we are as alone as Ishmael, if not as desperate—but only if we are capable of experiencing in some degree his sense of isolation. We join in asking inclusive questions of existence and do not expect to hear any answers except those the central consciousness offers. We are alone insofar as we fall in with Ishmael's sense of things, but it is also implied that those who attend to this lone voice are members of a company of those who share the sense of being isolated. When *Moby Dick* was published in 1851 they were not numerous.

The distinction between Melville's proffer of a world-engrossing consciousness through Ishmael and Hawthorne's invocation of a company of readers with whom he shares a sense of the way things go in their common world fades into insignificance for Emerson, Thoreau, and Whitman before the fact that both Hawthorne and Melville were writers of fiction, and as such dealt with a world of merely social selves. To attack that world directly was to involve oneself in it; the primary task, as Emerson, Thoreau, and Whitman saw it, was to put forward exemplary instances of the wholeness of vision which might conduce to the social world's conversion. Fiction, however, claimed a place in our imaginations that they sought to win for themselves. Fiction is opposed to the eternizing impulse of the imperial self; both history and fiction call on figured events and possibilities, bind us to the transient, and reinforce the belief that the self is vulnerable to change suffered at the hands of unassimilable human others. They felt that dramatic encounters with others were fatal to our chance to see things whole and unchanging.

The plural human world in which Emerson, Whitman, and Thoreau were forced to live did not offer them an acceptable way of knowing it; they made their own epistemological revision and offered it to others. They were hardly prepared to recognize that *Moby Dick*, a mere fiction, shared their individualism—the presumption that we see the world from a perspective that no other consciousness can affirm. For Melville, however, that solitary grasp of things was threatened by other people. The following chapter is devoted to the more firmly assured kind of consciousness which Emerson, Thoreau, and Whitman, often in surprisingly similar ways, ascribed to poets or makers, builders of their own world.

CHAPTER 2

Nature's Brothers

To realize the extravagant claims for the powers of the individual that we find in Emerson, Thoreau, and Whitman, one had to transform one's way of knowing the world, becoming one's own church and state, a source of authority about the nature of your most fundamental ties to the world. Your behavior conformed to, was sanctioned by, your innate capacity for moral judgment; no creed or publicly agreed-upon standards were required. The classical and Christian virtues were quietly assumed to be endowments native to the self. If most people were partial and fragmented, caught up in a web of merely apparent goods which ensnared them, the only remedy was a renewal of their capacity to see and act in the light of those inner powers which had illumined their infancy and childhood before the delusory pursuits of society had absorbed their energies and blinded them to reality. Since the practices and assumptions of a life in society had to be seen as if from without, the only way to convert others was to offer them an instance of life lived in an authentic relation to nature, a world correlative with our most inclusive vision.

Yet no matter how hard one tries to be a one man culture, to make a completely fresh articulation between oneself and the whole of nature, it will turn out that elements of the culture you wish to replace have been employed in the process. "Transcendentalists" did not of course transcend anything; what they did is much more accurately suggested by a term Orestes Brownson employed in reviewing Emerson's address to Harvard's Divinity School in 1838. Emerson, Brownson said, had deified the individual soul, positing a "psychological Christ" in each of us.[1] Since Unitarians believed that Jesus was the supreme example of a fulfillment of the most exalted possibilities of humanity rather than a god, we may put it that what Emerson had done was to demote him; he was simply the most noted among us and hardly unique. In Emerson's hands revelation was not part of a single providence, not part of one man's story, but a possibility for each of us at any time. Stories cease to account for us, become in fact bars to our realization of our own supremacy, attested in moments of visionary awareness. Our very own powers are potentially equal to those attributed to Jesus.

Having dropped both the story that was providence and the hierarchy beginning in man and capped by a deity, Emerson was forced to be a spiritual democrat, to find us all, at least potentially, capable of a vision of the whole of things. His practical sagacity informed him that most of us weren't going to make it, but his restriction of hope to the inward theater of individual seekers, enforced by his sense of the fragmented state of those imaginatively enclosed by society, precluded any aspiration felt in common with others. We must pull ourselves up by our own bootstraps. If there was what he called a "higher platform"[2] on which we might meet, a "One Mind"[3] whose workings we might all apprehend, each of us must beat his own way to it.

This perspective confined Emerson to an exemplary activity; neither he nor anyone else could actually display the sense of things he inwardly enjoyed at times, but speech and print could manifest what it was like to regard the world as if from one's own inaccessible watchtower, setting aside the grind and hustle of quotidian life, assured of a commanding separation from merely social dictates, and free to test all things in the light of the passing hour. To be "Emerson" before his readers and listeners was an activity, and it was this sense of a spirit playing over a spreading field of possibility which he managed to convey. He was sometimes bold enough to say that if we but took firm and full possession of our powers it would be apparent to us that we, that each of us, had made the world. We need not pause over the philosophical status of this assumption that the universe did indeed sing our song; what is of first importance here is that Emerson sees our capacity to chime with being as native to us and definitive of our humanity.

In the final decade of our century the intellectual atmosphere is hardly favorable to an understanding of Emerson's response to his own historical situation, a topic central to this book. The early assertive Emerson is assured that each of us has a window—largely obscured for most people—opening on a view of an all-inclusive and unchanging order of things. Those whom he finds significant are those whose activity testifies to a realization of this capacity, in whom moments of vision dissolve the distinction between creation and perception—those for whom the world is no longer distinguishable from their awareness of it. In our time various kinds of intellectual endeavor combine to undermine this focus on the capacities, indeed on the very existence of the individual. When language is reduced to the expression of differences, when accounts of society are reduced to investigation of its stifling powers of domination and a "new historicism" emphasizes the success of external constraints in forming our inmost selfhood, a grasp of Emerson's convictions is obscured. In such an atmosphere it is difficult to recapture a sense of how Emerson felt himself to be situated in his own time and to describe the resources he found in himself to become a distinctive voice in that time.

Standing aside from creeds and congregations, he nonetheless remained in many respects, ranging from his habitual behavior, the tropes he employed, and, most important, the emphasis he placed on individual souls, a Christian. An important instance of our habitual neglect of something endemic in his time and no longer taken for granted in ours is the phenomenon of conversion. We tend to elide the fact that Emerson was reorienting an existing body of religious feeling and practice. Emerson himself could hardly acclaim conversion, which was presumed to be a constitutive event for individuals, an experience which shaped their lives anew. Instead he steadily emphasized what may be described as the drawing of a curtain which revealed what the individual had all along possessed: a capacity for apprehension of the vast spectacle of nature and for the activity it provoked. Conversion was a joining up; withdrawal of the curtain made it wondrously clear that the world was already ours if we but brushed away the enclosure of worldliness. Yet for readers and hearers encounter with Emerson became an analogue of conversion, a liberation into a realm at once self-enhancing and distinct from society's claims upon them. The self did not, in Emerson's reading, have to undergo a transforming upheaval at once personal and social, since no such event could define us. It was not a story that defined what was central in our lives; rather it was our native powers, which membership in society had veiled.

The community in which Emerson lived, in which conversion was thought of as a transforming experience, granted an extraordinary potency to discourse, whether spoken or written. Emerson took full advantage of this vulnerability. His analogue of conversion, focused not on membership but on our original self-sufficiency, was a ministry which offered glad tidings: felt isolation was the condition of hope rather than despair, the only possible means of access to the universal—he had a ringing appeal to the unchurched.

Emerson's own conception of the effect of writing or speaking is suggested by his use of the term "publish" in the sense of making publicly known, a usage he may well have hit on because it was related to, and yet distinct from, uttering the good news or glad tidings of those who preached the gospel to a Christian congregation. He addressed himself not to assemblies as such but to the individuals of which they were composed, or to the solitary reader. His intent was to provoke in each hearer or reader a sense of his own "self union and freedom."[4] His insistence that each of us must follow a particular path was capped by the assurance that we would meet again on a "higher platform." In his most confident phase he was animated by the belief that each individual's realization of his powers would ultimately afford a vision of things common to all individuals. Emerson was not, however, anticipating a new social order arising among those who have reached his "platform."

Emerson's avoidance of any description of an earthly heaven is profoundly characteristic; what was to be "united"—that is, given an inclusive vision of things—was the self, not mankind. There would be no conversation on the platform; there would in fact be no need to say anything. Ultimate spiritual success left you as isolated as did the feat of making more money than all the rest.

Looking back from these chilly heights toward society,

we note that Emerson levels the walls of the fortress of domestic piety which was widely held to be the very matrix or seed ground of social order. By subordinating social ties to individual fulfillment Emerson created a difficulty for himself.[5] Even though he sometimes said that admirable men showed both feminine and masculine traits, he found it hard, nearly impossible, to imagine that women could escape being bound by the reciprocal ties both biological and communal which constrained them. Such spirited and intelligent women as Margaret Fuller were finally denied the possibilities he granted men, even when these women testified to a comparable sense of disaffiliation from the going social order.

In addition to this rather stringent limitation of his spiritual democracy—that men alone had access to the universal—Emerson, as has been suggested, made still another proviso: giving instruction to others demeaned them; writing and speaking were exemplary, a "provocation" rather than a means of instruction.[6] (Whitman is equally intent on showing us *how* he sees instead of asking us to respond to a made thing, a poem.) Writing as a kind of exemplary or witnessed activity may of course be hortatory in effect. In Emerson's essay "The Poet" it appears as the highest of all activities, but its value lies in its display of the possibilities of individually realized human splendor.

The title of the essay enforces a focus on the agent rather than the object produced. Since what is produced is not a message or a call to act in concert with others but an incitement to use one's powers in a fresh way, Emerson's hearers or readers are being told to listen to themselves, to awaken abilities which are dormant in them. Although many shared the emphasis on the inward "moral sense" we find in the early Emerson, he is asking for something more, for an inner revolution of the human subjects he addressed. History, an external record, meant little to him, but he somewhat inconsistently assumed that in the years of his youth an epistemological shift had taken place. As he puts it in a late essay, "mind had become aware of itself."[7] The inconsistency appears when we consider such dicta as "when a thought of Plato becomes a thought to me . . . time is no more."[8] That is, his view of things is not historically determined.

This emphasis on the agent's or subject's capacities doesn't simply defer the hope of a community of minds; it abstracts it from the temporal realm altogether. The only possibility of significant change was that more people would begin to employ a capacity native to the species. To invoke providence or history to account for a diffusion of such an awareness would deprive the subject of its present majesty, would make it a mere follower and subdue it to the past. Since we have always been endowed with the powers we may now come to enjoy fully, the fall into the merely social must be viewed as a persisting liability rather than an event within history. It could not be "social" since our primary relation was to a nature which, although it might exhibit change, had not undergone changes which affected our power to know ourselves as displayed in the natural order.

Emerson's assumption of the role of preacher to Americans did not involve any commitment to going institutions. He had no stake in the form our government had assumed, or in institutional arrangements in general, except in the degree to which they furthered the release of those individual human energies and individual capacities for a vision of things that he valued. Since the nation existed for the individual, there was no point in judging it from any other perspective. If the texture of the national life was in question, one could judge it in terms of the sort of individuals to be found within the national borders. One might have high hopes for the future, but they were not hopes for a collective achievement or beneficent social change; they were hopes for the realization of individual possibilities. When, in mid-life, Emerson wrote *English Traits*, he spoke of Great Britain as the best of actual nations, but this was by no means to suggest that any nation ought to serve as a model, since individual realization of individual possibilities was the standard. Nor could any church, a visible band of believers, serve as a model. The Christian heaven had been reserved for the chosen. Emerson collapses the notion in two ways: we need not posit a deity to elect us; we may choose ourselves, and we need not defer our choice; it is open now. An exemplary humanity would necessarily be comprised of individuals.

The insistence that works of art were at once the best available instances of realized human possibilities, and finally only symptomatic of their ultimate fulfillment, is accompanied by a set of breathtaking negations of the world taken for granted by Emerson's contemporaries. We are not to be constrained by family, history, institutions, the masculine sexual role, custom, and so on. These are clogs to the spirit which may be, momentarily at least, shaken off. The things we make and the actions of which we are capable touch us with the wings of such freedom from constraint, but we ought not to allow ourselves to be subdued to such symptoms; we can only be enlivened by the possibilities they intimate. This is Emerson at his highest pitch, the exigent demand he made of himself and laid on us if we can sustain it. In such a context works of art are like signs of grace; they are at best analogous to sparks thrown off by the spirit which has achieved vision.

Art is both exemplary and symptomatic; it does not, as Richard Poirier holds, function for Emerson as "a world elsewhere,"[9] consciously set off from an opposed region of daily affairs and commercial enterprise, since these last are simply not given that much weight, don't have the power to clog the spirit in that degree. If one grants that society bounds the creative power, the project of an imaginative appropriation of the whole becomes impossible and even unintelligible; the nub of the Emersonian stance disappears.

Much of this is familiar, but it is necessary as a preliminary step in characterizing the force of the claim for our individual creative capacities made by Emerson, Thoreau, and Whitman. It is so inclusive that scholars have emphasized the modifications and qualifications they find. When one does so, one winds up with a more genteel and accommodating Emerson than I find in the texts. The cultural radical is reduced, illicitly, I believe, to a writer who indulged in merely poetic extravagance. Taken quite seriously, as Nietzsche appears to have taken it, Emerson's demand for what amounts to an epistemological overturn, a fresh kind of tie between man and nature, doesn't go down so easily; it is an astringent which shrinks social bonds. For Emerson, who had no intention of addressing a tribe of "critics" which came into being as art separated itself out from the general culture, there was no such specialized office as he has often been given in our time; he was addressing all the Americans he could with all the force he dared to employ. When we consider Emerson's radical position in the light of the cultural pressure from the world of money and exchange that he and the other two felt compelled to deny, their extreme emphasis on the powers of the creator seems less eccentric; seems in fact an appropriate response to the countering extremity of selves so largely defined through acquisitive motives.

Since the claims these three made for individuals were indeed exorbitant, their claims invite comparison with those made for individuals by what is now known as "civic humanism" and, more plausibly, with those made for the romantic genius. The former kind of recognition of individuals was not a live option for the three. The republican ideal of a populace prepared to recognize those fit to rule, and to give a willing assent to their rule because it was seen to further the common aim of preserving the republic, meant putting the community first; but in their view no such community existed or could exist without an individual psychic overhaul for everybody. This sounds rather more like a demand that everybody take care of his own salvation than a preparation for civic life.

The more tempting affinity, that with European romanticism, has led, I believe, to an important misunderstanding. The notion of the genius is correlative with the recognition of extraordinary personal powers on the part of an influential body of admirers who trumpet one's claims, as in the case of Goethe. Emerson's familiar insistence on the "representative" character of human greatness is a protest against a dialectic or dramatic view of distinctive individual greatness; it is to be conceived as an aspect of the qualities that would be exhibited by all if the species achieved the goal we may now only glimpse. To make the human world an available object for the self Emerson first crumples history into the originating sources, great men, and then proceeds to give their greatness a merely exemplary character; having thus made all times his own, he may celebrate his moments of vision and urge us to seek ours.

The implied situation of those who are urged to try for the fullness of vision is seldom spoken of; it is desperate indeed. What occupies them—family, work, politics, acquisition—are all, by contrast, nullities. The representative nullity is money-getting, which is assumed to absorb and color all the rest. The massive emptiness of the lives of those deprived of their native powers as inclusive knowers is in accord with the featureless character of money, whose pursuit may best be understood as reductive of all that might serve to discriminate one man from another. Acquisition is, so to speak, less than meaningless; is the nullity of nullities because to gain money, to be suffused with possessions, is to pile nothing upon nothing.[10] If the lives of those whose pursuits thus testify to a lack, to incompleteness, are to be filled, it must be with a sense of the whole. In the world as Emerson, Thoreau, and Whitman envision it there are no half measures; one cannot be half filled, half empty: what is offered by the trio is a totality of meaning. All three have canceled the possibility of the most familiar sort of life, a life which accretes meaning over time, a life which composes a narrative even of the most commonplace sort, a life which might be a part of a history. It is striking that the emptiness of the deprived and the fullness hoped for by the visionary are conceived outside of time. Those who, as Emerson has it, are "dwelling in a relation,"[11] haplessly caught up in a network defined by getting and spending, live in a hell defined by mere useless repetition.

Had Emerson, Thoreau, and Whitman written in such a way as to exhibit this privileged position as knowers, they would have gotten only hoots and catcalls in response; such an overt condemnation of the concerns of those among whom they lived would have seemed simply insane. It follows that the exemplary mode in which they worked was a necessary acknowledgment that, although the ideal was complete possession of a world which complemented the individual, both their hearers and themselves must be thought of as only potential possessors of that world. They attempted to domesticate what common sense declared unattainable: the creative activity we undertook must exhibit the delighted absorption in the whole of the unconditioned knower; yet this exhibition—which was an effectual denial that people were limited by circumstance—necessarily took place in a world in which most people felt themselves heavily constrained by circumstance. Only those whose impatience with their spiritual plight took a wholesale form, who sought an inclusive disaffiliation, were likely to respond with enthusiasm.

Such enthusiasts must be distinguished from those who admired admitted geniuses, say, Byron or Goethe, and saw them in opposition to, or as superior to, the rest of the society in which they made themselves felt. These enthusiasts must also be distinguished from piecemeal reformers who sought to correct particular social ills such as drunkenness or who wished to abolish slavery. In Emerson a much more inclusive denial of the going society, a deep negation of its habit and outlook, was shrouded in a tremendous affirmation which made overt denial seem irrelevant and active contention with others demeaning and useless.

Emerson's mode of address to those who were prepared for wholesale affirmations by an impulse to what I call an "inclusive disaffiliation" was in one sense arhetorical. That is, having disavowed persuasion and having undertaken to address not so much our current state, which we might be presumed to share with our fellows, but instead to address our indistinct longing for another mode of seeing things, which he took to be latent in us, Emerson might be described as speaking in the presence of potential seers. If the spark leapt the fire would be ours, not his. All he could offer us was the example of that activity which was "Emerson." In homelier terms, Emerson sought intimacy with what he conceived of as our best selves. Disavowing address to a constituted "audience," he was singling out our putative inwardness. In Whitman the cognate expression is surely "I might not tell everybody, but I will tell you," which is to say that only a single consciousness can embrace the world as I do.[12]

A writer who adopts the relation to human others common to these three is necessarily absorbed in the possibilities of the moment of experience for readers and listeners. Recalling Thoreau's appropriation of the term "story" quoted earlier, in which it is applied to the whole course of providence, and his reduction of that sequence to the effect of a moment of realized vision, we may call the creative activity of Emerson, Thoreau, and Whitman "occasional" in a special sense: moments of individual experience are thought to spread to the horizon of human awareness and to roll up the chronological span of awareness so that it surrounds us instead of being antecedent to our existence. Their activity as writers is then an invocation of such moments and a repeated attempt to dissolve the linearity of the written. Since this is in any literal (!) sense impossible, they must be said to be bending language as far as it will go to invoke occasions of spreading insight both spatial and temporal.

An excellent illustration of the primacy of instances of making over things made, and of the conviction that what we see is what we have ourselves made, is found in a Whitman poem which was first published in 1855 and was later titled "A Song for Occupations." Whitman, like Emerson and Thoreau, cannot grant that he is in a state of opposition to anything; to do so would be to admit a limit to his power; and he therefore assures us—and himself—toward the close of his poem that "you and your soul enclose all things, regardless of estimation."[13] Estimation implies greater or lesser value and the possibility of exchange. Any such standard is impersonal and subjects the soul to limitation. The mode of consciousness Whitman means to displace is ruled by estimates of greater and less which in turn make mensuration possible. I quote the last eight lines of the poem.

> When the psalm sings instead of the singer,
> When the script preaches instead of the preacher,
> When the pulpit descends and goes instead of the carver that carved the supporting desk,
> When the sacred vessels or the bits of the eucharist, or the lath and plast, procreate as effectually as the young silversmiths or bakers, or the masons in their overalls,
> When a university course convinces like a slumbering woman and child convince,
> When the minted gold in the vault smiles like the night-watchman's daughter,
> When warrantee deeds loafe in chairs opposite and are my friendly companions,
> I intend to reach them my hand and make as much of them as I do of men and women.[14]

The extended catalogue of artifacts, institutions, and occupations which precedes the announcement that the soul includes everything or is the source of all we can name is, like all Whitman's catalogues, testimony to the active powers of a maker; it is never a celebration of the manifold goings on of the world as terminal or a simple delight in the landscape of being. Adam merely named what had already been created; consciousness in Whitman assumes the office of creator and assimilates naming to creating. What is celebrated is not things or occupations as such but our power to produce them. A full sense of our world is closed to us the moment we assume that one of our productions is to be esteemed more highly than another; to do so is to lodge power and authority in the things we have made rather than in their originating cause—in ourselves. Whitman names the glorious variety of things not to delight in discriminating but to catch them up into himself.

The massiveness of Whitman's assertion that our consciousness is the source of being, the insistence on the primacy of the act over its products, can hardly be exaggerated. We do not learn what is essential about our humanity through its representations in religion, scholarship, detached aesthetic objects, the use of money, or ownership. Language itself is suspect when it becomes a medium for the exchange of settled and therefore constricting meanings. As Whitman has it at the beginning of his poem: "I was chilled with the cold types and cylinder and wet paper between us. / I pass so poorly with paper and types. . . . I must pass with the contact of bodies and souls."[15]

It is not of course the physical means alone that are called into question. Whitman was even more concerned to escape recognizable literary forms. In a chapter of a book by John Burroughs which Whitman himself worked over, we find them repelling the charge that his poetry is vitiated by its lack of form with a counterattack: "And the critics are right enough as far as their objection goes. There is no deliberate form here any more than there is in the forces of nature. Shall we say, then, that nothing but the void exists? The void is filled by a Presence. There is a controlling, directing, overarching will in every page, every verse, that there is no escape from."[16] Confronted by the extravagance of such expressions, and similar ones employed by Emerson and Thoreau, we are tempted to resuscitate an outmoded expression and call it a "poetic" extravagance. It is in fact nothing of the sort; it is a call for a cultural revolution. The term is an oxymoron, but the internal contradiction is present in these writers; they wished to change their world by changing each individual within it.

It is helpful in this context to recall Tocqueville's presumption that egalitarianism presents everybody with the spectacle of the looming power of the state.[17] What he did not glimpse as a possibility is fulfilled in Whitman: each individual is invited to claim the power of a universal comprehension and enjoyment of all that has existed, now exists, or will come to pass in the future. The power of the eye, the fact that my vision of the world does not "countervail" another's "eyesight,"[18] becomes a master trope: the vision of existence of the "I," of each individual identity, offers a wholly inclusive vision of being to each of us. If we all adopt Whitman's stance toward experience we will all see that the world streams forth from each of us. We have created what we see. In Emerson's concise phrasing, "Perception makes."[19] To rejoice in the glory of the world is to rejoice in the power of the self to make the world. It may be objected that Tocqueville had imagined that egalitarianism had created a coercive power and that such beliefs as Whitman's left whatever power was in the field untouched. This is accurate: the very assertion of a universal grasp of existence on the part of individuals renders them passive, since what is claimed, an imaginative appropriation of the whole, makes particular actions taken within society quite meaningless. It will be necessary to return to the "eye," or "I," which both receives and creates the world, but I first give an extended quotation from Emerson's journal as an instance of the extravagance of the assertion of creative power which appears in all three writers.

> My brave Henry Thoreau walked with me to Walden this P.M. and complained of the proprietors who com-

pelled him to whom as much as to any the whole world belonged, to walk in a strip of road & crowded him out of all the rest of God's earth. He must not get over the fence: but to the building of that fence he was no party. Suppose, he said, some great proprietor, before he was born, had bought up the whole globe. So had he been hustled out of nature. Not having been privy to any of these arrangements he does not feel called on to consent to them & so cuts fishpoles in the woods without asking who has a better title to the wood than he. I defended of course the good Institution as a scheme not good but the best that could be hit on for making the woods & waters & fields available to Wit & Worth, & for restraining the bold bad man. At all events, I begged him, having this maggot of Freedom & Humanity in his brain, to write it out into good poetry & so clear himself of it. He replied, that he feared that that was not the best way; that in doing justice to the thought, the man did not always do justice to himself: the poem ought to sing itself: if the man took too much pains with the expression he was not any longer the Idea himself. I acceded & confessed that this was the tragedy of Art that the Artist was at the expense of the Man; & hence, in the first age, as they tell, the Sons of God printed no epics, carved no stone, painted no picture, built no railroad; for the sculpture, the poetry, the music, & architecture, were in the Man. And truly Bolts & Bars do not seem to me the most exalted or exalting of our institutions. And what other spirit reigns in our intellectual works? We have literary property. The very recording of a thought betrays a distrust that there is any more or much more as good for us. If we felt that the Universe was ours[,] that we dwelled in eternity & ad-

> vance into all wisdom we should be less covetous of these sparks & cinders. Why should we covetously build a St. Peter's, if we had the seeing Eye which beheld all the radiance of beauty & majesty in the matted grass & the overarching boughs? Why should a man spend years upon the carving an Apollo who looked Apollos into the landscape with every glance he threw?[20]

Emerson, at first cautiously avuncular on the question of property, is led to play with Thoreau's exploration of the ties of property to making, when the young man introduces one of Emerson's deepest convictions: that we reduce ourselves when we submit our vision of things to the constraints of expression in words. He goes on to develop the consequences of throwing forms into the world, the domain of the exchangeable, of possession. If we were entirely self-possessed we would not need to detach incomplete representations of ourselves, open to appropriation by others and subject to what Whitman's poem calls "estimation."

This withdrawal of the act of making from the assumed corollary of an audience may seem confusing. When we associate it with an emphasis common to all three writers on the hermaphroditic character of creation of the highest order we may be still more puzzled. Another quotation from the Burroughs/Whitman chapter of 1877 ties this assertion of a godlike creation by fiat to the conjunction of the self and the organ of vision: "Under the influence of the expansive, creative force that plays upon me from these pages, like sunlight or gravitation, the question of form never comes up, because I do not for one moment escape the eye, the source from which the power and action emanate."[21] We submit to Whitman not as to a poet but as we do to an environing natural condition; we are not his audience; we move in him as we do within the order of nature. Such passages lead us to ask whether Whitman is helping us to reconstitute our own vision of the world or is completely incorporating us in his own imaginative universe, but what I wish to deal with here is simply the claim to a creative power of a kind we do not ordinarily associate with poets.

This claim to the powers of *natura naturans*, nature in the process of conferring a nature on things—the scholastic term is employed by Emerson—or to be, as Thoreau puts it, "another nature, nature's brother," may be illustrated from Thoreau's journals.[22] He imagines, for example, that in transferring his glance from one flower to another he cross-pollinates them and produces a new species.[23] A forthright passage about the generative eye appears in Emerson's journals: "Poet sees the stars, because he makes them. Perception makes. We can only see what we make, all our desires are procreant."[24] And, once more from the journals, there is a passage reminiscent of the account of the walk with Thoreau in which he speaks of "casting Apollos"—that is, creating statues—into the landscape with every glance: "the entranced soul living in Eternity will carry all the arts, all art, *in power*, but will not cumber itself with superfluous realizations."[25] Fifteen years after the date of the passage about walking with Thoreau, he notes that Thoreau sees the farmer's field as his own, overlooking it "like a sovereign his possessions," and goes on to give a homely touch to the idea of individual generative power, saying, "Indeed it was the common opinion of the boys that Mr. Thoreau made Concord."[26]

Why should the connection of making with sexual generation be a problem for these three visionaries? The answer is clear enough once we have absorbed the thoroughgoing character of the rejections they were compelled to make in order to remove the obscuring screens of familial and social relationships. To step out of time and historical circumstance, one must discard reciprocal ties as constitutive of one's selfhood. To assert an identity released from a network of such ties, it was necessary to get rid of the expectation on the part of others that you were fulfilling an already established role, ranging from the role of author with an audience to that of husband with wife and family. Only an outlook cleared of these obstacles afforded glimpses of that totality to which the self was correspondent.

It is the pressure of this need to proclaim an independence of defined sexual role which leads Emerson to speak of a realized humanity as hermaphroditic and Whitman to think of his orgasm as giving rise to "landscapes projected masculine, full-sized and golden,"[27] or of the maker as rivaling the sun in defining things with a light beyond light.[28] The realized self "publishes" itself with the insouciance, the freedom from the constraints of our social conditioning, which the age conceived of as that of nature itself. A fully developed selfhood would feel that all that was seen and all that happened was wholly consonant with its own nature. Emerson writes of an entry into an enhanced awareness as quite free of any purposive intention; he has been not a conscious agent but an enraptured discoverer of that which complements him.[29] We are at such moments of discovery incapable of distinguishing seeing from making what we see. Unlike St. Augustine, who, in the *Confessions*, calls on the glorious spectacle of nature to speak for itself and hears it murmuring only, "He made us," Emerson refers the glory of what is seen to a consciousness which has no question to ask because it is not separable from what it holds; it is simply a brimming cup of delight.

Each such moment is terminal, something final and good in itself. It is also, strictly speaking, incommunicable; its quality may only be suggested. In 1866 Burroughs had remarked of a Whitman poem that it was "but one remove from silence," that the voice is almost as assuredly integral as silence itself.[30] Such moments of experience as Emerson reports render time and succession meaningless because they take us out of the everyday region of purposive activity. They enforce a standard of value incommensurate with those which govern a husband, father, householder, owner of bank stock, citizen. Since Emerson was all these things, since one could not be at every moment one of the "Sons of God" capable of creating statues with a glance, one had to content oneself with the partial and merely suggestive power of writing and speaking. The apparent contradiction, "Perception makes," is indeed fundamental for Emerson, yet it is not demonstrable to others, who must become aware of its truth for themselves.

A comparison of a sentence from an 1841 letter of Thoreau's with Whitman's poem "Crossing Brooklyn Ferry" offers a fuller instance of the way in which creation may be conceived as carrying us beyond our communal or—as Mikhail Bakhtin calls it—"dialogic" relation to language. Writing to Lucy Brown, Emerson's sister-in-law, Thoreau condenses into a sentence the character of his aspiration to a wholly "natural" creativity.

> I dream of looking abroad summer and winter, with free gaze from some mountain-side, while my eyes revolve in an Egyptian slime of health,—I to be nature looking into nature with such easy sympathy as the blue-eyed grass in the meadow looking into the face of the sky.[31]

Those flowers which bear both stamens and pistils propagate without assistance, exercising a creative power which confronts that of generic nature face to face. Thoreau habitually turns to flowers for comparison with human creativity: "Each human being has his flower, which expresses his character. In them nothing is concealed, but everything published."[32] Nature embraces the whole round of the seasons, and Thoreau imagines himself doing so as well, "looking abroad summer and winter." He will perform the act of transmutation he found so fascinating when considering the lilies which floated on the Concord; the mud uttered flowers, and, in the letter, his eyes will have the creative fertility of the mud deposited by the Nile.[33] In his journal he speaks of "the life of the gods" as wholly without drama or determinate roles.[34] In his letter to Mrs. Brown he asks why he may not be called *more* human than "any single man or woman," why, that is, he may not exercise a "free gaze." The freedom he speaks of is a freedom from a determinate sexual identity—a freedom like that of the blue-eyed grass or the generic nature into which it gazes. Stationing himself on a "mountain-side" above the scene of constrained social life, he undertakes to blossom in sentences, exercising a power indistinguishable from that of nature.

Whitman's "Crossing Brooklyn Ferry" opens with lines asserting a similarly exalted position, the stance of someone at once universally receptive and creative. It offers a colossal confrontation, more strident than that suggested by Thoreau's phrasing of it as "nature looking into nature." The voice in the Whitman poem encounters nature, manifested in the sun and the tide, "face to face," announcing itself as not simply a cognate power but a commanding one. Whitman proclaims himself a superior natural power in the twenty-fourth and twenty-fifth sections of "Song of Myself": "earth by the sky staid with" has given birth to the sun, now, at its rising, shooting "libidinous prongs" upward. "How quick the sunrise would kill me," he continues, "If I could not now and always send sunrise out of me." He has been born of a union which confers a power commensurate with that of the sun: that of his soul and the world, which he in turn illumines and, as if present to us, expresses in "Crossing Brooklyn Ferry."

> What is more subtle than this which ties me to the
> woman or man that looks in my face?
> Which fuses me into you now, and pours my meaning
> into you?[35]

In this poem's sixth section an escape from the world of "contrariety," of sexual longing, guilt, and the competing wills of others, is said to have enabled the speaker to achieve his status as a natural force. Following his enfranchisement from a reciprocally defined humanity, from, in Thoreau's phrase, that of "any single man or woman," Whitman is endowed with what he calls, in a sense precisely analogous with Thoreau's "free gaze," a "free sense."[36] Both have a creative glance which transcends the world of heterosexual reproduction, or, more generally, of emotional commitments to particular persons as self-limiting influences. The Whitman poem and Thoreau's sentence coincide in yet another important respect: both incorporate the cycle of the year in a moment of vision. The poet of the "Ferry" watches the flight of the "Twelfth-month" gulls above him.

> Saw the slow-wheeling circles and the gradual edging
> toward the south,
> Saw the reflection of the summer sky in the water.[37]

The December gulls enact the movement of the sun toward the south in winter, and the very next line lands the watcher in the summer sun. To become an infant god and wield primal powers one must stand outside time.

Eager as he was to be known as the "new man" capable of transforming the way in which Americans saw themselves and their world, Whitman was very much aware of the dangerously confining conception of the role of poets among his contemporaries. He avoided referring to himself as a poet in the poems of his first edition of 1855 and in his Preface to that edition tries very hard to give the term "poet" a very wide meaning. His work is to be the cause of a fundamental change in our conception of ourselves, not as a set of directives but as a new light on things which will enable each reader to see the world differently. Just as in Emerson and Thoreau, the impulse to transform the way the world was apprehended, the urgent need to become as gods in Brooklyn and Concord, appeared a practical necessity. "Poets" were expected to produce articles for consumption, furnished with morals and seasoned with familiar emotional stimuli. The rhetoric texts of Hugh Blair and Henry Home, widely used in the United States, may have been unfamiliar to Whitman, but the attitude toward the office of the poet and the function of poetry they fostered was not.[38] He not only stood out against it; he struck at its root: the confinement of the arts to a decorative function laced with tributes to convention and based on the manipulation of received elements.

Whitman's extravagant and illogical assertion of his literal presence in his works was made by a man who had found the most profoundly moving of his experiences of others in their vocalization in oratory or opera. He who lives breathes, and song, ringing out and momentaneously present, is what this poet presses toward. The horrified responses of a good many of his early readers furnish proof that he had obtruded on their sensibilities in ways they could not stomach. The very assertion that he had a body and sexual organs, and that he meant to touch us and to invade our very inmost convictions and transform them, was felt as a kind of "presence," welcome to a few, although abhorrent or at least disturbing to most people.

Although Emerson and Thoreau do not ask us to connect our sense of them with their bodies, they too make a curiously radical assertion of presence. It is not difficult to see that they must do so. Preachers contemporary with them could rely on the conviction in their audiences that they were voicing a providential order which lay behind everyday life and was supported by the biblical texts, traditions, institutions, the very shape and significance of the building in which they preached. Preachers were not therefore announcing that the order lying behind the world of the congregation's daily life was discontinuous with that life; rather they were asserting the order's articulation with it, and their words provoked scorn in all three men. In proclaiming that an access to reality was available only to individuals as individuals, they pointed to what they found the only means of truly breaking out of existing social versions of reality. In our century, those who try to break out in this inclusive sense come laden with intellectual equipment of various sorts; a Walter Benjamin, a Jurgen Habermas, a Jacques Derrida or Michel Foucault must address an existing order if they are to deny it; they do not attempt to do so on the basis of a native endowment which all have but most are obscuring or distorting because they have succumbed to society's sense of things.

Voices stripped of external social sanctions and of accepted roles, all three invoked impersonal conditions, natural conditions, asserting that what appeared special or peculiar in what they said summoned up a wider generality than the gregarious middle ground could offer. One of the most revealing remarks Emerson ever made, which occurs in his journal for 1830, indicates that he was aware that doing away with the middle ground meant attempting to marry the particular person to universal truth: "Then it seems to be true that the more exclusively ⟨individual⟩ idiosyncratic a man is, the more general & infinite he is, which though it may not be a very intelligible expression ⟨is⟩ means I hope something intelligible."[39]

Emerson's use of "idiosyncratic" here does not suggest quirkiness or eccentricity, although he employs the word in this negative sense elsewhere. He is attempting to enforce his belief that the private vision is far wider than the scene constituted by the assent of numbers of people. Those to whom others granted ascendancy because they were felt to be representative of publicly sanctioned values and powers were in Emerson's eyes mere "personages," like the character in a Henry James story, "The Private Life," who disappears when he is not on public view. Such people may be described, in Emerson's scornful phrase, as "dwelling in a relation."

This is a conception of the highest human activity as self-contained, terminating in its exhibition of powers independent of those of other agents, who, insofar as they were involved, were present only as elements in the picture you were making or the activity you were carrying on—since the world you grasped was, ideally, an object correspondent to your activity, a cosmic sandbox in which you could enact what occurred to you because its conditions were designed for you. Others might profit from the example of your activity but failed if they modeled themselves on you, since to model oneself on another was to blind oneself to one's powers as an originating source of creative vision.

When things were going well the world seemed to exfoliate out of the self, and at such moments the claim to what Derrida calls "presence" was absolute.[40] Whitman makes this explicit in his use of performatives which imply that in reading him you are witnessing what he does, as C. Carroll Hollis has shown.[41] But it is only less apparent in Emerson and Thoreau, whose prose often carries the suggestion that to write is simply to speak at one remove. This is the wholly expectable consequence of putting one's personal identity first. Starting with a fuller sense than others had that the qualities of the breathing person were constitutive of his world led to the assumption that the means employed were secondary when compared to the looming fact of the power to make oneself felt as a source. Whitman's lordly way with his texts in successive editions makes it plain that what counted was how he felt at the moment rather than what form had been assumed on the page by an earlier avatar, a superseded "Whitman." We may add that the journalizing habit of Emerson and Thoreau offers evidence that what was primary was the way they played on the world and the world played on them, the capacities revealed by encounter with things, rather than the creation of detached aesthetic objects, the use of forms or genres, the search for truths to return to—or any aspect of things which issued from prior agreement among their fellows. The means, writing and speaking, although important, came second.

On this score, what makes it hard to recover the attitudes of the three writers under discussion is not simply the technical point made by Derrida, that language can refer only to what is absent, but the widespread predisposition of our culture to focus on the means we employ rather than on those who use them. We tend to look first to the question: how have what means been employed? The question these writers asked is: who am I now addressing? Within the limitations that all three acknowledged, they felt assured that language worked to its presumed end. The work of Michael West on Thoreau shows that Thoreau thought of language as rather more clearly an aspect of human endowments than his fingers and toes, since the latter were closer to mud than the flower of speech was.[42] Whitman tries in his turn to collapse naming and creating into a single act, as if he were nature proclaiming let there be "crocodile"—or God pronouncing being as in "Let there be light."

Emphasis on the instant moment was required by the sense that we must be open to the reception of the due ray from every quarter. This meant catching up things past in our present, subduing all other tenses to the present tense. In his journal Thoreau refers to Homer, the Zendavesta, and Confucius as "a strain of music wafted down to us on the breeze of time," conferring on these classics the immediacy of the song of pewees and larks he hears about him. Of that "strain" he writes: "by its very nobleness it is near and audible to us."[43] This account of Emerson, Thoreau, and Whitman in their most radical vein, that in which seeing and making come to seem indistinguishable, is important because it is the aspect in which they converge most closely. The fact that they share a position so extreme is evidence that they are making a common response to a felt pressure from the culture around them.

Yet we must still ask: how could such a profound shift in awareness be brought about among those who heard or read them? I have described what they did as an exemplary kind of activity, which must be discriminated from offering an argument or proposing a systematic view of any sort. All three felt that direct instruction was a fatal concession to the interlaced worlds of discourse which characterized society.

One could not break out by speaking in one of its partial roles; any such presentation of one's views screened both the speaker and the hearer from awareness of the wider natural realm which alone corresponded to the fully realized powers of the self. As Emerson puts it in 1838: "It is with Society that Seeming comes in."[44] Distorted by its incompleteness, society produced only appearances.

It followed that a discourse directed to potential seers and creators, to responsive individuals, must be scoured of whatever was merely public or taken for granted. What could not be felt on one's own pulses simply had no sanction. Over the whole range from common sense to elaborated theory, our native responses must take precedence no matter how numerous the opposition party might be. The enthusiasm Emerson felt when, on his first European journey, he visited the Jardin des Plantes was not an admiration for the marvels of science but pleasure in a fresh imaginative dominion over existence.

An unalloyed expression of the radical position our three writers shared would have frightened off many who found an exciting whiff of spiritual assurance in their work, something which preachers and politicians had failed to provide. One could listen to Emerson and gain a sense that a felt lack was being supplied, without concluding that one must break all one's ties with the existing social order. The speaker clearly had not done so, yet he enforced the conviction that the hearer had a power and importance not acknowledged by preachers and politicians.

It is easiest to recognize the urgency of the appeal these writers made to those who found themselves in spiritual need when we emphasize its seeming discontinuity or avoidance of ordered development of any conventional sort. This refusal of the expected structure of argument or systematic exposition, accompanied as it is, whether in Whitman's poetry or the prose of Emerson and Thoreau, by an unmistakable continuity of tone, shows us how consistent all three are in trying to reach behind the group to the solitary listener or reader. There is no one else to address, because in the measure that we listen as members we hear nothing of any import or force. Emerson's not infrequent invocations of the distanced democracy, of those who may one day "be *members*, and obey one will"[45] or know what he means by the "One Mind," are references to those not yet on the scene. That scene is first of all the inward scene of each hearer, which is still dark, one which Emerson's example may one day help each of us to light from within. What appears discontinuous is a series of reiterated instances, so many examples which are meant to be adjurations that we make a similar leap toward a wider awareness.

But, it might be objected, Emerson gave lecture series on matters of contemporary interest; Whitman, at least in his second edition, gave his poems titles; and Thoreau put *Walden* together with extraordinary care! Yet no matter how much we emphasize the practicality, sagacity, and conformity these three exhibited, it remains clear that they had in common a pervasive undersong which was profoundly subversive.

Reversing Prometheus, these three stole the most heavily charged of the words current in their culture for their own use, as in the case of "friendship." A friend became not an additional link with others on the social plane but a sharer in visionary expectations. Emerson even speculated (referring, without naming him, to the death of a brother) that when the friend has fulfilled this office he "is commonly withdrawn from our sight in a short time."[46] The parallel with the eighth section of Whitman's "Crossing Brooklyn Ferry" is suggestive. Whitman is imagining a leap on his own part and that of others out of the world in which they have "knitted the old knot of contrariety," outwardly bounded by loves, hates, and greed, inwardly suffused by guilt, into a region of awareness of which he can exclaim:

> What gods can exceed these that clasp me by the hand,
> and with voices I love call me promptly and loudly
> by my nighest name as I approach?
> What is more subtle than this which ties me to the
> woman or man that looks in my face?
> Which fuses me into you now, and pours my meaning
> into you?
> We understand then do we not?
> What I promis'd without mentioning it, have you not
> accepted?
> What the study could not teach—what the preaching
> could not accomplish is accomplish'd, is it not?[47]

Those whom Whitman imagines greeting in this passage may not be able to outface the sun, but they are at least, in Thoreau's phrasing, nature's brothers and exercise a natural force quite beyond the scene of relative "estimation."

Did Emerson's hearers and those who later found solace in the detached and even godlike stance of Thoreau and Whitman actually emulate them? To do so would have been to become similarly independent, to manifest a capacity for creative vision, rather than assume the attitude of a follower and admirer. It is obvious that they did not, and could hardly have been expected to, and equally obvious that the response they did make, and that Americans continue to make to these three writers, is evidence that the writers had given voice to a need felt by others and had proposed a glorious fulfillment of that need. Those who listened had found the pronouncements of preachers and politicians hollow. The part Emerson has played in the history of our culture and those later given Thoreau and Whitman show that all three were directly responsive to a desire created by the character of the surrounding culture: a desire for a mode of self-definition independent of that enforced by the impersonal pressure of exchange and acquisition. Those who did listen were told not that they should or could help to change society but that they could find a fresh source of authority within themselves which would make it plain that the ties of family and society were subsidiary and provisional. The isolation and moral unease they felt were given a positive significance: the individual *qua* individual was the sole means of access to the universal order of things.

Failure to employ the splendid powers we possessed could not be blamed on the species; we had no original flaw. Yet Emerson could not promise that, to use his familiar phrase, we would all meet on "a higher platform" from which the universe would present the glorious spectacle correspondent with a full exercise of the human endowment. The hope for a universal spiritual democracy that we find in the elder Henry James did not accord with Emerson's focus on the isolate self.[48] The higher reality was there for those who found it; it could not be promised to all. Emerson's hardheadedness on this point is in accord with his highest hope for the self. Those who failed to make their vision of things correspond to reality failed indeed.

The imaginative displacement of authority from society to self appeared to democratize our potential godhead, but its fundamental effect was necessarily a shift in the view of the way in which individuals were associated with each other. The effort to bring about social change through the activity of groups with a shared goal, groups which acted within the existing social nexus, became meaningless. Emerson undertook a secular reenactment of the Unitarian shift which displaced Christ as redemptive figure with Jesus as the supreme exemplar of fulfilled humanity. But, in abolishing the church which had existed in parallel with the society, in democratizing the opportunity to become one of those "unnumbered supremes" who rise from the tomb in Whitman's "Song of Myself," he left the individual at the mercy of society. All institutions, even if they asserted values other than those society had adopted, were condemned; no group could set goals for individuals without fatally narrowing and distorting the consciousness of each of its members.

Yet the society's power to invade the self was undeniable. It was not simply on one occasion that, in Emerson's phrase, we paid "the costly price of sons and lovers" for "reality," but daily, and in many ways. Intrusions so numerous led to a sense that the self was split; as Emerson once put it, we had perforce a lesser ego which dealt with them and was opposed to our grand ego. Thoreau and Whitman, who also testify to their periods of incapacity to maintain the visionary stance, discard, as Emerson does, the vocabulary of sin and guilt. But all three make it clear that their view of the whole is often fragmented. They struggle not with society alone but with its intrusion on the self in the form of familial attachments, the business of getting a living, and awareness of crippling complicities—Emerson, we recall, questions himself because he owns stock in a bank.

An insufficient recognition of a split within the self in these three has contributed to a common misapprehension of their situation in their culture. Despite their effort to stand outside the culture, it was an inescapable ambient medium which necessarily conditioned their attempts to counter its ascendant power. Their response was, to a degree that may be described as peculiar to the United States, confined to carving out a reality founded on the use of language. This is not the commonplace it appears to be. These three were living, like all their fellows, in a nation which had founded itself through a set of written documents; they were also concerned, as many of their contemporaries were not, to direct themselves to Americans as Americans, working, that is, at the business of defining an American identity compatible with their high hopes for individual self-completion. We may put it that the quantum of taken-for-granted thought and behavior was not what one might expect in older societies; writing had to assume a heavier burden in a country in which much was fluid and at risk.

Both Emerson and Whitman cherished the idea of a presence so compelling as to amount to an irresistible moral and spiritual example but were in fact confined to the use of words. Any agency exercised on or within the society would have deprived them of the condition essential to vision, its inclusiveness. As I remarked earlier, one feels in reading these writers that there is no question of hearing a voice one may listen to and discriminate from others as one reads; one is either possessed or not by these "presences." Sometimes Whitman's verse betrays a breathy striving for this effect, but at its best his use of language is, like Emerson's, successful in absorbing our attention completely in its mastery—mastery over the bewildering multitudinousness of things, away from discriminations, from the need to follow arguments, from conclusions, from events felt as climactic, from the thought of irretrievable losses; here are voices which fill us like sound in an echo chamber or open our eyes on a landscape wholly satisfying. These voices fill our consciousness without ever hinting at the expectation of an interruption, a possible interlocutor, an open question, an insuperable difficulty—such is the effect of this simulacrum of presence. These voices are not appeals; rather we are led to see as they see, hear as they hear, resound inwardly as if we too had the power to make all things ring in accord with our note.

Those who respond are occupied by the force of the impression; when it ceases, when you draw back, you find that you have no sense of finality; if you have just now been raptly attentive, to draw back is to find yourself unsupported by any lingering thought. You are left alone as by a departure from the room. If phrases linger it is not because they have a separable suggestiveness or the power of a symbol to evoke further connections; rather such phrases are echoes of the total immersion you had experienced as you read. You must once more beat your way through your own thicket and hear accustomed calls summoning you along this path or that. The incapacity of Emerson and Whitman in their most powerful work to make a stop, to give us the effect of a conclusion, is one of the most directly revealing aspects of their work. What occupies them, what they offer us, is not a matter of when something happens or what happens; it is always and forever how the flux of things is to be felt and known.[49] A mode of knowing may be intermitted, but it may not be said to terminate.

What that mode seeks to establish for the hearer or reader may be illustrated by a familiar quotation from Emerson: "But the longest love or aversion has a speedy term. The great and crescive self, rooted in absolute nature, supplants all relative existence and ruins the kingdom of mortal friendship and love. Marriage (in what is called the spiritual world) is impossible, because of the inequality between every subject and every object. The subject is the receiver of godhead. . . ." He later adds: "Nor can love make consciousness and ascription equal in force. There will be the same gulf between every me and thee as between the original and the picture. The universe is the bride of the soul. All private sympathy is partial."[50] This is Emerson at the height of his aspiration; note that all that is "public" or shared by others has been appropriated and devoted to the use of individuals. It is only *their* landscape of being which has an extensive view. Just so does Whitman claim sovereignty over his "interior republic."[51]

What I wish to emphasize here is the way in which this passage affects our sense of our ties with others. In giving the subject this commanding position Emerson is not an eccentric celebrating his own uniqueness; rather, in substituting a splendid interior world for a displeasing public one he is at one and the same time acknowledging the isolation enforced by a world in which counting and owning play a preponderant part and affirming the possibility of something positive: the chance for an individual secular redemption. The sentences I have quoted mark the endpoint of his long drawn out struggle to find a gospel he could preach; the fact that it did not square with any existing or hoped-for civic order was not an issue for him. What he meant to offer others was an example of a mode of knowing, a way of knowing which he sought to convey through lectures and essays; writing was an imperfect way of doing so, but the only one available.

Emerson, in common with Thoreau and Whitman, found subversive competitors among writers of fiction, a mode which fragmented the inclusive sense of things they wished to exhibit. It is not only conclusions or endings which threaten the trio's sense of things; every aspect of a sequential account of change limits the completion of the self as knower of the world. For them fiction is an extension of the distorted vision imposed by society. Emerson speaks of society as the seed ground of "seeming" or illusion. The moment one man or woman offers a version of selfhood to another person marks a descent to the merely social, which is, for Emerson, "dwelling in a relation." One is tied to the social web or, as Whitman sees it, subject to relative "estimation." To accept a given role or to be classed as of greater or lesser worth distorts or shatters the lens through which we may enjoy an unobstructed vision of things. To accept another, even Jesus, as the prime example of a fulfilled humanity is to obscure one's own view.

Emerson's successive views of fiction give us a glimpse of the stages by which he arrived at this conviction. The early journals are quite conventional in their rejection of fiction as departure from truth, as made up or factitious. Emerson shows a not unusual inconsistency; his references to the novels of Sir Walter Scott, for example, are so offhand as to suggest that they were for him as well as for his contemporaries almost as much the common coin of discourse as the Bible itself. But the Emerson of the late 1830s and after has a deep-seated quarrel with fiction. His grounds are at bottom identical with Whitman's distrust of all writing which is thought of as constituting an aesthetic object distinct from the source from which it emanates. Those who are indeed sources, who persuade us that they have an inlet to truth, are not to be viewed as mere writers assembling objects for an audience; they are not enclosed by the going social presumptions about their limited office. The subject free of this enclosure has a different standing. I quote from the Emerson lecture on "Aristocracy" (1848) in which the phrase "dwelling in a relation" appears.

> The terrible aristocracy that is in Nature. Real people dwelling with the real, face to face, undaunted: then, far down, people of taste, people dwelling in a relation,

> or rumor, or influence of good and fair, entertained by it, superficially touched, yet charmed by these shadows:—and, far below these, gross and thoughtless, the animal man, billows of chaos, down to the dancing and menial organizations.[52]

To stand "face to face" with an inclusive reality, to claim the power Thoreau dreams of in his letter to Mrs. Brown, that of the blue-eyed grass confronting the sun, or Whitman's even more assertive confrontation, again "face to face" at the opening of "Crossing Brooklyn Ferry," is to occupy the only position from which one can speak or write with actual authority. In an earlier Emerson essay, "Character," that position is described as an activity congruent with the tides of being itself: "Man, ordinarily a pendant to events, only half attached, and that awkwardly, to the world he lives in, in these examples [those of the heroes he has been describing who dominate circumstance by their very presence] appears to share the life of things, and to be an expression of the same laws which control the tides and the sun, numbers and quantities."[53] The scorn for those who are describable as "dwelling in a relation"—for all persons who are definable through anything less than their vision of the whole—is withering. This long passage from the essay "Books" concludes once more with the assertion that it is our business to confront the world in its most inclusive aspect.

> Nature has a magic by which she fits the man to his fortunes, by making them the fruit of his character. But the novelist plucks this event here and that fortune there, and ties them rashly to his figures, to tickle the fancy of his readers with a cloying success or scare them with shocks of tragedy. And so, on the whole, 'tis a juggle.

> We are cheated into laughter or wonder by feats which only oddly combine acts that we do every day. There is no new element, no power, no furtherance. 'Tis only confectionery, not the raising of new corn. Great is the poverty of their inventions. *She was beautiful and he fell in love.* Money, and killing, and the Wandering Jew, and persuading the lover that his mistress is betrothed to another, these are the main-springs; new names, but no new qualities in the men and women. Hence the vain endeavor to keep any bit of this fairy gold which has rolled like a brook through our hands. A thousand thoughts awoke; great rainbows seemed to span the sky, a morning among the mountains; but we close the book and not a ray remains in the memory of evening. But this passion for romance, and this disappointment, show how much we need real elevations and pure poetry: that which shall show us, in morning and night, in stars and mountains and in all the plight and circumstance of men, the analogons of our own thoughts, and a like impression made by a just book and by the face of Nature.[54]

This is rather flabby Emerson prose; it is as if the consideration of fiction aroused in him a loathing which, because he is dealing with a mere representation of the bramble of desire and fear which he actually has trouble in avoiding in his daily life, licenses him to express a strong feeling; he gives way to his own fear of being invaded and fragmented. Fiction, if I may so put it, is condemned rather because it refers to what he feels to be a threatening reality than because it is so largely and so often poor stuff. Both fiction and what is for most people reality are suspect, and at the end of the paragraph he struggles out of the mood they provoke in him. In a more equable moment we find him describing an encounter with Scott's *Quentin Durward* without losing his balance.

> *Novels.* To find a story which I thought I remembered in *Quentin Durward* I turned over the volume until I was fairly caught in the old foolish trap & read & read to the end of the novel. Then as often before I feel indignant to have been duped & dragged after a foolish boy & girl, to see them at last married & portioned & I instantly turned out of doors like a beggar that has followed a gay procession into the castle. Had one noble thought opening the abysses of the intellect, one sentiment from the heart of God been spoken by them, I had been made a participator of their triumph, I had been an invited and an eternal guest, but this reward granted them is property, all-excluding property, a little cake baked for them to eat & for none other, nay which is rude and insulting to all but the owner. In *Wilhelm Meister* I am a partaker of the prosperity.[55]

In Goethe's novel, as he elsewhere explains, "The only power recognized is the force of [individual] character."[56] In praising the "noble natural man" in an essay in *The Dial*, one whose subjectiveness refers you not to himself but to "universal good," Emerson describes a mental landscape which renders all narrative a mere distraction from the inclusive significance of literature: "Of the perception now fast becoming a conscious fact,—that there is One Mind, and that all the powers and privileges which lie in any, lie in all; that I, as a man, may claim and appropriate whatever of true or fair or good or strong has anywhere been exhibited; that Moses and Confucius, Montaigne and Leibniz, are not so much individuals as they are parts of man and parts of me, and my intelligence proves them my own,—literature is far the best expression."[57]

Fiction, then, is a display of the fulfillments of fragmented men who try to make themselves whole by getting the girl and the money, as if possessions were finalities. But the noble natural man realizes himself through an imaginative appropriation of things so complete and totally absorbing that he can no longer distinguish seeing from making; it is in him that the morning stars sing together.

I have described this stance as desperate, a claim made in the face of a sense that the surrounding community was sickeningly absorbed in its fragmented pursuits; it seemed the purest possible opposition to a world suffused by possessiveness. Melville recognized and satirized what he saw as a ridiculously self-satisfied attitude in Emerson and Thoreau but could not himself escape an overwhelming sense of isolation which stemmed in part from the same cause. His struggle with his condition is described in the next chapter.

CHAPTER 3

Selfhood Beset

In the measure that the commercial culture, more pervasive here than in Europe, came to define the possibilities of relationships between Americans, it distanced them from each other by interposing the abstractions of the money network. It called forth the imperial claims of the three writers described in the preceding chapters. In its extreme form, their project was to get individuals to build their own worlds. Coupled with it was the assurance that if each of us did so we would ultimately find ourselves united in an apprehension of nature wholly correspondent with our inward capacities.

Since such wide-ranging claims for the self cannot be realized for others without a wholesale conversion to a fresh way of seeing the world, their appeal is not to those who call on others to change the existing society through the formation of parties or interest groups. It is an appeal rather to individuals believed capable of seeing the world as their oyster, that is, chiefly to those who are white, male, and eager to transcend the roles their society offers them.

Hawthorne, who saw all such appeals as attempts to divorce us from the reciprocal responsibilities which defined our humanity, is not of course the only well-known American writer to contend with these calls for the construction of one man cultures—individual efforts to define our relation with "nature" which put the middle ground of community to one side in order to seek fulfillment. James Fenimore Cooper, Mark Twain, William Dean Howells, and, curiously enough, Emily Dickinson, who made God himself a member of her social circle, together with Edith Wharton, William Faulkner, and Saul Bellow in our own century, may be counted among those who could hardly conceive of individuals who undertook to make their world unaided and unconstrained by their fellows. The list could be extended, but I name these writers here simply to recall their sense of immersion in society as an aid in defining the quite distinct position of Herman Melville, the subject of this chapter. He was neither an Emersonian nor one who assumed, as did these writers, that distinguishable personal existence could arise only within a given community.

Melville early came to feel himself a loner, and even culturally orphaned; he was pressed when very young to ask ultimate questions about the human condition. Pushing all preachers aside, he looked into an abyss which seems to have opened for him as a consequence of the financial failure, madness, and death of his father. He felt himself cast adrift on the world, became a schoolteacher, and thereafter took a place still lower in the social order as a seaman before the mast. Although he was never without ties to more fortunate relatives or a touch of self-dramatizing awareness of his class origins, his voyages gave him a range of experience leagues beyond that of any other middle-class writer of his time. Mark Twain observes that he is seldom surprised by oddities of human character and behavior, since he had met such a multitude of human variations during his years as apprentice and pilot on the Mississippi;[1] Melville had much more extensive grounds for claiming that he had encountered humanity in myriad guises under the most taxing conditions.

Melville's early literary success—*Typee* and *Omoo* were published when he was in his late twenties—seemed to overlie his sense of disaffiliation. Recognition in New York's literary coterie, publication in England, and a happy marriage and fatherhood combined to make it appear that he was launched into a world prepared to receive him. The mixed reception of *Mardi*, in which his preoccupation with ultimate questions prevailed over the seagoing yarn with which it begins, made for a momentary hitch, which *Redburn* seemed to repair. But Melville was far too variously intelligent and too much the cosmopolitan to feel at ease with the terms on which he had been received. His readers were pleased by tales of the exotic South Seas or angered by his attacks on missionaries, but in his own view they altogether missed his larger intentions; he was being praised for dancing in puddles; few noticed that he had dived into deeper waters, or, if they did so, told him to get back to his job. When, after another attempt at conformity in *White Jacket*, Melville really let himself go in *Moby Dick* (1851), his star fell, never to rise again during his lifetime or in the thirty years following his death in 1891.

Melville's importance for this book lies in the fact that his sense of things differs both from that of those who find themselves socially surrounded and from that of the aspiring world possessors, Emerson, Thoreau, and Whitman. He was neither able to believe that he had grown in a social medium nor moved to create an outsider's version of individual capacities to embrace existence. Alone in an arena constituted by the presence of other persons, who often agglomerated themselves into mobs, he struggled to preserve an identity, hunted by forces without and haunted by impulses which arose within. Melville took the world personally. As insistent as Emerson on the premise that each of us must shoulder the responsibility for interpreting existence and that institutions are but the shadows of those who profit by them, he is wholly persuaded that our identities are perennially at risk, that others have the power to invade us and deprive us of our full selfhood. He is adramatic in the sense that encounters don't alter relations between his fictional characters but rather issue in collisions which overcome the characters or enable them to swallow up other identities; his is a scene of instances; he is, like Emerson, Thoreau, and Whitman, an exemplary writer, but what he sees as our vulnerability cancels the Emersonian hope of arriving at a vision of things which neatly complements our inward powers. Melville shared the exemplary mode, which is essentially adramatic, without feeling assured that he could make the world square with his vision of it. What is viewed as a satire directed against Emerson and the practical consequences of Emersonianism in Melville's tale *The Confidence Man* (1857) amounts to condemnation of a desiccating impersonality which is as inhumane as the impersonality of ruthless money-getting. He makes bitter fun of the man who held that we can be friends with others only on the ground that they sympathize with our exalted spiritual aspirations. For Melville there was no such escape into abstraction; his was a world in which individuals encountered other individuals.

There is a pervasive oddity about *Moby Dick*, the book that has counted most heavily among us. The persons of this novel move about the decks almost as isolated from one another as so many sleepwalkers, who make of the people and objects they meet the subjects of their dreams. What qualifies this comparison is of course a shared absorption in the crafts of whaling and sailing a ship. Practice flows in to fill the vacancy of the middle ground of human intercourse. We are led to accept this because it accords with our sense of the strict regimen of shipboard existence, here intensified by the scorching will of Ahab. The effect is pervasively felt, so that snatches of colloquies and inner ruminations seem like murmurs among the groundlings who catch only distant glimpses of the cosmic spectacle which Ahab and Ishmael are in different ways confronted by. It often seems that each speaks out of his own isolate preoccupation. The illustrative set piece is of course the series of quite distinct reflections on the doubloon Ahab nails to the mast as a prize for the first sighting of Moby Dick. The two visionaries, Ishmael and Ahab, share the world of practice with the rest, but they alone, barely limited by the presence of others, press toward ultimate judgments of the human condition.

The interactions between characters don't have the property of shaping events and determining actions; they too have the character of illustrative generality. Before Ishmael and Queequeg board the ship one may cling to the notion that one is reading a conventional narrative. Once on board, if we except the tie between Ishmael and Queequeg, the expectation of such a narrative diminishes. Conversations between Ahab and the carpenter, Ahab and Pip, Ahab and Starbuck exemplify dissonances in the way experience is construed by each character, although Ahab has the power to constrain the behavior of all of them. We find such snatches of narrative as do crop up chiefly in passages which deal with encounters with other whalers. These serve to highlight the social vacuity of the *Pequod*; intertwined human needs and purposes reach its decks from other ships but in that vacuum gasp and die like so many flying fish landing on deck. The ship's crew, through whom the impulses of Ahab's will dart like electrical shocks, seem not to share any collective awareness, save in the surreal Shakespeareanizing of "The Forecastle at Midnight" (chapter 39).

Given our sense of the separateness and isolation which attend the putative "characters" on board, how are we to see them as constrained to sail on the same ship, or to appear on the same page? One is led to feel that they do so only as manifestations within the consciousness of Ishmael or in that consciousness to which we must submit as long as Ishmael does, that of Ahab. The others do not—again with the exception of Queequeg's bond with Ishmael—contribute to a developing action of which they are a part because they seem mere appearances fleetingly entertained by Ishmael and Ahab. Even Stubb's cruel taunting of the cook about the preparation of a delicate portion of whale meat suggests that the cook is simply a foil for Stubb's exhibition of what goes on in his head, a miniature reduplication of the ampler appropriation of the existence of others in the consciousness of the visionary characters, Ishmael and Ahab. The reader in turn must wholly submit to Ishmael; he is master of our awareness. It would be ridiculous, for example, to call him the "hero" of the book we are reading, because others appear to him as aspects of an inclusive reality rather than agents on a scene he shares with them.

Those who seek or claim a global reach for their sense of things are minimally associated with the conventional uses of the term "character" in fiction. Yet Ahab, who has such a world-engrossing vision, has undertaken to be an agent, an actor on the universal scene he has envisaged. He has turned a commercial venture into a quest as fantastic as that of Gilgamesh in pursuit of immortality. Extrapolating the absolute authority conferred on the captain of a ship, he conscripts his crew as accessories of his fantasy and hunts down a beast which personifies all that is irrevocable in human existence. If Ishmael, both comprehending witness and threatened individual, were not present the book would hardly engage the reader; it would simply be a fable about a mad sea captain who tries to avenge the loss of a leg to a sperm whale.

The part played by Ishmael in *Moby Dick* affords the best example of Melville's conception of individual existence. The devil-may-care Ishmael whom the reader first meets takes to the sea as an alternative to "pistol and ball," that is, suicide; he is at odds with himself and the world. He alone of those who board the *Pequod* is prepared to apprehend the pitch of desperation which leads Ahab to aggregate all human ills in Moby Dick and seek to destroy them, as if the whale was the incarnation of whatever was adverse to humanity. This project can only be referred to as an effort to enact a metaphor. Since whales had in fact been known to attack ships, the action of the whale in the story represents no breach with possibility, but it does take an Ishmael or his fellow to give the yarn significance for the reader, since his is the only consciousness capable of embracing the measure of Ahab's colossal disaffection. When you attempt to universalize your relation to the world, as Ahab does, human others recede, become bit players in the mythology you are creating. Because Ishmael too has been impelled to ask inclusive questions about the meaning of existence, he is vulnerable to the peculiar grandeur of Ahab's legend. He is also fearful of the consequences of a voyage on a ship "rushing from all havens astern."[2]

What distinguishes Ishmael from all other major characters in Melville's work is simply his points of attachment to the world, to his "dear Pacific," to which he writes a paean, to the spectacle of the whale nursery, to his pleasure in everything in nature that beguiles him.[3] One might almost call him Emersonian, until we realize that "nature" is never the self's all-inclusive window on the world for him; his is the natural world of a particular sensibility with chosen loves, and he is wary all the while of its dangers. Melville does not, in most of his work, give this much weight to such moments of rejoicing in the being of the world; Ishmael's capacity for pleasure is significant by contrast, and his relatively assured sense of his situation is not found elsewhere in Melville's writings.

What sort of man is Ishmael? An acquaintance with the bulk of Melville's work makes this question loom because this extraordinarily loquacious character, whose address to us makes up much of *Moby Dick*, seems almost assimilated to the exercise of telling us about whaling and the voyage of the *Pequod*, so that we find it difficult to conceive of his having had a precedent life or a subsequent one. More important still is the unparalleled exuberance he shows in universalizing his immediate experience in the book. His emphasis on the way he takes the sensations that pleasure him, frighten him, shock him—the degree to which he is played upon by the world instead of trying to shape it—might lead us to compare him to a blank canvas which images and ideas are unremittingly filling in, or to a participant observer reporting on the passions, skills, and employment of the cultural artifacts of his own species.

Is it extravagant to say then that *Moby Dick* seems to be what happens *in* Ishmael? That he is aestheticizing his response to what happens to him in order to incorporate it? If so, in what way does he differ from the conventional narrator? Ishmael's account of the composition of the crew, now "federated along one keel," emphasizes a separateness, a fortress-like apartness. "They were nearly all Islanders in the *Pequod*. *Isolatoes* too, I call such, not acknowledging the common continent of men, but each *Isolato* living on a separate continent of his own."[4] The matter-of-fact statement of the crew's origins immediately gives way to Ishmael's characteristic emphasis on the isolation of individual consciousness, of which he is the prime example, although to us he talks all the while. So again, in the chapter called "The Mat-Maker," we find him saying, "such an incantation of revery lurked in the air that each silent sailor seemed resolved into his invisible self."[5]

Ishmael departs from the stance of the conventional narrator by appealing to those who feel themselves sundered from society—to those as isolated as himself. No such audience had yet been constituted; few people were prepared to read Melville's book at the moment of its publication. Only later would Americans feel alone enough to accept it. An acute reviewer of *Typee*, Melville's first novel, had made a stab at suggesting that Melville had cut himself off from any existing audience in portions of that book. Failing to notice the desperation which leads the hero to flee from the Typees, he nonetheless calls Melville a traitor to his western kind: "He [Melville] writes of what he has seen *con amore*, and at times almost loses his loyalty to civilization and the Anglo-Saxon race."[6]

The exuberance of the prose with which Melville endows Ishmael, a voice sounding like a trumpet at the gates of other fortress selves imagined as similarly responsive to a rendering of the universal plight—aware of their isolation and unbounded by "civilization"—must have been the product of the high-water mark of the writer's personal integration. In this book Melville's writing masters a split in his sense of himself which shows in much of his other work. His Ishmael is both witness to and participant in an enterprise which serves to figure not civilization but the human condition at large as

Melville conceives it. We can hardly account for his triumph as a writer, but it is possible to point to some of the contributing aspects of his success in this instance.

To write in what I have called the exemplary mode common to Emerson, Thoreau, Whitman, and Melville is to write from a conviction that the self, whether for good or ill, for enlightenment or ignorance, is the sole judge of our experience. The opposing view may be suggested by Kenneth Burke's term "dramatism," which entails a growth of our sense of things grounded in interplay with others.[7] My contention here is concisely stated by Diana Trilling in the Foreword to a collection of her essays: "Far from believing that the self is best comprehended or realized apart from society, I am of the older opinion that it is society which provides the self with its best possibilities of ascendancy, even of transcendence. My opinion includes the belief that when we are implicated in society we are the more, not the less, likely to exist in all our personal variousness; . . ."[8] Since these sentences were published, in 1964, our conception of something we might call "society" has grown more attenuated. The power of market economies over our minds and hearts has been ever more deeply interfused with our sense of things, but the root contention that the growth of distinctive individuals takes place in relation to the presence and influence of others remains, I assume, inescapable.

Melville, however, had little interest in the process of growing up which such a conviction involves, yet he remained free of the claim that the self could create a world congruent with its vision. The grounds on which, isolato that he was, he nonetheless resisted the Emersonian claim to the self's sufficiency arose from his sense that the integrity of his being was threatened by the power of others, expressed through force, or arbitrary authority, and the command of wealth, and by his own deepest erotic need: a loving tie with another man. He felt himself an outsider on both counts and wrote as if on guard against threats, studied other men for dear life, took the world personally because he was beset from within and without.

The energies released in the creation of *Moby Dick* are first of all brought into focus by the use of a declared outsider as leading figure. Second, and most obvious, it invokes the heroism, a heroism democratized, of those who hunt whales. Third, it accords the widest possible imaginative range to Ishmael as spectator not simply of Ahab's quest but of all the attendant natural circumstances—Peleg and Bildad have signed on an Ishmael who is licensed to play philosophic observer of a miniature reenactment of the plight of mankind. Fourth, and at once least prominent and actually essential in freeing Melville to write as he does in this book, is the establishment of Ishmael's bond with Queequeg.

Before I turn to the significance that bond had for Melville, something should be said of the place of Ahab, whom I am effectually subordinating to Ishmael in my view of Melville's fable. Ahab does not lose, nor is he a tragic figure, since tragedy demands an audience, and he is, so to speak, incorporated in Ishmael's account of the possibilities of action over against the universe. Ahab surrounds his defiance with rhetorical splendor, makes his point by dying without surrendering his purpose; seals, we may say, his affirmation that he cannot be deprived of his identity, even though his affirmation of it is fatal. In the upshot, Ahab is Ishmael's delegate, who explores the alternative Ishmael had considered in the first chapter, that is, "pistol and ball." Since Ahab transforms himself out of the possibility of recognition by another, becomes inhuman in attempting to affirm himself, he is not, in short, an answer Ishmael can accept. Ishmael is altogether too comprehending a witness to constitute an audience for tragedy all by himself. Ahab's is a rejected choice for him; the right worship of whatever powers there may be is not defiance.

When Ishmael pops up from the maelstrom caused by the sinking *Pequod*—and before he is absorbed in the further ruminations of Melville on man's fate—he grasps one of the ropes attached to Queequeg's coffin, and we are reminded that he has at least that much personal history: he is attached to Queequeg.

The condition which gives Ishmael a wider horizon than any other Melville character is an episode we may think of as minor: his encounter with Queequeg at the beginning of the book, an encounter which goes far to explain the momentary equilibrium Melville had achieved in the period when the book was being written. To suggest how the meeting of these two counts in establishing Ishmael's imaginative economy as Melville represents it, it is helpful to go back to Melville's first novel, *Typee*, based on a brief sojourn among a cannibal tribe in the Marquesas Islands, a novel in which the writer's relation to experience of the world is epitomized.

Typee may be said to answer the rhetorical question posed in *Moby Dick* in grander terms: were the spheres formed in love or fright? The answer, for all human purposes, is, according to Melville, that they were formed in both. Both love and coercive power such as Ahab's are invasive, threatening to our sense of ourselves; our very identity may be swallowed up by love as well as by the coercion or domination of others. *Typee* presents this version of our condition without equivocation: Tommo, the seaman living among this savage tribe, must either be totally absorbed, must accept and reciprocate the loving attention the members of the tribe offer each other, that is, internalize the tribe's outlook on the world, or be destroyed as alien, unintelligible, as much outside the tribe's collective superego as the enemy in the next valley, the Happars, whom they kill and literally devour. If Tommo is to remain himself he must escape.

Typee is, in this central aspect, an exemplary tale. The Typees treat Tommo as one of themselves, but he will be stifled if he stays and no doubt eaten if he rebels. Western society presents a hazard less dramatic but almost as stifling—enclosure in domesticity and crippling social constraints, which are countered by the impulse to "landlessness," celebrated in the chapter called "The Lee Shore" in *Moby Dick.* Bulkington, a supreme example of landlessness, regards the whole western community as if it were almost as oppressive to him as the valley of Typee is to Tommo; he takes experience wholesale, is wholly unfettered by domestic ties or shared communal convictions, is a seaman before the mast who nonetheless exhibits an imperial independence. I will come back to the part he seems to be playing for the author after considering the relationship between Ishmael and Queequeg.

I have said of Ishmael that he somehow stands clear of the danger that besets other central figures in Melville's work, that of being enslaved by external force on the one hand or by love on the other. It often appears that for Melville the loner who takes on the whole job of defining the world for himself—who does not become a participant with others in the creation of a shared sense of reality—must necessarily regard others as threats to his liberty or as irresistible seducers. For him, succumbing to others amounts to a loss of selfhood. Melville's representations of this threat may well be the result of his erotic response to other men. However, his fictional representations of irresistibly attractive male figures assign the responses they provoke not to individual lovers but to a mesmerized group who become followers of a supremely independent man. Such a man is a kind of tribune of the people, who disdains rank but is tetchy as a lord over any invasion of his rights—a commoner who exhibits a wholly native nobility. Shared with others, affection for such a being blunts the suggestion of a passion the age saw as shameful.

Melville's disposition of his erotic impulses is writ large in his work, but powerful forces in the culture have worked to obscure it from his day to our own. The most pervasive and widely felt of these is so much a part of our cultural baggage that it is almost invisible: the presumption that the artist is another breed of cat altogether. Even though much contemporary criticism seeks to overthrow this presumption by claiming that language is simply an instrument in the hands of those who hold power or that it is too slippery to perform the office of effectual communication, it remains true that most of the discussion of this writer singles him out as artist and excludes his own intention, more plausible in his century than our own, to address us as fellow creatures. Another barrier has been interposed by the relative crudity of our categories for the discussion of sexual impulse. Such terms as "homosexual" or "bisexual" often work to obscure the individual case. I prefer to ask Lionel Trilling's question, "What does the poet want?" and to supplement it with the question: how, and with what deflections and transpositions demanded by his time, does he set about getting it?

An episode near the opening of *Moby Dick*, Ishmael's "marriage" to Queequeg, is the most directly revealing of the character of the all-too-brief equipoise Melville achieved in writing this novel. The term "marriage" is gamesomely employed; it carries no hint of sexual consummation. Nonetheless, the union between Ishmael and Queequeg is, for Melville, a kind of anchor for the whole book, a representation of a bond between males which did not threaten the masculine identity of either man.

Forced to share a bed in the crowded Spouter Inn, Ishmael awakens to find that Queequeg, the savage harpooneer, has thrown an arm over him while sleeping, and he recalls a terrible awakening of his childhood. Condemned by a harsh stepmother to go to bed in full daylight, he had wakened in the night to find that his hand was being clasped by an unseen presence in the darkness, and he had lain rigid with fear. Melville's comment has a suggestive incompleteness: "Now, take away the awful fear, and my sensations at feeling the supernatural hand in mine were very similar in their strangeness to those which I experienced on waking up and seeing Queequeg's pagan arm thrown round me." Nothing in Melville's work seems more suggestive of the involution of his feelings about other males.

In what is described as a childish memory, the overwhelming need appears to have been a loving and comforting male presence, yet the hand clasped in his provokes overwhelming terror; need is bound to danger. Nonetheless, in the peculiar and touching occurrence at the Spouter Inn Ishmael is not threatened; the embrace of a "pagan arm" assures him that this is a white, an asexual marriage—a comradeship without the danger of invasion on either side. As in the tale of Tristan and Iseult, in which a sword lies between the lovers, so here Queequeg's "tomahawk" lies between this fond pair. The chapter is called "The Counterpane"—from the French *contrepointe*—and Ishmael can hardly distinguish between the patchwork of the quilt which covers them and the tattooed squares marked off on Queequeg's arm. Ishmael has met a "strangeness" devoid of danger. The squares are joined yet distinct, as are the squares on the homely New England quilt and those elaborate emblems of another culture marked off on Queequeg's arm.

The weapon lying between the two sleepers guards the otherness of each of them; the quilt and the arm indicate the possibility of a bond in which the otherness of each man is preserved. The couple achieves a mutual recognition which involves a measured participation in the culture of each party. Ishmael is content to take part in the worship of Yojo, Queequeg's little carved idol; Queequeg at a later stage cedes to Ishmael the choice of the ship on which they are to sign on for a whaling voyage. The union the two form has a character which transcends the culture of both. They enjoy a fellowship glimpsed nowhere else in Melville.

The Ishmael who boards the *Pequod* is secured against a threat to his identity by the bit of social space created by his mostly tacit tie to Queequeg, a tie which secures the identity of both; they revolve about each other like twin stars. For Melville this was not simply a matter of an independent spirit. He had too much experience of shipboard life not to know that one could be subjected in other ways than through seaboard discipline. Those who went to the wall, like poor Doughboy in *Moby Dick*, were subject to anal penetration, in which force and the very erotic impulses Melville himself felt were dismayingly mingled. Ishmael's universalizing authority of vision was sealed by his assumption of a humanity which was beyond any given culture. He had become, so to speak, that ideal anthropologist who was not culturally bound, nor in danger of being eaten, like Tommo in *Typee*, or buggered, we may add, though Melville could not of course say this.

I have not yet noted another incident of the stay at the Spouter Inn at the beginning of the book. When Bulkington arrives with his shipmates, fresh from an extended whaling voyage, their behavior underlines an important contrast with the bedroom scene involving Ishmael and Queequeg. Discovering after an interval that Bulkington has left the inn, his fellows are overset by his absence and run about calling for him as if he were not simply their leading figure, even on shore, but an influence which ordered their lives. They dash out in pursuit. The reader of Melville is led to recall Jack Chase, captain of the maintop in *White Jacket*, likewise a central man, who polarizes his mates about him but is himself wholly free. Bulkington seems almost a character from Melville's own life—as Jack Chase literally was—and the author's introduction of a character endowed with an identical magnetism indicates that Ishmael is to be both saved from a consuming love and, as he is in the end, freed from the spiritual domination of Ahab.

The white marriage with Queequeg, a bond which involves mutual recognition and equality, a bond which transcends the constraints of the culture of both men—exists beyond culture and is appropriate to a vision of human existence at large—serves as a guarantee that Ishmael remains human. He will not break all ties as does Ahab. We may nonetheless suspect that in introducing Bulkington aboard the *Pequod* Melville is serving personal psychic needs as well as giving Ishmael an identity which differentiates him from White Jacket, one of Jack Chase's followers. Having brought Bulkington on stage, Melville is required—or is it licensed?—to kill him off with the rest of the *Pequod*'s crew; one might surmise that Melville, in an exuberant mood, disposes of Bulkington not simply to emphasize Ishmael's independence but covertly to proclaim his own, leading us to suspect that Melville's memory of Jack Chase is alive in him and may safely be memorialized only if the man is dead.

Although this much is supposition, it is clear that Melville has provided Ishmael with a more assured standpoint from which to contemplate a wider horizon than that of any character he subsequently imagined, or, as I have observed, has healed the split in himself which is manifest in later fiction, in which a basic contention between two characters as to how the world is to be conceived is dominant. No spectator is thereafter so widely empowered as is Ishmael; many are caught in a struggle which threatens to undermine their very identity.

In characterizing the relations between characters in *Moby Dick* as adramatic, as chiefly exemplary, I have emphasized its departure from novelistic convention in which constitutive events lead to transformed relations between the characters. Yet one such event, the formation of the tie between Ishmael and Queequeg, is indeed constitutive; it frames the reader's sense of Ishmael throughout, incidental though it may appear as a part of this enormous fable. We might recall Scott's careful schooling of his hero in *Waverley*. The youth who grows up at Waverley Honor is endowed with just the sort of romantic sensibility which prepares him to enter into the daring and extravagant fantasies which animate the conduct of the Jacobite rebellion. Or, to take an instance nearer Melville's own intention, when Ishmael and Queequeg become blood brothers they achieve the sort of bond between two men which D. H. Lawrence describes Birkin as seeking, and failing to achieve, with Gerald in *Women in Love*.

Roped together, Ishmael on the deck and Queequeg standing on the carcass floating alongside while fending off the ravenous sharks with a cutting pole, or jointly engaged in weaving a rope mat—an activity which figures the interplay of chance and necessity—these two are joined in a fashion symbolically reasserted at the end of the book when the coffin, prepared for Queequeg during an illness from which he recovers, and now functioning as a life buoy ringed with depending ropes, proves the salvation of the lone survivor of the *Pequod*. Ishmael is indeed attached to Queequeg, even, we may say, in death. He had met the living man at the portal of the book and is last seen grasping a relic which survives him. Ishmael's humanity is thereby attested; he and Queequeg had been a commonwealth of two, citizens of the world. Their communion had been largely tacit; they were, so to speak, outsiders but together. (We cannot, however, attribute Ishmael's awareness that Ahab was trying to enact a metaphor for the destruction of all human ills to Queequeg.) One is led to question the author's need to hold his book together with an encysted idyll, a guiltless love affair between two men. Was it not in fact what lay behind the release of Melville's energies that we find in *Moby Dick?*

A selfhood both hunted and haunted is common in the fiction that follows *Moby Dick*. The crucial nature of the struggle in one group of short stories is emphasized by titles which make phallic references—recalling Tommo's injured leg in *Typee* or the dismasted Ahab with his wooden leg. "Cock-a-Doodle-Doo," "The Lightning Rod Man," and "I and My Chimney" are examples. But a fuller and more revealing pair of instances in which fatal encounters with others take place is found in "Benito Cereno" and "Bartleby the Scrivener."

In the last two we find variations on a repeated pattern: Don Benito Cereno suffers, as does Ahab, a fatal psychic wound; in his case the result is not the enactment of a trope incommensurate with humanity but an overwhelming recognition of the horrors of which mankind is capable, horrors in which he, like Joseph Conrad's Kurtz, is implicated.

Ahab's figured opponent is a whale, who with his jaws and his battering ram of a head wreaks physical destruction, but Benito Cereno's is the wily black, Babo, a demonic virtuoso of cruelty and deceit, who reveals the abyssal possibilities in our very humanity. Both Moby Dick and Babo come to figure what is intolerable in the human condition. Don Benito dies not out of fear of Babo but of an overwhelming recognition of the horror which has welled out of our very humanity—a history of slavery and cruel aristocratic insularity in which he and Babo are inextricably bound up.

Instead of Ishmael, the universalizing spectator, who is both constrained and assenting participant in an almost fatal quest, Melville offers a version of the generic American, Captain Amasa Delano, whose absorption in practice immunizes him against history and such awareness of its terrifying weight as visits the Spanish captain. Delano lives in a sort of pragmatic eternity in which the encounter with what Benito Cereno and Babo represent is but a temporary untidiness. He counts his own vision of things as sufficient, is a sort of human lighthouse seeing only what he illumines. Unconscious of the possibility of drama and the irrevocable in human affairs, he finds life itself a matter of daily housekeeping.

When Delano comes to offer assistance to Cereno's storm-battered ship, now in the hands of the slaves who had been its cargo, they carry on a masquerade to convince him that Benito Cereno is still in command. Yet on a number of occasions the pretense breaks down. Delano feels an obscure disquiet. There are alarming anomalies in the behavior of those on board. Delano comforts himself with the reflection that nothing so out of the way as mutiny is occurring—he has a cheery confidence that everything can be managed if one but reckons with accepted rules and conditions. What he hasn't thought of as possible is unthinkable. Not until the desperate Don Benito hurls himself over the side into his departing boat does Delano begin to realize that all is not what it seems. Even after the whole grisly story of revolt and murder has been told, he is puzzled that Don Benito cannot greet the rising sun of a new day as a chance to take up the daily round—to make an Emersonian fresh start. Before his blank gaze the author has paraded a miniature enactment of what has marked human history: abuses of power, the bitterness of slavery, the savagery of the slave revolt—an array of horrors which provoke only a momentary disquiet. In this story the question of the distinction between the kind and range of the consciousness of Benito Cereno and Captain Delano is clear: the Spaniard dies of an insupportable burden of awareness arising from a sequence of events, while Delano's horizontal consciousness appears to have spread (without constitutive moments of growth and alteration) from the narrower circle of little "Jack of the Beach" to its present assurance that the life of his so far successful practice—which might be compared to the nineteenth century's assumption of the spreading plain of scientific knowledge—is the only sort of knowledge which makes sense. The execution of Babo concludes the episode for him; it is the proper sequel of a mutiny.

"Bartleby the Scrivener" is the most masterful of Melville's uses of an account of a wounded consciousness, in this case the narrator's own, but it works to wound the reader as well. "Benito Cereno," we may assume, was not felt as so direct an assault on the reader; few can be assumed to have been shrewd enough to perceive Melville's thrust at the ahistorical and blindly pragmatic character of Delano as a judgment on Americans, although, as an account of a visit to the United States in *Mardi* testifies, it is in fact such an assault. And the reader of the 1850s, agitated though he might be by the question of slavery, pro or con, would have found it distanced, almost exotic, as a tale of events affecting a Spanish aristocrat. The writer of "Benito Cereno" exercises a disposing authority in the course of his exposition of the radically different views of the action exhibited by Benito Cereno and Amasa Delano. No such possibilities of detachment exist for the reader of "Bartleby," who finds himself implicated in the story.

Melville spoke scornfully of the two books which preceded *Moby Dick, Redburn* and *White Jacket.* Each of these two books had been conventional in its assault on convention: Redburn's account of the suffering poor he encounters when his ship lands at Liverpool and White Jacket's outrage at the cruelty and stupidity of navy discipline are both instances of societal oppression which demand redress. But Melville thought them potboilers because his central concerns were at once more personal and more general; a focus on social reforms, no matter how appealing to the public, blanketed the wider issues about our lives which had been posed in *Typee.* He was haunted by preoccupations akin to the biblical query "What is man?" and by persisting wonder over the governance of the universe. He felt too much alone to throw his heart into causes, and his best work has grown on American readers as they have increasingly felt their distance from each other.

Moby Dick, "Benito Cereno," and "Bartleby the Scrivener" come close to inverting the perspective on the situation of the central character found in the two earlier novels whose merits Melville questioned. These two are ostensibly directed toward the social spectacle. (There are of course striking exceptions, such as the account of White Jacket's plunge from the yardarm.)

But the three works just named aim at general views of the plight of individuals and show a progression as regards the involvement of the reader in assessment of the situation. Ishmael is a comprehending witness of Ahab's pursuit of an imagined embodiment of the source of human ills; Delano in "Benito Cereno" is unable to imagine what has overcome

Benito Cereno, and this forces the reader to serve as interpreter—the reader is further engaged. In "Bartleby" the ancillary characters in the lawyer's office in which the scrivener is employed and the lawyer's professional colleagues are so encysted in their own habitual preoccupations that the lawyer-narrator is essentially alone in his efforts to cope with the scrivener. The isolation of the lawyer seems in fact to illustrate the distancing of each human being from all others which was spoken of at the beginning of this chapter: the relations between those in the lawyer's circle of acquaintance, both those in his profession and those he employs, are governed by questions of property and profit. The greatest figure who had appeared on the lawyer's horizon had been the country's richest man, John Jacob Astor. But Melville pushes beyond the spectacle of a society engrossed in profit, beyond the social ills the reader is prepared to condemn, to the question of mortality, so regularly elided in Emerson, Thoreau, and Whitman, in whom the irrevocable full stop gives way to an attempted immersion in the flow of existence.

Bartleby, engaged to copy legal documents, is initially a paragon; he copies assiduously and correctly, showing none of the failings which mar the work of the other two clerks. Turkey, Nippers, and Ginger Nut, the office boy, are lightly and amusingly sketched as characters of a Dickensian singularity. Bartleby, however, is wholly assimilated to his office; pale and silent, he writes indefatigably, but, as the lawyer discovers with growing exasperation, he will not do anything else, repeating, whenever he is asked to assist in comparing duplicate copies or to run an errand, "I would prefer not to." Despite the lawyer's inward reflection that there is a point beyond which sympathy fails, the narrator cannot rid himself of the impulse to find a way of arresting the progression of Bartleby's negations.

The scrivener determines not to copy any longer, yet insists on remaining in the office and, after the lawyer in his desperation has moved his office elsewhere, refuses to leave the building itself. Fears for his practice—others find his tolerating Bartleby so long suspicious—do not deter the lawyer from making an effort to extricate Bartleby from his whirlpool of negation, even after others have had him sent to the prison known as the Tombs as a vagrant. When the lawyer visits him there Bartleby varies his formula, saying, "I know you and I want nothing to do with you." On his last visit, his former employer finds Bartleby curled against a blank wall; by refusing to eat he has willed an utter negation of identity itself.

The lawyer's own identity is, as the story presents it, rather tenuously based. His ties are external; all have to do with his profession. The increase in his business which leads him to hire Bartleby has been occasioned by his designation as a Master in Chancery, but subsequent legislation abolishes the position, and his report of his loss of its emoluments may be taken as an account of a shrinkage in his sense of himself. He has no other source of assurance in the story, no wife, no friends—indeed the response to his persisting activity in Bartleby's behalf is so totally uncomprehending as to suggest that anyone who departs from the conventions of his world will fall between its cracks unnoticed. He speaks of unavailing efforts to discover Bartleby's origins, yet his own are hardly less obscure to us. But the literary origins of the narrator are apparent: he is one more of a familiar line of whimsical, bachelorish commentators in a current convention stemming from Ik Marvell,[9] discussed by Ann Douglas in *The Feminization of American Culture*. Melville's lawyer is both frantic and flustered over the spectacle of Bartleby's steady movement toward extinction, but his final reflections are grating in their shallow inadequacy to his experience. Asking Bartleby to take heart because a patch of green grass and a blue sky are visible in the prison yard is to invoke a tattered remnant of the Emersonian faith in nature; reporting a rumor that reaches him after Bartleby's death that Bartleby had been employed in the Dead Letter Office, as if to suggest that this had led Bartleby to conclude that there was nothing to live for, and the lawyer's final exclamation, "Ah Bartleby, Ah humanity," are all touches of what Ann Douglas calls "magazinish" sentiment, plastered over Bartleby's choice of death.

If the lawyer, despite his being moved and engaged by Bartleby's dignity and steadfastness, proves a deficient "reader" of the momentousness of this choice, what is the situation of the reader of the story? Allan Silver has argued that in the measure that we judge the action correctly we judge that this is a story about a society which fails to institute felt bonds of obligation and fellowship among its members, and it is certainly true that these are lacking in the story.[10] Nothing in the customs of those who appear in the story furnishes an assurance that property and profit are not motivations outstripping all others, save among those who can look forward to nothing except their scanty wages.

Yet one more qualification is required before we can attempt to answer the question of the situation of the reader of Melville's story. What Allan Silver's analysis suggests is that the lawyer's helplessness before the behavior of his clerk is that of his society at large. But the lawyer does not resemble a Gradgrind, the character in Charles Dickens's *Hard Times* who is solely moved by economic motives. The observations of the narrator on Bartleby's fate are not those of a man of affairs; they are akin to those of a detached observer of the foibles of his fellows. The narrator is the voice of such putative expressions of fellowship as were current in polite fiction. But may we then call the lawyer the central character, central in that he alone has the opportunity of action and that he finds neither means of action nor appropriate emotional responses to his clerk's determined movement toward nonexistence?

I think we must, and that Melville's shrewdness in imagining the situation is disconcertingly complete as a commentary not simply on the society that surrounds the lawyer, and of which he is a member, but on what most deeply concerned Melville himself: what are the conditions of being human, of being born, living, and, inevitably, dying? Melville was bold enough, enough of a loner, to believe that he could comment on the generic situation of humanity and on the fatuity of conventional responses to it. Bartleby is, in more than one way, exemplary. First, Bartleby is conceivable; such a view of the desirability of concluding with existence can hardly be dismissed as a fantasy. Second, for those who feel themselves isolated, cut off from the assurance provided by satisfying ties with others and deprived of any overarching faith, the spectacle of Bartleby leads to a deeply invasive fear. "Mind," as William James later put it, "is preference," and Bartleby's preference for death makes us alarmingly intimate with our mortality. What holds on life do we have? This may well have been Melville's own question; it is evaded by the narrator, and Melville seems to have been persuaded that the reader would try to evade it as well.

The reader sufficiently moved by the story would blame the nature of the society around him. The deficiency Melville felt in *Redburn* and *White Jacket* was precisely this: both books catered to the impulse to blur or elide the harsh conditions of human life by shifting the blame to bad social conditions. In this story Melville exploits what he knows about the vulnerability of his readers with unprecedented harshness. He knows what we cannot bear, has known it in himself. We cannot bear the irrevocable, cannot face directly what he views as the human condition. Storm and earthquake produce results we cannot hope to affect and are therefore able to accept, but we find ourselves dismayed by Bartleby's whirlpool of negation as if it had an irresistible seductive force.

Melville was indeed invaded by the Emersonian presumption of our essential isolation, but it had a sharply different meaning for him. His sense that one had to work outward from a wholly personal center was always colored by his fear of our liability to be swallowed up by an equally inclusive countervailing sense of things held by another or others. While Emerson, Thoreau, and Whitman had hopes for a transformed humanity, Melville had none; isolated as the three knew themselves to be in the present, they were able to look to the possibility of a shared vision. The high price they ask their readers and hearers to pay is the necessity of making it alone until all have acknowledged their isolation and achieved a gloriously complete apprehension of the whole which lies about them. Then, and only then, will they realize that the order they celebrate is common to all men.

For Melville this invocation of a common future was without content; he saw it for what it was in essence, a claim to the possibility, realized at moments, of dwelling in eternity. He saw and denounced the link between what we call "transcendentalism" and pragmatism, before the latter term had been employed as William James employed it. That link is the assumption that individuals can start over, begin afresh, quite as if they were self-begotten. Kierkegaard had observed that with the coming of the Christ the eternal came in time; it was this assertion, democratized, that Emerson had put forward, but for him the temporal qualification was not the announcement of a unique saving mission; we were all enjoined to be our own redeemers.

I have described this effort to make us aware of the possibility of making a self correspondent to an inclusive order as a reaction to the suffocating impersonality of a commercial culture. Melville, however, saw himself quite differently, saw himself as surrounded by human others, whose power over us whether erotically attractive or brutally coercive might leach away our identity or, more insidiously still, as in the case of the narrator of "Bartleby," expose us to a realization of the comparative nullity of our selfhood. What grounds does the lawyer have for preferring life to death? Emerson, Thoreau, and Whitman block out what Melville sees, the irrevocable aspect of our end. The figures they hold up to us are those whose grasp of the world is as imperial as they aspire to be.

It was because he had himself faced death that Melville had such an acute sense of the vulnerability of his audience. I have so far emphasized his sense of being beset by others, with the proviso that *Moby Dick* exhibits a Melville who enjoyed a confidence in his powers which appears to have been sanctioned by an instance of fellowship which dissipated his fears of invasion—the tie between Ishmael and Queequeg. But what that confidence engendered was something more: *Moby Dick* is an attempt at wholesale seduction. The writer clearly felt that he might himself become a central man, a very Jack Chase of the pen, and win an audience to his sense of the world and their common plight.

This novel is not an attempt to wound us, as is "Bartleby the Scrivener" or *The Confidence Man.* To pursue all the involutions of Melville's rage and frustration with his audience is hardly possible here; others have documented it, and Melville's own letters and journals show it in undisguised form.

He had early learned that readers whose preferences and expectations were scorned might turn on one like the culturally outraged inhabitants of the valley of the Typees.

Moby Dick was written and published in a time unprepared to receive it; it is an appeal to an audience of isolatoes, to persons emotionally disengaged from engrossing social ties, odd men out. The novel's scene and atmosphere largely lack a provision for a set of holdfasts to secure individual identity. When this sense of being adrift in a world one could neither control nor feel safely enclosed by became much more widely diffused after the Second World War, Melville's novel became a national classic, an experience akin to the reader's sense of homelessness, provided the reader was male. Thereafter, as the seventies wore on, women too became sympathetic readers, quite as if part of the price of their claim to equality had been a feeling of rootlessness, of being disjoined from a settled order of things.

But Melville's delayed recognition is also part of the history of other nineteenth-century writers whom we came to call "major writers" in the 1940s and 1950s; this fact has worked to obscure the importance of a distinction between his individualism and that of Emerson, Thoreau, and Whitman. Their claims to possess the human scene married vision and creation so completely that lapses from it could issue not from the influence of others but only from a failure to employ the individual's full powers. What holds of the early and most assertive phase of the work of Emerson and Whitman does not apply to Melville; the persons in his fiction are beset by others, must, like miniature nations, defend identities threatened by alien powers and betrayal from within by their own impulses. In short, they cannot hope to command the impersonality which attends all-encompassing vision. The Ishmael who pops up from the sea at the end of *Moby Dick* has found no ground for all-inclusive visions.

One must be wary of a writer who commands so many voices, but one generality seems safe: whatever threatens our sense of ourselves wears a human face. Melville has no doubt about the power of individuals to shape our lives as conclusively as rejection by readers shaped his own. When we look back from the austerity and harshness of the prose which imperfectly encloses the erotic sentiment and even sentimentality of the manuscript posthumously published as *Billy Budd* to other voices such as the shifting disguises and recurrent oxymorons of *The Confidence Man* or the apparently open "social" novels, *Redburn* and *White Jacket*, to the agonized stressfulness of *Pierre*, or to the heady rhetorical assurance of *Moby Dick*, we are led to marvel.

Is it plausible that all these voices, including the play with the accumulated baggage of western culture in *Mardi*—a sort of lecture course often more informative about the writer than the world he is traversing—were responses more and less exacerbated to the spectacle of a single culture conceived *en bloc?* Or, pushing this presumption to its limits, as Wai-chee Dimock does in *Empire for Liberty, Melville and the Poetics of Individualism*, is Melville himself the most articulate voice of a completely commodified culture in which identities are bought and sold?

That the market mentality is indeed constitutive of a social macrocosm so pervasive as to threaten our construction of distinguishable identities I have argued throughout; that we in turn comprise parallel microcosms, market monads whom Dimock calls "imperial" selves, is a position which only a methodmonger can maintain. The result is a sophisticated echo of the position common to so many nineteenth-century visitors to this country: that Americans were essentially greedy.

Since I have emphasized Melville's status as an isolato, a perennial outsider, this once more raises the question of his escape from the world envisioned by those other outsiders, Emerson, Thoreau, and Whitman. What does it mean to say that Melville took the world personally? We may put it that he refused to make it an object open to his possession, as did Emerson, Thoreau, and Whitman. Any such grasp as these imperial selves claimed was necessarily impersonal. Emerson, Thoreau, and Whitman shared a call for a wholesale conversion, an epistemological overturn. This dictated a theoretic democracy; mankind might hope for a future unity in its vision of things. For Melville the assertion that our sense of things was fragmented, chiefly through the translation of our pursuits into commercial terms, had no such meaning as it had for the other three. Neither reform nor the attempt at wholesale conversion on the part of the hopeful trio seemed primary to him. The basis for his dislike of such generalities about our associated lives was his own experience. What he had met in his eight years of knocking about the world did not answer to any of the categories others proposed to justify their hopes for the future.

The cannibalism he had encountered in the Marquesas Islands was only the most forthright of the modes in which men sought to dominate other men. I use a cant phrase to suggest what Melville seems to have felt: civilization, wherever encountered, wore a human face. The face, if it had a meaningful part to play, was male. The only sharply etched female figures one is likely to recall are Annatoo, the termagant schemer who appears in *Mardi*, and the proud and intractable Mrs. Glendinning, who attempts to keep Pierre in leading strings in *Pierre*. There is no hint that Melville can deal with women except as temptresses who unman men, or as objects to be pursued, or as shrews, or as witches like Hautia in *Mardi*. This is curious, since Melville was passionately fond of his wife, at least early in their marriage, but the burden of the fiction suggests harsh or churlish attitudes toward women. Pierre is extraordinarily perspicacious about the shaping power our parents have over us but remains incapable of imagining the process of growing up. Melville clearly satirizes sugary sentimentality in the opening scenes between Pierre and Lucy, and there is no intimation that Pierre is capable of anything but the most fictionally conventional responses to women, a deficiency which robs his sticky end of any weight it might have for the reader. There is not enough felt human circumstance to establish grounds for Pierre's employment of grandly general views of his situation.

The book's failure is most massively accounted for by Melville's inability to find women anything but incomprehensible hindrances to male thought and activity. A juxtaposition of the women in his fiction with the men, with Jack Chase, Bulkington, the John Paul Jones of *Israel Potter*, or with Queequeg, reveals a disparity between the imaginative authority accorded male and female existence which goes well beyond the conventional subordination of female figures in his own day. In reading "The Paradise of Bachelors and the Tartarus of Maids" we encounter a distinct queasiness about female sexuality; Melville's red torrent of menstrual blood and his pallid maids in the mill may remind us of the saying in *Moby Dick* that candles cost blood,[11] as the making of paper does here, but these exploited maids are distanced, as if indeed seen by a visiting bachelor who means to keep himself warm and well fed in the company of other men. It appears that it is only men who act and confer meaning on the blank sheets of paper by writing upon them. Women play accessory roles in his fiction; erotic intensity is reserved to relationships between men.

This apparent limitation is in fact a condition of the magnificent success of *Moby Dick*. It frees Melville to write about a world in which there are no conventional consummations in encounters with human others. His Ishmael shares this trait; he is one of the most wonderful witnesses in literature, but, as if in a courtroom, he presents his evidence without coming to conclusions about its significance.

What we learn of Melville's meetings with the Hawthornes in the spring of 1851 and from his letters to Hawthorne suggests that he longed for a white marriage, a twin star relationship with Hawthorne, after the pattern of Ishmael's marriage with Queequeg, with the exhilarating difference that, as his essay on Hawthorne's *Mosses from an Old Manse* seems to indicate, their juncture would signalize the mutual recognition of America's greatest literary talents.[12] Sophia Hawthorne's account of Melville in that period reflects her admiration and proposes a cause for Melville's turbulent and unsettled state.

> [His] fresh, sincere, glowing mind . . . is in a state of 'fluid consciousness,' & to Mr. Hawthorne speaks his innermost about GOD, the Devil, & Life if so be he can get at the Truth for he is a boy in opinion—having settled nothing yet—informe [unformed]—ingens [vast]—& it would betray him to make public his confessions & efforts to grasp,—because they would be considered perhaps impious, if one did not take in the whole scope of the case.[13]

For Sophia, then, it is immaturity which leads to Melville's failure to reach conclusive views, although Hawthorne himself, when Melville visits him in Liverpool five years later, finds him still debating large questions of this order and still unable to conclude. Is Sophia altogether wrong? She certainly recognized the high, perhaps overwhelming, intensity of Melville's admiration for "Mr. Hawthorne"—she may have thought it akin to a schoolboy's crush on his teacher. But there is an earlier passage in her journal, written just after her marriage to Hawthorne, which suggests that she may have sensed something more than immaturity in him. Sophia's nuptial journal rejoiced in Hawthorne's "corresponding part" (her phrase) both spiritual and bodily. Sophia writes: "The truly married alone can know what a wondrous instrument it [the body] is for the purposes of the heart."[14]

This entry is echoed in a passage in *The Blithedale Romance* in which Hawthorne describes the kind of defeat Zenobia meets in dealing with Westervelt: "she ultimately finds that the real womanhood within her has no corresponding part in him. Her deepest voice lacks a response; the deeper her cry, the more dead his silence."[15] We can hardly imagine a more striking instance of Hawthorne's ability to see what Melville, preoccupied with our isolation, is less aware of, that it is the dramatic character of our relations with others that shapes the world for us.

The pathos of the encounter in *The Scarlet Letter* between Hester and Dimmesdale in the wood had a more immediate meaning for the Hawthornes than we seem prepared to admit. They found the familiar motif of parted lovers, of sexual consummation denied, profoundly moving because the union of body and "heart" had been constitutive for them, had indeed freed Hawthorne from his almost cloistered sense of the world. They had a proportionately keen sense of the emotional investments of others.

I conclude that they sensed the quality of Melville's feelings for Hawthorne; for Sophia this suggested incompleteness, or immaturity. For Hawthorne it must have meant a demand that he could not answer. Lacking the letter of praise for *Moby Dick* Hawthorne wrote, we must simply infer its content from Melville's exuberant and extravagant response. The impression he made on the Hawthornes was clearly overwhelming, and just as clearly the writer was aroused to this pitch by the presence of Hawthorne, author of *Mosses from an Old Manse*, the only work mentioned in the essay he published called "Hawthorne and His Mosses." The omission I find significant is that nowhere in the record does Melville mention *The Scarlet Letter*. This well-known omission may not have puzzled Sophia Hawthorne as much as it has puzzled Hawthorne's later commentators. Melville had little interest in love stories involving men and women.

This much is supposition; the indubitable fact is that Melville's work is adramatic, exemplary, rather than comprising a sequential narrative in which an action turns on events which change the relationships between the characters who figure in it. Of such changes the progress of the love affair was, in Melville's time, what it no longer is in ours, the central instance.

Both the subversive convictions which arose from Melville's knocking about the world as a young man and his cherished encounters with superb masculinity affected his sense of those who read him. Clearly he had no patience with tales that found marriage matter for a conclusion, nor could he subscribe to the contemporary cult of domesticity. Feeling isolated, he sought like company; *Moby Dick* is the widest net he cast, and it brought him the letter from Hawthorne but little else that he could count as comprehension. He had the pain of knowing that he had done a great thing and that it had not been acknowledged. When he subscribed himself a "Virginian" in the essay in which he praised Hawthorne to the skies, his generic pseudonym carried an association with some of the noblest characters the nation could boast of; he had undertaken to do something heroic in writing *Moby Dick*, and he was succeeding. "Hawthorne and His Mosses" is in retrospect one of the most touching documents we have from his century because its writer was rejoicing in his discovery that he had a fellow in accomplishment; in their persons the new nation might take pride. Melville's letters to Hawthorne at this time are full of hyperbole; in associating Hawthorne's powers with Shakespeare's he was himself claiming powers which gave him the right to make such comparisons with authority.

When readers recoiled from what he had done, Melville seems to have turned his energies against both himself, the momentarily triumphant isolato, and the familiar enemies, domesticity, hack writers, moral falsehoods, and, most harrowing of all, the sense of the possibility of realized greatness ignored. All this and much more is to be found in *Pierre* (1852), which was issued in the year following the publication of *Moby Dick*. But the writer was a genius—I use the word Richard Poirier has been bold enough to restore to criticism—and, in the process of attacking himself and all about him, uncovered rather more about how we achieve a discriminable psychic identity than any other American writer had even glimpsed.

He was permanently scarred and never recovered his buoyancy, but he achieved a kind of health—the endurance notable in the eponymous hero of *Israel Potter* (1855), that hard nubbin of a man who is permitted a glimpse of human greatness in John Paul Jones—and something more, a piercing insight which called his readers to account, as he does in "Benito Cereno" and "Bartleby" and in the last of his novels, *The Confidence Man* (1857). Those who had misread him had done so because they had the insular vision of things he sketched in "Benito Cereno" and "Bartleby," and he lashed them mercilessly in *The Confidence Man*.

Melville, isolato that he was, was peculiarly well situated

to appraise the inadequacy of those who, like Emerson, Thoreau, and Whitman, likewise stood apart from shared communal aspirations but proclaimed the possibility of possessing the world imaginatively, as if the world order they glimpsed might one day become a common possession. For Melville the scene that mattered was composed of human others, variously streaked and striped by their distinct ways of taking their experience. Melville, who respected Emerson as a voice among others, could not countenance essentially impersonal efforts to imagine counterworlds. It is not surprising to find Emerson and Thoreau caricatured in *The Confidence Man*; the moment a view claimed universal application this bitter book sees it as one more swindle. "Transcendentalism," as popularly perceived, made such an insupportable claim.

Melville, who saw himself not as a visionary seeking to embrace the whole of "nature" but as hedged about by human others, each enacting his character, was nevertheless an exemplary and fundamentally adramatic writer. He was also a man whose sense of self was always at risk when faced by the seductive or socially sanctioned coercive powers of other males. The success of his fiction was the result of what might have been seen as a series of deprivations by those whose fictions embraced the conventional motifs of narrative in his day. The use of the love affair, the very foundation of social order as the prelude to marriage and domestic life, was not available to him, since he granted priority to emotional ties to other men. Nor could he employ the motif of descent, family history, to recall the discrimination made by Werner Sollors in *Beyond Ethnicity*, in which the love affair and marriage are said to function as an epitome of the founding of a new nation, while an emphasis on descent enforces tradition, continuity, the old order. Melville's treatment of the latter theme in *Pierre* doesn't convince us. Since the alternative of a commitment to Emersonian vision is also ruled out, what is left?

What is left is what Melville had himself hoped to realize, what he had on occasion tried to image, the possibility of sharply individualized human greatness. It was this ambition and this hope which distinguished Melville from those who, in response to the pervasive influence of the commercial culture, tried to create a blanketing universal scene. When Melville sat down to write he appears to have been confronted by hazards; the represented situations in his fiction involve twin dangers to the vessel of his selfhood: unsanctioned love or arbitrary power. The only escape was to write one's way through, to become in effect an irresistible power oneself. When his mighty effort at mass seduction appeared to have failed Melville was deeply wounded. No such assurance as Ishmael commands in telling his story appears after the crushing blow of *Moby Dick*'s reception. Melville's own readers, those who felt as lone as he, were few; the culture was not yet prepared to cherish him as he has been cherished in our time. The vigor and mobility he showed in response to public failure is extraordinary, but it is pervaded by his sense that readers might be as merciless as cannibals if one strayed from their customs or expectations. Yet he never resorted to impersonal condemnation or aggregated his world into an object to be condemned.

He saw, in fact, a connection between such judgments and the ahistorical sense of things he had skewered in his description of Captain Delano in "Benito Cereno." In *Mardi* (1849), a visitor from that fabulous archipelago calls the vociferously assertive Americans "sovereign kings" and insists that, despite their boast that history culminates in them, the United States is just as subject to cataclysmic change as was the Roman Empire.[16] The remark is attributable to Mardi's king, and is precise. These Americans are making claims to unlimited sovereignty, and such claims must be called atemporal in the measure that the self is universalized, that is, thinks of present conditions as unchanging. Related appropriations of the world are treated in the following chapter.

CHAPTER 4

Wholesale Appropriations: John Dewey and Henry James

The cultural conditions which led to the individual stance of those who first reacted strongly against the creeping tide of commercialism were of course the very conditions which precluded all efforts to bring about changes within the society. These writers construed this incapacity as a positive: since society fragmented the self, it must be thought of as a set of hampering conditions. One called on others only in the hope that they might realize their fragmented state and achieve what Emerson called "self union."

Emerson, Thoreau, and Whitman have a primary importance because they were the first to see their society as a block society in which distinctions between public affairs and personal or private activities were insignificant. They tried to blanket the situation by viewing all substantive human endeavor as taking place within the theater of the self. They abandoned any hope of bringing about change except through an internal conversion of each of their hearers and readers. They at once recognized what they saw as a cultural reality, denied its power over them, and offered others heady examples of the countering activity of universalizing the self.

American historians have come to the sensible conclusion that the search for the essence of things American can be of little help in treating the past of a country as large and various as this one. Yet if there are no detectable essences, there may well be important differences which distinguish us from other countries. David Hollinger's title for a book of essays on our cultural history, *In the American Province*, makes this point neatly; provinces are related but distinct. The need to take the world *en bloc*, or to see nature as the object of our awareness at the expense of our implication in the human community, arose out of the apparent sameness of a scene dominated by considerations of profit and acquisition. Present-day historians offer us a more complex view of the mid-century; this should not blind us to the fact that our visionaries were claiming far more for their vision than history ever warrants and that they had an imperative motive in doing so.

The effect is reciprocal: the historian who ignores the testimony offered by Emerson, Thoreau, and Whitman that their social world appeared to be pervaded by acquisitive impulses is also likely to see their declaration of their power to transcend it as an aberrant arrogance. It follows that the very notion that individualism was a significant presence among nineteenth-century Americans ceases to have any force for the historian. It is not hard to see why those who write our history are impelled, when dealing with the nineteenth century, to discard Emerson's picture of himself as subject and the world as object. The picture of things that Emerson presents is largely static—it is the transformation of the self that counts—and history is nothing if not an account of change. An early solution was to say that Emerson lived in an agrarian period, that his response to that period consorted with its characteristics, and that the industrial period which succeeded Emerson's time necessarily changed the way in which society was perceived. But to see the world as Emerson did is to disavow the meaning of historical change altogether; his vision rolled up past, present, and future into the moment of awareness. This way of taking things, in which the visionary transcends the possessive, corresponds to our world as well, one in which the focus on the possessive may be thought to have intensified but not to have changed. We cannot recapture Emerson's ample faith in the powers of the individual, but we obscure the facts when we overlook the persisting demand for a similarly inclusive picture of existence in our own day.

An apparent revision of their views by Thoreau and Emerson might lead the historian to think of them as having acknowledged membership of a constraining sort in the society. They conceded the necessity of an effort to get rid of slavery because slavery effectually forestalled the possibility of individual self-realization. (Whitman, however, had begun the retreat toward citizenship which was to culminate in *Democratic Vistas* before the war broke out.) The violent response of Emerson and Thoreau to the Civil War was provoked by their realization that slavery violated individual rights rather than by a concern for the Union. Emerson called down blood and destruction in his journal. Yet subscription to any collective cause posed a difficulty which Thoreau's action illustrates. He wished to be seen as acting on his own beliefs. He sought out an antislavery group which emphasized the individual moral convictions of its members, and he found a hero in John Brown, whom he saw as acting on such a conviction. Brown could not, as Thoreau put it, be tried by a jury of his peers because he had none.

The period following the war is usually discussed as that in which the attitudes and institutions fostered by capitalism prevailed. No such inclusive attempt to give primacy to the powers of the self as had been manifest in the first generation of visionaries recurred before the time of Henry Miller, the Beat generation, and the uprising of the middle-class young in the 1960s, and when it did it took the form of overt attempts at personal disaffiliation from a society viewed as actively inimical to individual development rather than as clearly subordinate to visionary claims. Scores of attempts to change the society from within had been made during the intervening century, and many, chiefly those of the labor unions, had measurable effects. But such wholesale efforts to stand outside the society on the part of individuals as are found in the work of Emerson, Thoreau, and Whitman are not prominent until after the mid-twentieth century, when individuals once more announced that the United States must be seen in the lump and *explicitly* condemned.

The two figures treated in this chapter matured and did their work during the interregnum. The first half of John Dewey's career was largely devoted to an effort to domesticate Emersonian individualism in the democratic order. For Henry James the relatively barren cultural landscape of the United States came to be seen as chiefly animated by business concerns. Despite the apparent gulf which separates the philosopher and the novelist, they share both the view that the United States was to be thought of as a single entity and Emerson's ahistorical conception of human affairs. For them the past had to be reseen in relation to present needs and values, almost to the exclusion of its power to limit and determine what we now see and do. Both were blind to the actualities of politics and believed that our preeminent duty was to expand the horizon of individuals to further what James called "consciousness" and Dewey "experience."

I am chiefly concerned here with the first half of Dewey's career as exhibited in works published from 1882 to 1916, the year in which his enormously influential *Democracy and Education* was published. One of the first of our philosophers to be trained in the borrowed German mode at Johns Hopkins, Dewey was—as he continued to be—extraordinarily productive during this first period. Read in sequence, his writings suggest that he was the most socially engaged of our thinkers at the time, yet it may be said that until well into his fifth decade he was clearly absorbed by a problem set him by Emerson.[1]

In 1903, speaking at a celebration of the centenary of Emerson's birth, Dewey praised him as "the philosopher of democracy."[2] Yet how could a *community* composed of individuals as Emerson described them be imagined? These self-authenticating persons, ever seeking a wider awareness, might one day hope to gain a common realization that the universe was informed and animated by a single cause, but meanwhile their capacity to join one another in the day-to-day activities which would further the common good was not provided for by Emerson.

One may also ask: how can Dewey, the philosopher of practice, be associated with the abstract and visionary Emerson? In part because Emerson and the pragmatists share an ahistorical sense of things. A story told of John Dewey that may well be apocryphal is nonetheless exemplary. The philosopher was sitting at his desk in his Long Island farmhouse when water began to drip on his papers. He went upstairs and opened the bathroom door. In the overflowing tub sat a child, who said, "Don't just stand there, John! Go get the mop!" The story may be compared with an episode in Rousseau's *Emile*. The tutor wishes to give Emile a sense of the impersonality of natural conditions. When the child breaks a window, the tutor puts off having it repaired. Emile will learn that when one breaks a window one is chilly. No intervention of the human will is visible. But of course the tutor is stage manager; authority is present though masked. The story about Dewey takes us a step beyond Rousseau; the youngster in the bathtub is functioning in a world that is not conditioned by authority; child and father face a situation common to them both. They can start from scratch. Here is a matter that demands an appropriate means-end resolution—water is in the wrong place; clean it up! Responsibility and the need to demand it are not in question—the histories and passions of the two characters are stilled and sterilized by the child's definition of a problem and a solution.

Dewey offered an account of human relationships in which people had no personal histories to color their encounters with one another. One could find a true beginning, a still point in time, a false present in which it was possible to start over. No reverberations of earlier moments affect this one. The intertwined, internalized elements of the human condition are eliminated; no sense that our peculiar histories play a part in every action is allowed to intrude. Pragmatism, when applied to human affairs, is a fairy tale of energies magically released from the conditions we know into what Dewey called the "situation," jointly apprehended by the problem solvers involved. But pragmatism is utterly helpless before the encounter of two or more live persons. The philosophy that tries to make the method of inquiry a matter of daily practice has only a tangential relation to human actuality. This must be emphasized because of Dewey's well-known insistence that his thought aimed at reporting how things go among us and because he often tells us that what he has to say about experience is designed to work *within* experience, to reconstruct it and make it more successful in bringing about desired consummations. At the turn of the century, when Frank Norris, Theodore Dreiser, Jack London, and William Vaughan Moody saw their fellows as driven by unbridled appetite or beastliness boiling up from within or as helpless before natural and economic forces, Dewey stoutly maintained that we were in the saddle, that there was more day to dawn, that, as in Emerson and Whitman, this very moment was as full of possibility as any antecedent moment.

An ahistorical attitude such as this is not simply a concomitant of individualism; they mutually entail each other. It is precisely the individual who experiences the sufficiency of the present moment, incorporating or rolling up history as having a significance fully displayed in his own present vision. Again, it is individualism which grounds the American's view of his society as an object rather than a various or plural spectacle. The correspondingly universal view of society is held by those who give imaginative ascendancy to commercial relationships.

Dewey's passionate devotion to the democratic ideal led him to pursue an articulation between the Emersonian individual and a democratic order which might be worked for right now. Emerson's repeated assurance that "we shall meet again on a higher platform" required a supplement. Dewey set about building the "platform," a method for securing a common vision. He did not alter Emerson's individual; what he altered was the conception of the means available to him to achieve a union with his fellows. Viewed from the outside, the two men's accounts of our humanity are alike, equally fantastic in their denial of the primary significance of our sexuality, our propensity to conflict—both within and with others (and hence of our capacity to resolve conflict as well)—and the stubborn facts of instituted power within any given society. Both believed conflict and power would vanish in the common awareness of wholly attainable ideals. Putting it positively, they hoped everybody could be transformed through a shared perception of universal conditions.

Three sentences from *Democracy and Education* illustrate the assumption Dewey shared with Emerson: "This common understanding of the means and ends of action is the essence of social control. It is indirect, or emotional and intellectual, not direct or personal. Moreover it is intrinsic to the disposition of the person, not external and coercive."[3] These sentences are fairly staggering, whether read in context or out. Dewey is followed easily enough if we understand him to say that society does not function by giving orders all day long; that people do what they are expected to do because it is their impulse to do what is expected of them. When we ask, however, whether this is indeed the result of something "intrinsic" which is at the same time a "common understanding," we may well feel that the sentences bridge a chasm with a formula. Dewey has fantasized a tie between individuals and groups; there is no such magical consonance between self and society, nor do these terms refer to any imaginable psychic organization in which such transactions can take place. These are drastically edited or mutilated conceptions of both individuals and groups. Dewey's notion of communication as a literal making common of the information possessed by two or more people can be realized only within a system as impersonal as that of a computer. All political philosophy could be inserted between what is said to be "intrinsic" in a particular mind and what is said to be a "common understanding," and the gap would still remain largely open. In such flat and determinedly innocent sentences, couched in a prose meant to be widely available to teachers, we hear the nineteenth-century echoes that lead us to look back to Dewey's earlier work. Both Emerson and Whitman had insisted that our ties to others must be those created by "indirection," by our common apprehension of things, which simply cancels the often harsh encounters of alien wills, groups, and interests.

We are accustomed to think of Dewey in connection with a scientific positivism current in the 1920s that, we have been told, was actually a mask for power, for covert economic domination. But the early Dewey, who explicitly disavowed Comte's positivism, is working in a quite different American vein, in which the connection of the individual with his inward vision operates as a sufficient guarantee of reality. Such a persistent effort to view the world solely from one's own perspective precludes a full recognition of human others; it leads ultimately to an emphasis on what can be universally apprehended, like the periodic table of elements. This is true whether you try to possess the whole in vision or simply see it as an order which you as an individual can profit by. In this formal sense, a John D. Rockefeller who perceives the possibility of using rebates from the railways in order to organize an oil trust and an Emerson are alike; they have both seen the world as an impersonal order by seeing it as an object for the self that is susceptible to definition and, in Rockefeller's case, manipulation. This is an American phenomenon; not every social world seems open to apprehension as a whole. In France or England it would have been impossible during the nineteenth century to be either a Rockefeller or an Emerson. One would have had to reckon, like the hero of a *bildungsroman*, with a plurality of persons and institutions and to choose a path in relation to them.

To be an individualist in this sense is distinct of course from being a crank or an eccentric: it is to encounter the object of your experience as a whole, whether for the purposes of vision or of acquisition. What looks like a paradox in Emerson is not, as he saw it, a paradox at all. To repeat a passage from Emerson: "Then it seems to be true that the more exclusively ⟨individual⟩ idiosyncratic a man is, the more general & infinite he is, which though it may not be a very intelligible expression ⟨is⟩ means I hope something intelligible."[4] Or, as Dewey put it in an ambitious early essay over half a century later: "Transcendentalism was incomplete till it recognized that the universal content can be realized only in an individual bearer."[5] Dewey is referring not to what is called transcendentalism in this country but to the whole German tradition from Kant to Hegel and beyond, and he is revising it in the Emersonian mode. In this essay of 1886, "Psychology as Philosophic Method," he wrote what Emerson was too consistently inconsistent to write, a sketch for an Emersonian metaphysics. Dewey's commentators have distorted the whole question of Dewey's primary focus in the eighties and nineties of the last century. They speak of the first important phase of his development as Hegelian, as qualified by his attachment to the idea of the universal mind, and simply fail to note that "mind" had to have an "individual bearer"—precisely the Emersonian position.

Again, his commentators use philosophic vocabularies that simply do not engage the area of Dewey's most personal concern in these years: his passionate absorption in the idea of democracy, which he held to with religious fervor. If the individual could be brought into communion with society without losing his unique access to the universal, Dewey's problem would be solved. What Dewey got from Hegel in the years following 1886 was, as he saw it, continuous with what he got from Darwin. To enable the "individual bearer" to join his fellows, he needed a conception of a social process in which the bearer figured. Hegel offered an account of society in which a developing truth was immanent, and for

Dewey this development had a basis in the plasticity of our biological endowment that he found in Darwin. This movement toward union was adumbrated in his favorite Emerson essays, but the idea of a developing and self-correcting body of scientific inquirers offered what seemed to him a more satisfactory model for tying individuals together in a society. Each individual would have access to a developing body of truth rather than to that static vision of the whole that Emerson frequently fell back on. Instead of being the puppet of universal mind, as in Hegel, each citizen would be potentially a possessor of all that was known and knowable.

Dewey hoped for individuals who would be both free and capable of recognizing and acting on a shared perception of reality. In his book on the seventeenth-century philosopher Leibniz (1888), Dewey describes Leibniz's monads as "a true democracy, in which each citizen has sovereignty."[6] How could Dewey bring about such a democracy in the United States? The monads, whose form is individual and whose content is universal (that is, each is a recapitulation of the whole), together with the simpler conception of the individual in the elder Henry James—in which the form is once again particular, the content incipiently universal—are far more relevant to Dewey's work in the 1890s than is Hegel. Dewey's ambitious essay of 1886 had as its core the sentence already quoted: "Transcendentalism was incomplete until it recognized that the universal consciousness can be realized only in an individual bearer." It provoked a withering retort from William James's English correspondent, Shadworth Hodgson, who, replying in the same British journal, *Mind*, called Dewey's position "a shortcut indeed to the Deification of the individual."[7] (This charge recalls Orestes Brownson's assertion that Emerson had multiplied psychological Christs.)[8] Dewey was stung and shaken, as his later work reveals. Hodgson had no sense of the cultural extremity that Dewey's subscription to democracy imposed on him—the unsolved Emersonian problem of the union of the citizens—nor did his fellow Americans, William James or George Santayana. A brief account of Dewey's career helps us to see how different his situation was from theirs.

The young Dewey was exceedingly able; he could master philosophic systems with ease and had an obvious gift for philosophic exposition and a prose often far more lucid than that of his later work. Nonetheless, beside the more sophisticated William James and Santayana, Dewey must be described as having a tin ear, both for the distinctive qualities of things and for the ways of language. He was, and remained, a provincial, yet a peculiarly representative one. At the same time he had a fire in his belly—the appetite to prevail. And how much more he had seen of the United States than James or Santayana! Dewey had grown up and been educated in Burlington, Vermont. He taught high school in Oil City, Pennsylvania, attended graduate school at Johns Hopkins, and subsequently taught philosophy at Michigan. Thereafter he moved to Chicago, as professor of pedagogy as well as philosophy, and there he encountered, in the university, at Jane Addams's Hull House, and in the city's schools, the problems of creating a democracy in urban America. He finally settled at Columbia, where he taught until 1930. Dewey had an extraordinary insight into the generic situation of the intellectual heirs of Emerson's period, but he was, as Neil Coughlan has shrewdly noted, simply unaware of the "richness and density" of the social and intellectual life led by his English contemporaries.[9] No American could call him a hick, but a cultivated European would have found him ineradicably provincial.

Unlike William James and Santayana, whose upbringings

had fostered a measure of detachment from a country undergoing an industrial transformation, with all its consequences for the democracy, Dewey seemed to feel that the whole country was in some way his affair. It was his inner imperative that American reality be brought into accord with the democratic vision. He adopted the ways of the professors—and it should be noted that he was a member of the first generation that profited fully by the founding of actual universities across the country. He tried, within the terms exacted by his professorial status, to fight for the people at large; he denounced economic tyranny and said repeatedly that our hopes lay with the nascent democracy. Santayana's transplantation to another culture must have seemed inconceivable to Dewey. Precisely because he was so caught up in his time and place (he even found a way to be a Christian, a social gospeler, as late as the 1890s), his impulse to implant his demanding dream in the minds of his fellow citizens and his success in doing so make him representative of an important strain in the national consciousness.

During the late 1880s and the 1890s, that is to say his late twenties and his thirties, Dewey put most of his energies into texts and course outlines in psychology and ethics. He emphasized these over the metaphysics and logic that preoccupied his contemporaries because, as he put it, "Psychology is the democratic movement come to consciousness."[10] In other words, those whom Melville had called "sovereign kings" had to become aware of the nature of their responsibility in a democracy. In an encyclopedia contribution of 1894 Dewey says that Hegel had shifted the basis of morality from Kant's abstract reason to the "unified life of society," and Dewey meant to do nothing less.[11] What has been ignored is that what Dewey had on hand when he set about trying to unite us was not a complex image of society derived from

Hegel or anyone else; it was a stock of Emersonian individuals. His society would be a far cry from Hegel's, since it looked toward a future in which individuals had assumed the full burden that fell upon them with the disappearance of every external authority.

Dewey paid a heavy price to bring about the union of Emersonian individuals. His individuals had extraordinary powers as communicators and joint actors with their fellows; they shared a "common understanding" of such impersonal, ahistorical concerns as technology. But, unlike Emerson's, they had no consciousness of a struggle with a recurring inner division in the self. Emerson (in this respect still a Christian) had acknowledged an internal difficulty in sustaining his vision of things; Dewey's individual bearer had none. He had to grant, as Dewey often put it in the 1890s, that he was "partial" or "incomplete"; but he need not admit, as Emerson so often did, that he had a built-in doubleness, that there was an abiding encounter between his lesser worldly ego and the grand ego of his widest vision. Dewey was apparently able to suppress the relationships that occupied Emerson's lesser ego.

The essay that most conveniently exhibits the consequences of Dewey's willingness to sacrifice distinctive ties to human others, to wife, to child, to neighbor, is called, somewhat misleadingly, "The Significance of the Problem of Knowledge," published in 1897.[12] It seems to foretell an imminent secular apocalypse. Like most of Dewey's uses of history, it tacitly assumes that we have now overcome what was limiting about the past; history for Dewey is generally an account of the resolution of false dualisms that keep us from plunging into that ongoing wave of experience within which we are—or are just about to be—immersed. Although ostensibly about epistemology, the essay actually deals with epistemology as symptomatic of a struggle between conservative rationalists and progressive empiricists, now happily resolved. Dewey begins by telling us that philosophy had been born in Greece when "the time of direct and therefore unconscious union with corporate life, finding there stimuli, codes, and values, has departed." Dewey says this led to Socrates' practical questions about the proper goals of life, but unfortunately these practical concerns gave way to the work of theoreticians. Theory was split off from practice, and under the Roman Empire and the medieval church knowledge was purveyed exclusively by external authority. When, during the Renaissance, the individual arose, he had to take matters into his own hands. In the passages that follow, Dewey tells how the individual became qualified to cope with this new and overwhelming burden, which is to say, how democracy became possible.

> The entire problem of medieval philosophy is that of absorption, of assimilation. The result was the creation of the individual. Hence the problem of modern life is that of reconstruction, reform, reorganization. The entire content of experience needs to be passed through the alembic of individual agency and realization. The individual is to be the bearer of civilization; but this involves a remaking of the civilization which he bears. Thus we have the dual question: How can the individual become the organ of corporate action? How can he make over the truth authoritatively embodied in institutions of church and state into frank, healthy and direct expression of the simple act of free living? On the other hand how can civilization preserve its own integral value and import when subordinated to the agency of the individual instead of exercising supreme sway over him?

After noting that epistemology cannot provide the method the individual requires for doing what he must now do, Dewey continues:

> Admitting that the practical problem of modern life is the maintenance of the spiritual values of civilization, through the medium of the insight and decision of the individual, the problem is foredoomed to futile failure save as the individual in performing his task can work with a definite and controllable tool. This tool is science.

Science, it is important to note, comes on stage as enabling the creation of a community composed of those I have called, using Melville's term, "sovereign kings."

> Given the freed individual, who feels called upon to create a new heaven and a new earth, and who feels himself gifted with the power to perform the task to which he is called:—and the demand for science, for a method of discovering and verifying truth becomes imperious. The individual is henceforth to supply control, law, and not simply stimulation and initiation. What does this mean but that instead of any longer receiving or assimilating truth he is now to search for and create it? Having no longer the truth imposed by authority to rely upon, there is no recourse save to secure the authority of truth.

The self-corrective method of Charles Sanders Peirce's community of scientific investigators, who had to answer to each other for the results they published, has been widened and distorted to serve the democracy. Dewey uses that method as a sort of social cement: since the results of inquiry will be apparent to all, all will be bound by those results. Of course this assertion becomes far more sophisticated later, in Dewey's new logic of inquiry, which took its first form in the *Studies in Logical Theory* of 1903. Yet the initial assertion stands: democracy must depend on a common method of knowing and of testing its knowledge; citizens are to be associated not by what grows out of their shared lives and histories and the ideas and hopes that grow out of these but by a method of discovering what is here called "truth." History is as definitely transcended as it is in Emerson.

To focus exclusively on Dewey's shifting engagement with systems of thought is to lose any sense of the urgency of his situation in the culture. His principal shift of emphasis must be described in terms that relate him to that situation. In order to unite the individual with a hoped-for community, Dewey had to give a new content to the "Absolute" to which the individual bearer of the 1886 essay "Psychology as Philosophic Method" had been tied; by which, in fact, he had been constituted. In this essay we are told that to know *as* he knew was the only way to know and that he was the only authority. As Dewey put it, "But that the universe has no existence except as absolutely realized in an individual, that is, except as self-consciousness, is precisely the result of philosophy, and can therefore be no objection to such a consideration of the universe: in fact, such a statement only amounts to saying that psychology considers the universe as it really is."[13] No wonder Hodgson had charged Dewey with deifying the individual!

Dewey is carrying forward both Emerson's assertion of self-reliance *and* the access to universal truth that ultimately justifies self-reliance. To say this is an idealist position once held by a man who became a pragmatist or instrumentalist begs the important question. Dewey's use of the term "psychology," which looks so strange to us, is warning enough that what he wants is a way of tying Emersonian man to his fellows, to the democracy, and this is why he must substitute science and a self-corrective method of finding truth for the absolute. Dewey's own account of this shift is quite as external and misleading as those of his commentators.[14] But we can get a sense of what happened by juxtaposing the essay of 1886, "Psychology as Philosophic Method," which had provoked Hodgson to scold him for deifying individuals, with the essay "Psychology and the Philosophic Method" published thirteen years later, in 1899. Here Dewey responds unmistakably to Hodgson's attack. Referring to an earlier historical period in which all authority was imposed on the individual from without and the individual as such was subject to a "low valuation," Dewey goes on:

> As against all this, the assertion is ventured that psychology, supplying us with knowledge of the behavior of experience, is a conception of democracy. Its postulate is that since experience fulfills itself in individuals, since it administers itself through their instrumentality, the account of the course and method of this achievement is a significant and indispensable affair.
>
> Democracy is possible only because of a change in intellectual conditions. It implies tools for getting at truth in detail, and day by day, as we go along. Only such possession justifies the surrender of fixed, all-embracing principles to which, as universals, all particulars and individuals are subject for valuation and regulation. Without such possession, it is only the courage of the fool that would undertake the venture to which democracy has committed itself—the ordering of life in response to the needs of the moment in accordance with

> the ascertained truth of the moment. Modern life involves the deification of the here and the now; of the specific, the particular, the unique, that which happens once and has no measure of value save such as it brings with itself. Such deification is monstrous fetishism, unless the deity be there; unless the universal lives, moves, and has its being in experience as individualized.[15]

The "tools for getting at truth in detail" (the method of science) enable Dewey to say in effect, "Take that, Shadworth Hodgson!" Dewey has replaced his earlier version of the universal with the moving front of perennially reconstructed vision that science makes possible. Immersed in this sense of things, we can all apprehend reality in the same way.

Dewey has a much feebler grasp of human actuality than Emerson, who had celebrated the moment of experience but remained aware of an element in himself, a petty ego, that militated against the total coherence he tried for. But Dewey was never to have any way of describing internal struggle. The following passages from his ethical writings of the 1890s suggest how scoured of negations and limitations his individual was. He speaks of the emotion of anger as taking two forms: simple hostility against another person diminishes you by making you feel less "complete," but anger at a piece of meanness "serves to do away with that meanness and to brace the self."[16] Dewey goes on to make it plain that the effect on our inner kingdom rather than the effect on others is the basis for the judgment of an impulse: "*The completest possible interaction of an impulse with all other experiences, or the completest possible relation of an impulse to the whole self constitutes the predicate, or moral value, of an act.*"[17]

The criterion for the discrimination of right and wrong, he holds, is their effect on the interrelated experiences that make up the self; as in Emerson, we do not have to go outside or consult an external standard to make a judgment of what we have done. He writes:

> The basis for discriminating between "right" and wrong in the judgment is found in the fact that some acts tend to narrow the self, to introduce friction into it, to weaken its power, and in various ways to *disintegrate* it, while other acts tend to expand, invigorate, harmonize, and in general organize the self.[18]

What is primary for Dewey is the extension of our inner kingdom. One of his ways of describing our relation to society in these years is to say that this expansion of the individual is a fulfillment of the society's truly democratic self, what all would hope for when they came to see what democracy implied.

Dewey values the intimations in certain of Emerson's essays, in particular "Fate," "Compensation," and "Spiritual Laws"—intimations that Emerson shared his own sense of the self as growing, moving forward, and generating its ideals internally instead of putting them ahead of us as something forever unattainable. And Dewey finds the ethical position of the elder Henry James akin to Emerson's. He echoes the elder James when he writes, "The consciousness of goodness is the consciousness of a completely unified self. If the agent is thinking of his own glory, or credit, or moral worth, or improvement, he is by that fact *divided*; there is the deed to be performed and the reflection of it into himself." What Dewey is saying is that to enter into the moving wave of continually reconstructed vision we have to be internally coherent to a degree that Emerson himself would have found beyond belief. Dewey's attempt to incorporate the practical affairs of life *within* the visionary's possession of the "universal" led to the most extravagant and most nationally influential of his fantasies, his conception of the school. This was the work of his Chicago years.

It was preceded by Dewey's curious involvement with Franklin Ford, which occurred while he was still at the University of Michigan. Dewey found a way to diffuse awareness of the fashion in which we were all joined together: the thing could be done by publishing a newspaper! Ford, who, as a journalist, was dazzled by the possibility that a wealth of information about the workings of the economy could be digested and presented to the public in such transparent form that everyone would see just how the interests of the people at large were being betrayed, got Dewey to agree to edit such a paper. Everyone would be able to see that the activities of pork packers, senators, and railway barons composed a pattern inimical to the welfare of the people. As some might have put it in 1970, a complete and totally persuasive democratic counterculture was possible. The newspaper, as Dewey wrote William James, would be the only organ of the society with an unbiased interest in the common welfare and, at the same time, a commodity indispensable to the majority; it would inevitably make money.[19]

Historians of ideas, or of pragmatism itself, who treat Dewey's career as if its significance depended wholly on his handling of recognized philosophic issues, or who neglect the way in which his positions in philosophy or educational theory were overdetermined by emotional needs that corresponded to socially diffused needs, can make little of the Franklin Ford episode or of Dewey's involvement in the culture in general. The Ford scheme aroused Dewey's intense and quasi-religious sense of his mission to the democracy. All the readers of his newspaper would simultaneously become aware, each on his own hook yet all together, of the truth about the society at large. Each a monad, then—the form individual, the content universal! But Ford was an odd chap; perhaps the glitter in his eye warned Dewey. After actually announcing publication, Dewey drew back, and the matter was silently dropped.

It was at Chicago that Dewey founded the Laboratory School. What Dewey asks of the school, as George E. Axtelle, one of his editors, remarks, is incredible. As we might put it now, a space station frees us from gravity; Dewey's school is an earth station—freed from the effects of sexual determination, externally imposed authority, "economic stress," class and status, and every form of conflict—yet all the information children need for growth is said to penetrate the walls. In *The School and Society*, speaking of what happens to the child's imagination of the world when studying the beginnings of life on earth, he remarks:

> Where we now see only the outward doing and the outward product, there, behind all visible results, is the readjustment of mental attitude, the enlarged and sympathetic vision, the sense of growing power, and the willing ability to identify both insight and capacity with the interests of the world and man. . . . When nature and society can live in the schoolroom, when the forms and tools of learning are subordinated to the substance of experience, then shall there be an opportunity for this identification, and culture shall be the democratic password.[20]

For Dewey the schools became the cutting edge of democratic advance and the primary means of social reform. That he got so many people to share this fantasy is one of the most interesting clues we have about recent cultural history. "In education," Dewey writes,

> meet the three most powerful motives of human activity. . . . Copartnership of these three motives, of affection [he means of course for children], of social growth, and of scientific inquiry—must prove as nearly irresistible as anything human when they are once united. And, above all else, recognition of the spiritual basis of democracy, the efficacy and responsibility of freed intelligence is necessary to secure this union.[21]

No attempt is made here to assess the meaning of the public response to the philosopher's educational writings or to try to say in what ways the schools that sprang up in Dewey's wake were little substitute worlds built with taxes. But it is clear that he had once more envisioned such a world—as he had in the case of the abortive newspaper project—had envisioned, that is, a scene in which individuals could be united to other individuals through their grasp of something universal.

John Dewey's American democrat was originally conceived as an answer to the problem Emerson had set: that of making a democracy of individuals whose solitary and unlimited visions had guaranteed their identity. If we are properly naive, we ask: "But won't their visions overlap if we bring them all together?" And Dewey in effect replies: "I have found an all-purpose vision in the method of science; everybody can use it; it is universal!" A child sitting in the classroom is offered an ever-widening dominion—mastery of the way things go in nature—on the condition that we all share the same light. A phrase of Whitman's helps us to understand Dewey's hope. Whitman says that one eyesight does not "countervail" another eyesight; we may all possess the world in vision without interfering with each other.[22]

But the major books of Dewey's later career do not succeed in preserving the individual bearer, who becomes all bearer and loses all individuality. To read *Experience and Nature* is to be simultaneously aware of Dewey's mastery of technical philosophic issues and of a pervasive undersong, the tone of Faulkner's Benjy who is "trying to say."[23] Dewey tries to immerse us in an experiential continuum that is clearly a fantasy unrealizable at any time because it depends upon ironing out all the differences between those who are to be immersed in it. They are abstract people who all receive the same messages rather than people with histories like ourselves. Dewey in fact says that to conceive of experience one need not posit a self at all.

Yet this is the Dewey who in 1938 headed the commission to investigate the fabricated charges preferred against Leon Trotsky at the Moscow trials and who had a long and honorable record as a scrapper for the rights of citizens of the democracy. He had split his Emerson, yet he did not discard either the man with access to the universal or the individual as citizen. Horace M. Kallen, a longtime associate of Dewey, describes this split in an admirable essay in which he shows that Dewey's holistic, perhaps even "transcendental" version of existence simply ran alongside his persistent assertion of the indispensable worth of the individual.[24] This rather empty assertion represented his fidelity to the attempt to realize the democracy he had earlier undertaken.

Dewey's present obscurity is, in one important respect, testimony to his success. People are disinclined to admit that anyone has helped them to see what now looks like common sense. Dewey's vision of a shared and continuously reconstructed existential continuum was adramatic, ahistorical—

asserted a world more continuous in its character than the species has ever known or will know—but it did, as Richard Rorty insists, help to dispel the kind of thought which saw mind as a mirror of the world.[25] Yet if we ask who is ready to share knowledge and to reconstruct it, to acknowledge our immersion in experience while stilling the voices from his past, and to be born as a fresh register of the needs of the moment, the whole vision fades.

To turn to Henry James, widely considered the first of our modernists in literature, who nonetheless found an enclosing armature in his father's and Emerson's sense of individual existence, is to confront a figure who seems both to come from an earlier time and to embrace a later one than John Dewey. Dewey's focus on practices which might give reality to democracy, on dealing with experience as it came, seems altogether apart from James, who offers no standpoint from which change in human behavior can be estimated—whose image of our humanity was founded on the unending struggle between those who took and those who gave.

Both for scholars and for the wider public, Henry James began to come into his own after 1943, the centennial of his birth. If, as I believe, James has had a cultural function, we can tell approximately when he assumed it. The writer who is discussed in Frederick Dupee's collection of critical essays on James written before 1945 had, generally speaking, been regarded as one interesting novelist among others.[26] It was in the decade following the mid-1940s that he enjoyed a distinct position that set him apart and attracted a wider audience. He was often spoken of as the artist prized by other artists, although this did not of course explain the vogue that led to the reprinting of so many of his works and the absorbed reading they frequently got from those who had no interest in the character of James's innovations in fictional technique.

Did James answer a need felt by his readers at the time, and, if so, what was it? Assuming that the novels, as Lionel Trilling once put it, read us—assuming, that is, that James supplied something we badly wanted—what clues about us does this offer?

My most general response is that James shifted the focus of the novelist's concern from the question, what is to be known about the world in which we live? to the question, what are the highest capacities of the knower of that world? We may put it that the novel, which in the nineteenth century had been the great avenue leading toward life in society, was in the work of Henry James made to serve needs that may fairly be called Emersonian. The demands Emerson had answered for himself and for others were felt with a special intensity after the Second World War. Art might provide what Emerson had promised, a sense of the infinitude of every man,[27] a sense of things that was at once general and coherent yet clearly removed from a public scene that had opened abysses of horror. One didn't escape to James—one never of course escapes from one's needs or desires—rather we should put it that James animated and enlivened a space one had already occupied. In an introduction to a collection of James's stories published in 1950, I tried to account for the appetite for his fiction.

> We are in fact hungrier than we acknowledge; hungry to the point of indiscriminate excess, for the substance of the moral life. What would it be like so to act that each thought, each gesture, floated on the tide of passionate conviction; that the very shapes and colors of our day were judged and assigned a place in the measure that they contributed to our unique yet communicable sense of the world? The texture of the prose of Henry

James answers this question. It is the result of just such passionate absorption and conviction.[28]

There is a flavor of the 1950s about the phrase "the substance of the moral life"; yet I can recover its meaning easily enough. What I was saying was, in a particular context, very familiar, and is so today. I was saying that James was playing a role in American life much like that of Emerson, who had assured us that to recognize our own powers was to find ourselves articulated with a universe that was designed to greet and confirm those powers. In speaking of "indiscriminate excess" I was referring to the heavy cost to our sense of the variousness and complexity of our ties to other people which indulgence in such an extrasocial appetite involved. I was in fact running against the view then current that art and politics were to be sharply separated and was suggesting that the experience of reading James provided emotional returns not available in a world fragmented by Hitler and Stalin. James offered us a satisfyingly complete perception of his fictional scene; it was exhilarating, a liberation from a crippling social scene, yet it was suffused with complication and intensity. What showed in his fictions was the qualities exhibited by individual consciousness—just as in Emerson and the Whitman of the first two editions of *Leaves of Grass* what counted was the range of one's perception or vision. Like Emerson's nature, James's social world was open to the inclusive grasp of consciousness; what counted in it was *how* one saw.

But there was a highly engaging difference. Emerson invited emulation but not participation; in James the reader participated in a widening process of perception and discrimination. Within the fictional situation James had defined, principle shone ever more clearly through appearance. Whether you won or lost in worldly terms was inconsequential; you came to know the imagined situation with the completeness of an ideal Emersonian vision. We may even surmise that James's art became a stand-in for what, in the period when many cultivated Americans were entranced by the Soviet Union, they had called "politics." The actuality of politics was, for many of these people, hardly in question. For the group of readers I am positing, the Stalinism born of the depression was not so much a politics as a desperate grab for a picture of the world that would satisfy the Emersonian demand for a complete imaginative possession of things. The Soviet Union was not a political phenomenon for such Americans; it was the objective complement of their need for the totality of vision that characterized American individualism. This demand overrode the distinction between public and private worlds, a distinction that, as I shall try to show, disappears in the fiction of Henry James.

How, and with what modulations, interferences, quickenings, or delays of pace, one took things in: this was the activity James registered, to our delight. Ian Watt's explication of the first paragraph of *The Ambassadors* catches this perfectly.[29] The moral possibilities of this use of the activity of centers of consciousness opened toward Emerson rather than Balzac. In Balzac what all Paris is at the moment pursuing, scorning, proclaiming is felt with the force of a blow. Everyone is immersed in the social medium. In James the individual command of the scene is all. Authoritative judgment within the circle of awareness stems from the perceiver who is seen to prevail over others. Whatever all Paris or London does is of no intrinsic interest, effect, or worth. It is shared or ossified insight from the past, dead thought. What crowds think or feel is mere psychic weather for the fully aware; they must navigate through it. Milly Theale's sense, in James's novel *The Wings of the Dove*, that the copyists in the National Gallery are living underwater is prototypical; they are immersed in a world in which things are merely reproduced or exchanged.[30]

The focus on the quest for awareness in James's fiction sets up a relation to the reader that will help us to understand how we have employed him and how he serves to reveal our interests and needs, in short, how he has read us. In James the novel answers Emerson's requirements.

Had the Emerson who found himself cheated by fictions like *Quentin Durward* been able to read James's novel *The Ambassadors* he would have had no ground for complaint. In James the gains accrue to the reader rather than to the lovers in the tale. Our participation in a widening circle of awareness is direct; through that participation we confirm our powers, and when we have finished we are in possession of an enclosed world in which what we have seen and how we have seen it take precedence over the coupling of boys and girls and the possession of the money. If this were not so, other stories might loom on the horizon of this one; our consciousness would be wholly subservient to the daily scene that occupies what Emerson called his lesser ego. What we get instead is assured possession, a full consciousness of the whole situation, something that may be compared to the totalizing quality of one of Lévi-Strauss's accounts of a body of myth. We realize the claims of Emerson's grand ego. Of course what we grasp through Strether in *The Ambassadors* is less than the whole. Every center of consciousness within James's fiction is a deliberately circumscribed lesser author and must know less, and in more restricted modes, than James himself. But the breach Emerson felt between Scott's novel and himself is, in a work such as *The Ambassadors*, almost closed. James's novel is not about events or fatally separate others; it is about the process of taking possession of the world constituted by James's situation.

But I have so far left out something that distinguishes James from the unqualified visionary of Emerson's sort. Emerson finds us all endowed with consciousness to begin with; but in James it is achieved, or, more accurately, realized, when a subscription to love and creativity supplants our initial self-centeredness. Laurence Holland called this sacrifice of personal claims on the world the "expense" of vision.[31] Theodora Bosanquet, James's amanuensis, in characterizing James's sense of the human world as making a division between the "children of light" and the "creatures of prey," made an omission that we can supply from Holland: one must abandon self to become a child of light. The encounter of those who seek awareness and the greedy is, then, found within individuals, as well as in the society at large, because the division is, at least originally, present in each of us. Characters of these two kinds have different ways of experiencing the fictional worlds James creates.

Because Henry James renders the way a character construes experience, there is a temptation to find a likeness or an identity between the way James conceives experience and the way his brother William does. This turns out to be fundamentally misleading. For William James personal existence, the unique inwardness he describes in *The Varieties of Religious Experience*, is the most important datum of all. He speaks of the "darker, blinder strata of character" as the "only places in the world in which we catch real fact in the making, and directly perceive how events happen, and how work is actually done."[32] For the philosopher, our distinctive personal qualities are very nearly sufficient to explain what happens in human affairs; and this is wholly consonant with his emphasis on individual agency, on the will, and with his belief that novelty leaks into the universe in the persons of gifted individuals. But for the novelist and his father characters in fiction appear as grace notes on the limited scale defined by the generic human condition.

In Henry James's fiction, representations of distinctive personal being of the sort suggested by Ulysses, Falstaff, or Huck Finn are, with a few notable exceptions, absent. Such figures are intractable; they don't appear in the works of James that offer a unified vision because they are in themselves sources, proposals of human possibility obstinately unassimilable to a unified consciousness. Such a character as Kirilov in Feodor Dostoevski's *The Possessed*, whose plan to shoot himself in order to affirm himself sticks like a burr in the mind, would burst any formal mold James could contrive. A world into which such people erupt between center and periphery cannot be grasped as a whole. James's impatience with Dostoevski's novels, which he called "fluid puddings," is wholly explicable: if vision cannot penetrate everywhere, the edges waver, perspectives multiply, unleashed authors wander about and make claims to define the scene that clash or overlap.

James, however, assumes a dominion over his imagined scene as complete, lordly, and masterful as his conduct of his daily life. No foreign bodies intrude. He achieves this by becoming wholly conscious, first of all, of himself. To this extraordinary man the entire tract of what he has known seems wholly available for rendering, for statement. He expresses doubts, fears, uncertainties; yet it is hard to think of anyone who has set himself a more rigorous standard of coherence in every respect. The incapacity to be, as he put it in his unfinished autobiographical volume, "immersed or engaged," his withdrawal from action that would fatally engage him with others, results in a complete linguistic command of the scene.[33] He marshals the language as Napoleon marshaled armies, and as he does so it appears that the world abandoned as a scene for one's very own drama has become the world totally repossessed by an unfailing intelligence.

Those who were "immersed or engaged" were thereby narrowed and distorted, as James suggests in this sentence from *The Tragic Muse*: "If the affection that isolates and simplifies its object may be distinguished from the affection that seeks communications and contacts for it, Julia Dallow's was quite of the encircling, not to say the narrowing sort."[34] Encounters between these two loves define the human scene. All art, all speech, every aspect of manners are for James expressive either of the effort to widen consciousness or of the opposed effort to seize on its bearers or their goods as possessions. These encounters of the children of light with those who are materially, sexually, or aesthetically acquisitive and, not least important, those whose self-righteousness amounts to a moral acquisitiveness can only be indirect, because the two classes have wholly different desires. Nonetheless, works of fiction can represent an unqualified victory for those who try to widen consciousness over those who want and try for everything in the form of possessions.

In constructing his fictions James employed the energy of the acquisitive characters as an impelling force in his situations. Like the nakedly sexual and imperial desires of Goneril and Regan, which provoke the magnificent outbursts of Lear on the heath, these displayed energies are the inciting conditions of the transcendent triumphs of James's centers of consciousness. It is the imperious cravings of Julia Dallow, Kate Croy, Madame Merle, and Charlotte Stant, a company of the "immersed or engaged," that keep the action going.[35] They are actors in a melodramatic underplot who are regularly subsumed by an inclusive vision in which James and his reader share a triumph over the acquisitive in themselves and others. James, more effectually than any other American writer, assuages the fear of Americans that they are condemned to self-definition through possessions.

As I have noted, characters based on generic impulses, as James's are, cannot figure as individual sources or independent origins, as do Charles Dickens's Silas Wegg, Jane Austen's Elizabeth Bennett, or Gustave Flaubert's Emma Bovary, each qualified by a distinctive construction of the world, each in movement in a public world shared by others more or less distinctive. Another consequence follows: the fiction of James does not simply abolish character as a source; it also abolishes the distinction between the public and the private world. This amounts to saying that his characters have no distinctive inner life. The term "psychological novel" is hardly applicable to those of James. The novelist's characters are inhabited by the situation in which they move; as on the Elizabethan stage, they have a recess upstage in which they may reflect on that situation, and they encounter the other characters on the apron, but it is the constituted situation that bounds them both within and without. In this "melodramatist," as Jacques Barzun called him,[36] the grand ego of the perceiver encounters the lesser egos of those who follow everyday pursuits, who are immersed or engaged with other persons in the pursuit of wealth and status.

The James I have been describing is the writer of works now treated as central by his admirers: *The Ambassadors, The Wings of the Dove, The Golden Bowl,* "The Jolly Corner," and "The Beast in the Jungle"—all works that cater to Emersonian impulses. But he is also the author of *The Bostonians,* a novel that clearly and fully belies everything I have been saying about his work. Moreover, *The Princess Casamassima, The Tragic Muse,* and some works with American scenes, such as *Washington Square*, seem to a greater or lesser extent to invoke the world as it is seen in more conventional novels.

Because *The Bostonians* is most unlike the works I have named that are nowadays treated as central, I shall try to characterize its differing qualities. In this novel James conforms to the conventions about character and the relation between public and private worlds that inform most nineteenth-century novels. What clearly distinguishes *The Bostonians* and best accounts for its occurrence among James's works is that it grows out of a world James came to know as a member of his family. It was only as a citizen of the James family that the writer was ever to know a social world from within outward. Within the family he was in fact immersed or engaged; was inescapably a character himself; and was defined and defined others through loyalty, affection, and the free and ironic social play of family discourse, which is so copiously illustrated in F. O. Matthiessen's *James Family* and R. W. B. Lewis's *The Jameses: A Family History*. In this novel James comes astonishingly close to rendering the difficulties and ambivalences that attend the attainment of a sense of selfhood, which the family at once nourishes and threatens. *The Bostonians* also employs assumptions about the culture that are incorporated in the fiction of its day, notably in the treatment of its hero and heroine, Basil Ransom and Verena Tarrant. This presumption of the existence of a public world whose manners and artistic conventions are antecedently known by both the reader and the author deprives James of that total authority over the scene which is characteristic of the late works. To distance himself—and also, we may suspect, to guard himself—James uses irony in *The Bostonians*. Because the reader shares an awareness of the presented scene with the writer, he is prepared to see the foible or contradiction the irony enforces.

This is in sharp contrast with the works in which almost nothing may be assumed by the reader. The reader's participation in the widening process of vision characteristic of the late works—say, with Densher in *The Wings of the Dove* or with Strether in *The Ambassadors*—is not found in *The Bostonians*, in which the reader and author share a relation to a public world; the author's handling of character and action is therefore open to our scrutiny, and characters may appear as sources, independent perspectives on a common scene. Fine Dickensian oddities crop up on the firm ground created by a shared public world; in *The Bostonians* we have Selah Tarrant, Mrs. Farrinder, Doctor Prance, and so on, each a terminal effect, a separable delight for the reader, and, however modestly, a source. The hero is a noble defeated Southerner charged with a wholly conventional masculine energy, and we have as heroine a femininely gifted yet, in accordance with convention, deliciously passive Verena. It is a fictional scene Marx and Freud would find recognizable because it employs social class and inward psychic conflict.

The most startling thing in the book to people who have read only James's late novels is Olive Chancellor, a character almost unique in James because she is endowed with an inner life. Olive finds it difficult to live with herself. She is beset by her scruples, agonized taste, the pull of family pieties, her alternations of impetuosity and regret, her conscience. She is not one of James's "supersubtle fry," as he called the exquisitely aware, but a woman in a fix. She makes us sweat with sympathy, and she provides no Emersonian balm.

In short, *The Bostonians* has a public world set off from private worlds, has a character harried from within as well as from without, and is held at a certain remove from the writer and his readers by its ironic tone. Because there is no privileged center of awareness, we are not allowed to participate in the active pursuit of knowledge; we are readers of a story, that is, inhabitants of a social world, fictive though it is. *The Bostonians* does not serve the desire for disengagement from society I call Emersonian, a desire felt by Americans long before the discovery that Henry James gave it a scene and a voice. That appetite was satisfied by the late works I have named. These supply the only simulacrum of action on a social scene that remains available to readers in their detached state; that is, a focus on an individual vision rather than a socially environed sense of things.

But I have not up to this point filled in the last arc of my argument. Why should Americans wish to withdraw from society and from stories that plunk them down on a social scene? Numerically speaking, most of them did not express any such desire; but I have assumed all along that the turn to James on the part of the most literate among them has a wider significance. I have already hinted at my answer. The triumph of consciousness in Henry James is a triumph over acquisitiveness, over the world suffused by the money network. The kind of individualism apparent in Emerson, Thoreau, and Whitman had the same base; one withdrew from a world dominated by the money network in order to possess it in vision. James's late fictions constitute a series of legends in which we can participate in such a process. James's father provided him with the essential point here. We did not begin, as in Emerson, with the power to seize the world as our oyster; we set out with the desire to grab things for ourselves; only after we have surrendered our tainted social selves can we possess the world in love.

Three commentators have undertaken to give James a place in the history of American or of western culture so often denied him by his critics. The three books I have in mind are Laurence Holland's *The Expense of Vision*, Leo Bersani's *A Future for Astyanax: Character and Desire in Literature*, and Stephen Donadio's *Nietzsche, Henry James and the Artistic Will*. These three books differ in tone and method, but they share the presumption that James is a writer whose engagement in important movements of western thought and feeling cannot be questioned. All three have penetrating things to say about the nature of his artistic accomplishment; but they are not, as in so much of what is written about the novelist, confined to a universe of discourse created by James himself. In both Bersani and Donadio, James is made to count in our inquiry into the western past.

Leo Bersani finds in James examples of the possibility of smashing what he considers the stifling and repressive rigidities of the conception of "character" in literature, thus freeing desire through art. Bersani's work clearly derives from those French thinkers who stress the power of language to enforce structures of social domination. The approach he employs is, however, that of a critic concerned with the form and effect of particular works. Although I find Bersani much too insistently apocalyptic, he is surely right when he says that James's work dissolves traditional conceptions of character.

Stephen Donadio, who has no such impulse to wholesale condemnation of the western past, gives a masterful account in his opening pages of the effort to come out of society that I have described as Emersonian. He writes of Emerson, Thoreau, and Henry James that they undertook, as he puts it, "to break out of the net of social relations and to experience an existence unmediated by social forms." He finds in James's successive experiments in form a parallel with the process of self-overcoming in Nietzsche. Although I feel that, unlike Nietzsche, James did reach a limit prescribed by his most general sense of things in *The Golden Bowl*, I can only concur with Donadio's conclusion that James's attempts at imaginative disengagement from his society justify a juxtaposition with those of Nietzsche.

Laurence Holland's *Expense of Vision* works out the completeness of James's commitment of his very being to the creation of literary forms, a process Holland details with great subtlety. He conceives of what James does as a sacrifice of every personal demand on the world, drawing his evidence of this large intention chiefly from the prefaces of the New York Edition. The antithesis between making personal claims and devoting oneself to selfless creation parallels the antithesis I had earlier described in *The American Henry James* (1957). In that book I conclude that the opposition between every form of selfishness and the love that expresses itself in creation is common to the novelist and his father. (Holland, however, denies that the elder James is involved.) The point I wish to stress here is that Holland finds that James assumed a broad cultural and political responsibility. He concludes that James's sacrifice of his selfhood was made in the effort to bring about quite specific transformations in the attitudes of his readers toward such institutions as capitalism and marriage.

Considered in isolation, the theses of these three books are startling: Bersani tells us that structures of domination mark not institutions alone but also the very conceptions of character. Holland tells us that James attempted nothing less than the remaking of attitudes toward western institutions by committing himself utterly to forms he hoped would transform them. And Donadio, working as a cultural historian, assures us that the imaginative enterprises of Nietzsche and Henry James are cognate, and are equally radical in their impulse to transcend the western past. If these three contentions seem startling, I would insist that they are no more so than what provoked them: the work of Henry James himself.

If it appears that we have long concealed from ourselves a measure of detachment from our culture in James that is much too great to be covered by the mantle of artistic detachment, it seems equally clear that certain familiar ideas in the criticism of James's work have also worked to conceal important aspects of his view of the human condition. The early criticism stressed the idea that James's characters go in for renunciation. This would certainly be true provided one looked at James's work from the point of view of the "immersed or engaged," which was that of novelistic convention as well. But what appears to be renunciation functions as a way of screening the fact that characters such as Densher and Strether do not really want what convention and James's melodramatic subplots suggest they ought to want. Their choices are made in behalf of their wider conception of the situation. They stand outside the world of the immersed or engaged to answer a demand for loving and creative comprehension of the whole scene akin to that of the author himself. To call this "renunciation" now seems about as plausible as Leon Edel's proposal that James, who had no least interest in marriage, *chose* not to marry.

A second critical position, still frequently employed, is that James is ambiguous. Those who take the conventionally novelistic character of *The Bostonians* as a standard call James's other novels ambiguous because they have a coherence of an unfamiliar kind; they present a world which can be fully grasped by a single consciousness instead of constituting an invitation to enjoy the fullness, variety, and inconsequence of the great feast of life.

Our problem with James is not his ambiguity but resistance to what he has done. Delighted, for example, by the very qualities in *The Golden Bowl* that prove it is removed from the plural social world, these critics have often set about showing that it is a conventional novel, or would be if James had not made certain errors or had not had certain lapses of taste, such as giving a favorable account of a millionaire. In fact *The Golden Bowl* gives Adam and Maggie Verver the apocalyptic job of registering the final triumph of consciousness over acquisitiveness, of sopping up the whole world of the immersed or engaged. Those who refuse to acknowledge this find refuge in the charge of ambiguity. I haven't plumbed James to his depths, but I don't think we have any more ground for thinking he fails of an exquisite coherence than we do in the case of Dante. I can think of nothing ambiguous in Henry James except *The Turn of the Screw*, which he deliberately designed as a trap for readers.

In the 1950s, when Americans embraced Henry James as the very figure of the artist, they were hardly aware that they were also granting themselves a holiday characteristic of their individualism from the constraints of society and history, a disaffiliation from communal life, and a fulfillment of their need to see the world as a field for the exercise of their powers, the scene of their total realization of themselves. What they got was a celebration of the power of individual vision, a vision, in William Troy's inspired phrase about James's work, of "the body of humanity stretched out in imagination in time and space."[37]

What we must now learn to see is that this farthest reach of American individualism, a visionary possession of the world, is only another possession after all and has not cracked the money firmament under which we walk. What I did not see in the 1950s was that Henry James, more than any other American writer, had, by exposing the connection between public and private possessiveness, revealed both the nature of our confinement and what I now see as the self-defeating character of visionary capitalism as well.[38] We shall not crack the money firmament or attain to the freedom we want until we see that such liberty always comes from the quality of our relations with other people, and in no other way.

Chapter 5

Detached Critics and Engaged Novelists

The preceding chapters describe the United States as a nation more vulnerable to the imaginative incursion of exchange and acquisition than other western nations and discuss representative figures who were led to counter the effects of that incursion in ways which mirrored it in their universality. Hawthorne and Melville were viewed as exceptions of differing sorts: the former was assured that the identities we achieved issued from the character of our ties to others rather than from an inclusive vision of things; the latter was seen as a brilliant diagnostician of the preoccupations of visionaries as well as the self-interested, who was himself isolated by erotic desires the society did not countenance. His experience of internal conflict saved him from abstraction but condemned him to see human encounters as posing the danger of a loss of identity; love and dominating power were equally threatening to his sense of himself.

What has up to this point been neglected is the possibility of opposing a money-saturated scene head on. Aside from becoming a money crank and proposing such schemes as attracted Ezra Pound, how is this to be done? Among literate Americans there was no scarcity of people who were intensely aware that there was a widely diffused weakening of classical props to identity, both moral and institutional, in a society in which counting was coming to count more and more heavily and in which having things or claims to things was attenuating ties to other people.

One way of avoiding direct criticism of such a society takes advantage of the opportunities presented by the appearance of art as a separate realm, with a history and a distinctiveness which enable one to think of it as, in Lionel Trilling's phrase, a "unitary thing." (It is a wholesale attack on this separation which has led to the current proclamation, equally misleading, that all art is expressive of politics.)

Before offering some cases of the attempt to give fictional form to frontal assaults on the money-saturated scene, I offer brief descriptions of the treatment of Emerson by writers who have assumed his centrality in ways which are both illuminating and, I believe, disturbingly incomplete because, while focusing on Emerson's achievement as an artist, they neglect what was of the highest importance to Emerson himself. They disregard the aspect of his time that he found compelling: the fragmentation of human aspiration which attended its immersion in getting and spending.

Emerson is the primary figure in our literature for Harold Bloom and Richard Poirier, and Stanley Cavell gives Thoreau and Emerson an unequaled importance among our thinkers. I hope to give Emerson a somewhat wider meaning in our own cultural history than he has if he is treated chiefly as an artist or a thinker. In doing so I am bound to make him seem less grand and resonant a figure simply because I see him as conditioned by his times. A sketch of the attitudes of

Bloom and Poirier will indicate how difficult it is to think of the Emerson who appears in their work as temporally conditioned.

Bloom, like Northrop Frye, conceives of literature on a millennial scale, although his emphasis falls on individual strugglers rather than on genres. Bloom's poets, theologians, and philosophers are both absorbed by and contending with their predecessors in an empyrean above the dusty roads of western history. For him Emerson is a writer who frames the possibilities open to his American successors, not the greatest of them but nonetheless inescapable. He is most "American" in his discovery of something beyond the self within the self. He thus founds what Bloom calls an "American religion" that he also finds—with expectable modifications—in Whitman, Robert Frost, Wallace Stevens, and Hart Crane.[1]

Bloom and Poirier approach one another in their attention to what Bloom, speaking of Emerson's prose, calls "breaking," "crossing," or achieving "Transition" and what Poirier thinks of as the activity of "turning and troping" which manages to escape from "the institutional force of words." Indeed Poirier seems more concerned with what Emerson may now do for those who cherish literature than with his place in our common history. Attention to Emerson may, he holds, free us from what he thinks of as the feverishly historical and oppressively hermetic pretensions of modernism, as well as from humanism and the Arnoldian fret about the fate of the ongoing culture. In Poirier's treatment, Bloom's imperatively ancestral Emerson becomes something quite different: an exemplary "come-outer" who escapes the tyranny of an enclosing culture. Poirier is especially successful in associating Emerson with William James, and in doing so he supplements our sense of the relation of individualism to pragmatism.[2]

His chief contention about Emerson, however, runs counter to the argument of this book. He finds Emerson's genius manifest in the writer's effort to defeat the fatally constraining, fatally social, character of language itself. This is a sharp swerve away from Poirier's earlier position (in *A World Elsewhere*) and from any context in which Emerson may be seen as significantly American, and it distracts our attention from the historical Emerson by bringing him forward as a judge of our recent literary enthusiasms.

Although Poirier and Bloom limit their conception of Emerson's role in the culture to what he accomplished as writer, they are in accord with the traditional view that the writer and what he writes cannot be dissociated, as they so often are in contemporary theory. Poirier is especially persuasive on a point I have long sought to emphasize: Emerson's work is best understood as an activity, a performance—which I see as unintermitted, as inconclusive as the flow of a stream. Yet neither Poirier nor Bloom contributes any sense of Emerson's relation to the urgencies of his historical period. They accord him weight against other users of language but hardly help to answer the question posed here: under what circumstances did American individualism arise, and what aspects of the culture fostered it?

Because these two highly penetrating readers stay within the bounds of literary discourse, they do not touch the extremities which attracted Emerson and Whitman, who were coping with a cultural situation which imposed a definable stress on their activity. The first of these extremities is the belief in the possibility of a visionary grasp of things which affords an ultimate authority, although it is only partially communicable. The second was the cognate idea that art was only a crutch, an imperfect means which would be supplanted when our race reached its full stature, a view which Henry

Miller later noted and subscribed to. Any position less radical than this is threatened by judgments of relative value, open, then, to acquisition, exchange, the kinds of valuation regnant in the money realm.

Emerson, preacher to the Americans, is hardly more assessable in purely literary terms than is the Bible. He had a faith which engaged hearers and readers and reflected the consequences of his immersion in his time. It is clear that he wavered and that he retreated, but it is his extravagance that mattered and still matters. We cannot, however, speak of his peculiar faith as persisting over the generations in an unchanged form. His hearers and readers—those who responded with interest and sympathy—were indeed like him in feeling that they did not wish to enter into the prevailing interests of the society. They felt alone in that respect, and he spoke to them in their felt isolation. But in urging them to see their isolation as a precious and unique opportunity to brush away their entrapment in relations to a chaffering world and accept their potentiality for "self union and freedom" he could not escape the fact that it was he, Emerson himself, who was painting that opportunity as glorious or escape the fact that they were far more like followers or disciples than creatures of infinite potentiality.

Emerson could and did induce a mood, at least while one was hearing or reading, in which one might feel that one was experiencing a view of things unconstrained by ties to others, or in which others and their interests did not blur one's sense of one's power of seeing experience as somehow unified. But encounter with him did not culminate in that epistemological overturn which Emerson said was essential to a continuing sense of one's self-sufficiency. Yet the hunger for such a sense of one's experience was there, was steadily generated by the character of a culture which did not feed it. This means that when we speak of an Emersonian impulse in Americans we are concerned with a sense of a lack on the part of people who felt isolated, a lack which could be filled, or seem for a time to be filled, by generalities wide enough to seem satisfyingly inclusive.

We can specify many ways in which those who sought to oppose one or another aspect of the commercial society organized for that purpose. But, given our premise about the widespread sense of being cut off from others by the pervasiveness of money-tinctured relationships, given, that is, a feeling that one was alone and in need of a persuasive sanction for making an independent claim on reality, inclusive ideas about a transformation of one's social world could be entertained without leading to overt action. The appropriation of ostensibly public ideas or causes for personal use is one of the marks of the American difference.

One could be a single taxer of the school of Henry George, just as later one could be a Stalinist, without doing very much or feeling that one's vital interests were directly at stake. Among literate or cultivated Americans such apparently inclusive allegiances often passed for a politics, without ever assuming the dimensions of an active involvement. An important indication that people are making a personal use of public ideas is the habit of taking the instance or example as a clue to the character of the whole. The case of Sacco and Vanzetti became representative for many people who never asked themselves what had actually happened. An exemplary use was also made of the case of Alger Hiss. Without examining the circumstances, many assumed that he had been charged with perjury by officers of a state that *habitually* accused innocent people of having Communist ties. Once more we find that individualism, the view of one who feels detached, dictates wholesale judgments.

Save for recurrent depressions, the period from the 1850s to the 1950s was marked by the spectacle of a material success so overwhelming as to push an extrapolated individualism of this passive kind to the periphery. A nationalist fervor was generated by what was taken for unlimited progress. Public forms of protest and countering proclamations of loyalty to the going order gave American politics a closer resemblance to affairs in Europe, in which the sentiments of groups and parties were central. There were indeed expatriates in Paris in the 1920s, and this was the period in which H. L. Mencken was making fun of the "booboisie," but it was also the period in which "The Man Without a Country," depicting the terrible fate of an American condemned to statelessness, aroused shivers; it was a familiar anthology piece in the schools.[3] It was hardly thinkable—as it became thinkable in the 1950s—that one could, *simply as an individual*, undertake a thoroughgoing disaffiliation from the nation itself and be widely identified and honored while doing so. In the preceding period the complex effects of the Civil War, a vast tide of immigration, and a rapid industrialization had resulted not simply in a growing nationalism but in a pluralism of visible and often opposing interests, which effectively delayed the return of anything like the total disenchantment which had led Emerson, Whitman, and Thoreau to propose an inclusive reseeing of American existence.

During this great interregnum, in which individualism was at once everywhere and far less visible as a reaction to the character of the culture, opposition to the world in which the money network was ascendant took social forms in associations of farmers or laborers. This interregnum did not fundamentally alter the character of American individualism; rather, it shrouded the situation Emerson, Whitman, and Thoreau had encountered during a time in which it was far easier to think of the United States as a single and rather recent phenomenon on the human scene. (Thoreau, though a child, might well have recalled the deaths of two of the founding fathers, John Adams and Thomas Jefferson, in 1826, when Emerson was twenty-three.)

When the sense of a deadly sameness spreading across the land supervened at the end of the Second World War, a situation analogous to that of the pre–Civil War period came about. T. S. Eliot and Ezra Pound, whom we number among our "modernists," may be said to have anticipated such a revulsion against what they saw as the block character of our culture in the second decade of our century, but it was far more widespread in the 1950s. We may surmise that those who found the cultural landscape flat, undifferentiated, adramatic had a corresponding impulse to withdraw which reinforced their individualism.

The assertion that individualism is an essential American trait has long been common, but the contention that it has its origin in conditions enforced by the commercial character of the society—that commerce has tended to isolate us from each other—proposes a historical cause rather than a defining trait. The overwhelming character of commerce as it bears on the formation of American selfhood is argued in a book of the 1950s, Norman O. Brown's *Life Against Death.* And David Riesman's *The Lonely Crowd,* which also appeared at mid-century, makes the complementary claim that Americans find themselves cut off from each other and engaged in the pursuit of identity.

Neither book deals with the historical genesis of American individualism. Brown uses Freud's analysis of the workings of the human psyche and inverts its conclusions about the goal of psychoanalysis. For Brown the state of health is that of the polymorphous perversity Freud attributes to the infant. Without intending to do so, the author has produced a representatively American book, more closely allied to the attitudes of Emerson and Whitman than any other work of the 1950s I can think of. Brown's subject is western civilization's betrayal of the highest potentialities of humanity. Correctly observing that the United States has committed itself to exchange and acquisition, which he finds emotionally equivalent to absorption in feces, Brown sees this devotion to the money network as blocking our hope of attaining the supremely individualized state of the polymorphously perverse. Every countervailing aspect of western civilization is disregarded. Only an apocalyptic realization of private delight can fulfill the highest imaginable human goal. What is hoped for is a realization as all-inclusive as what Emerson sought in his most exalted moments. Brown, earlier a Communist fellow traveler, did not, like some who abandoned Communism, turn to an extreme conservatism; instead he adopted a goal so completely asocial that it defies parody: each of the polymorphous persons he imagines would be a single universal consciousness. His later shift to the religion of art in *Love's Body* is less Emersonian, precisely because he focuses on things made rather than on the state of Emerson's realized man, who is beyond the need to make things.

Riesman's book was written in an epoch in which the assessment of social situations generated more hope than it now does. It succeeded in going beyond the limits of the sociological discipline at the time, first of all because it enforced the awareness that most Americans were indeed isolated and sought, particularly in adolescence, momentaneously fulfilling modes of association. To this group, trying for clues to an identity offered from without—those he called "outer-directed"—he opposed the "inner-directed"—those in whom a Freudian superego was apparent. Riesman was shrewd in pointing to the loneliness of his crowd, but he did not connect that sense of isolation with the American past, a connection which is afforded when we consider the representative character of the way in which Emerson, Whitman, and Thoreau had earlier responded to the American plight.

In retrospect it seems clear that Brown, for all his extravagance, was addressing a reality which Riesman was avoiding. Having found Marxism inadequate, Brown turned to modes of analysis which involved judgment of the psychic fix of individuals, as well as the groups to which they belonged, and demanded a psychological and epistemological overturn, drawing on Luther and Blake as well as Freud to describe a world in which the money context was eating up all others.

The persisting difficulty Americans have in taking this in is of course an index of the measure in which we have all been invaded by or have found ourselves immersed in that context. Protest against commercialism is so old and so familiar a complaint that being troubled about its effects seems as foolish as complaint about wearing clothing. Yet if Europeans have been more brilliant in teasing it out, especially in the nineteenth century, the litany of American complaints, ineffectual as they have been, has been repeated generation after generation. Jefferson, who had high hopes for those not involved in trade, wrote John Adams that "our greediness for wealth has degraded and will degrade the minds of our maritime citizens. These have the peculiar vices of commerce." In 1783, Hugh Henry Brackenridge, falling into a delusion, still to be met with, that art may be separated out and nonetheless may serve to anchor values distinct from those of trade, writes:

> Why is it that I am proud and value myself amongst my own species? It is because I think I possess in some

> degree, the distinguishing characteristic of a man, a taste for the fine arts, a taste and characteristic too little valued in America, where a system of finance has introduced the love of unequal wealth; destroyed the spirit of common industry; and planted that of lottery in the human heart; making the mass of the people gamblers; and under the idea of speculation, shrouded engrossing and monopoly everywhere.[4]

It would be easy to make an anthology of such remarks, but those that have a particular bearing here have to do with the effect of the money-saturated consciousness on individuals. Van Wyck Brooks makes the conventional charge: writers, he says, "have not had the power to move the soul of America from the accumulation of dollars." This response is endlessly reiterated, but the work of Kenneth Burke on the way in which money affects thinking is far more incisive. I quote two observations from *The Grammar of Motives*. The first is on the way in which issues are discussed in print: "the monetary references is [*sic*] over-all *public* motive for mediating among endless diversity of occupation and private (or 'preoccupational') motives." The second has to do with the kind of imaginative authority which replaced the belief in God: "And the experience of an *impersonal* motive was empirically intensified in proportion as the rationale of the monetary motive gained greater authority. . . ."

Overt denunciations of the world in which money is ascendant are not of much use or significance for an inquiry into individualism and money. Even a dramatic rendering of encounters between people whose ties with others are primary and those whose imaginative horizons are bounded by money is hard to realize in the United States simply because dense social settings in which money values are secondary are difficult to establish in history and fiction. Allen Tate and William Faulkner afford glimpses of the possibilities and limitations of such fictions.

The Faulkner short story "Shingles for the Lord" takes us about as far from Emerson as we can go without leaving the country. The title juxtaposes the measurable and the immeasurable. The church in Frenchman's Bend needs a new roof, and Parson Whitfield engages his parishioners to give a certain number of days to do the work. Man is a sinner and owes God all, more than all he can give. To reckon this debt in hours is formally, though not, as we learn, practically, impossible. The story is a comic parable in which the interplay of mensuration and desire, abstraction and impulse, seated infinitude and human virtuosity, are all reflected in the consciousness of a child of ten or so.

This absorbed observer reports actions and speeches in the past tense, without any determinate marking of the moment of his telling the story, quite as if he were running through a segment of an internal record that he could play back at will, including his judgments of the significance of adult behavior based on earlier experience. Yet the scroll he runs through participates in the timelessness of the child's world as we are prone to imagine it; it is a pageant of existence in which eating, milking, the presence and behavior of mother and father form a spectacle more inclusive than that available to adult actors committed to facing a shifting flow of circumstance and to acting on its eddies and changes in order to hold their world together. The child, in other words, edits his world in behalf of his need for stability; the adults—fictional convention permits us to assume—are those who cannot avoid drama and constitutive events—those which change the tenor of our lives.

If the awareness of the teller of the story is circumscribed, so too is the community he lives in. Faulkner has invented a tribe in which the imaginative horizon is bounded to a degree approaching that of one of the South American tribes in Lévi-Strauss. Yet this horizon is not wholly impenetrable; much of the fun in Faulkner's fable derives from the intrusion of impersonal measurement on the question of work and its value.

As it begins, Rex Grier, father of the boy who tells the tale, is confronted by an instance of the extravagance of the imagination. The neighbor of whom he meant to borrow the tools he needed to assist in splitting shingles for the church isn't at home. Although the neighbor is totally deaf, he has been out all night sitting on a log while his hounds, whom he can't hear, are barking on the trail of a fox. Grier has to wait for his return. When, tools in hand, Grier approaches the church, he finds the preacher holding his watch and his fellows sitting waiting for him. He is two hours late, and Quick and Bookwright have waited for him instead of going to work without him. Solon Quick, who has had some experience with Roosevelt's Works Progress Administration, takes the position that what had been agreed was that the trio would supply what he calls "work-units" toward the production of shingles. Since Grier had failed to make up the agreed crew, they are now six units short. Grier remarks that work is work and is done when it's done, but Solon Quick persists; he is willing to exchange some of his labor to make up for Grier's lost time if Grier will agree to sell him his half of a valued hunting dog which Grier owns in common with Vernon Tull. Grier is savagely angry and sees that the work-units have in actuality been "dog-units."

Quick's reference to "modern ideas of work" is an effort to mask his motives with an abstraction; it is also a tactic in the familiar southern folktale genre of the story of a horse trade—here a dog trade. The abstraction Quick introduces has no place in the tribal mores of Frenchman's Bend. (It is even conceivable that Faulkner is slyly referring to the labor theory of value, or the campaign of Josiah Warren [1798–1874] in behalf of labor scrip, a document which obligated you to give a unit of labor, say an hour of work, which Warren proposed as a basis for the exchange of goods.) The community Faulkner has imagined is one in which hourly wages are a foreign notion.

Quick had earlier gotten Vernon Tull's consent to sell his half of the dog for two dollars; Grier has held out for five dollars apiece. He leaves during the noon hour, adjuring the boy to say nothing, no matter what his father does or says when he returns. While away he buys Tull's half of the dog in exchange for a half day's labor on the church roof as Tull's substitute. When he returns he offers to make a new deal with Quick. Quick is to pay him two dollars and to contribute a half day's work to pulling off shingles in the morning. Grier afterward explains to his startled son that Quick will be unable to consummate the deal because father and son will pull off all the shingles that night. They set out to do this but drop their lantern into the highly combustible interior of the church, and, despite Grier's desperate efforts and those of the gathered neighbors, the church is wholly consumed.

But as the boy, with his faith in things as they are, and the indomitable Parson Whitfield, who presides over marriages, births, and deaths and is determined to drag his sinning brethren into heaven, are well aware, the church itself has not been consumed; the tribe gathers in the morning, and Whitfield announces a call to raise a new church to which all respond. Whitfield denounces Grier as an "arsonist," but it is plain that Grier will insist on his right to participate, despite

Whitfield's denunciation; he is a member of the tribe. Two points that bear on our concern in this book are at once apparent in this story. Grier's wiliness in trade succeeds in reducing the impersonal usages of exchange to a contest of wits, which he wins, and the gathered community exhibits a collective conviction that their lives have a common meaning which transcends individual advantage.

But reflection on what the writer has done in this delightful yarn leads us to see that the child's way of taking the world is essential to its success; that the way he knows his world is both privileged and limited. We note that it is limited when the reader must take the writer's hint that Grier, who had been lacerated and knocked out while fighting the fire and been denounced by Whitfield, will make his first assertion of his manhood and right to membership after the fire by expelling the boy from the bedroom and making love to his wife. But aside from this moment, it is the child's fascinated spectatorship which makes the story an experience of a remarkably wide span for the reader, ranging from the dog trade, in which speech and significant movements and expressions are enacted for us, to the child's unquestioning acceptance of the preacher as spokesman for man's eternal concerns. In "Shingles for the Lord" consciousness is *of* what other people are saying and doing, a world social beyond the dreams of our televised world—a very bath of social engagement in which one must be incessantly adjusting oneself, measuring possibility, assessing character, and recalling personal histories.

In his most assertive early work Emerson often refers to the unclouded fullness of the child's view of the world and is even naive enough to say that small children clamor for new stories rather than the repetition of familiar ones. The contrast with Faulkner's narrator in this story is almost total.

The writer's young narrator is busy learning the ways, manners, and personal idiosyncrasies of people firmly ensconced in a community. To be at home there is to be aware of the play of discourse and activity about him among a set of people whom Faulkner has endowed—not without warrant in his own experience—with the indirection and cunning reflected in the speech of peasants for whom conversation is an art. In such a setting, one listens and observes with care or one is lost. "Shingles for the Lord" is not, however, intended as a slice of life. Faulkner has deliberately exaggerated and isolated those aspects of the community which indicate the human capacity to give personal meaning to the apparently impersonal; there is no mention of tenancy or the need to make a crop which will suffice to pay one's debt at the landlord's store.

The intrusion of the issues of counting and measuring into Frenchman's Bend furnishes a link with Allen Tate's novel *The Fathers*,[5] in which the narrator notes on an early page his "introduction to the world where people counted and added." This narrator is recalling, after the lapse of half a century, the period immediately preceding the Civil War, and his narrative concludes with the battle of Bull Run. In part his story, like Faulkner's, does not confess to being retrospective but unrolls as if it were an instantaneously recorded present, a reliving of events. Since we learn nothing of the narrator which bears on any subsequent moment, we are led to think of him as wholly preoccupied with these events he has so long survived.

This son of Major Buchan, of Pleasant Hill in Virginia, is, when we first enter his consciousness, on the day of his mother's funeral, coping with an event which cracks the surface on which his life has been lived. It is an encounter with a denial of the whole fabric of his world as it has heretofore been understood. The splendid George Posey, his sister Susan's fiancé, arrives at Pleasant Hill early on that day, but he inexplicably rides away before the meal, avoiding any participation in the ceremony which attends the death and burial. This action has a riveting effect on the young Lacy Buchan. Posey is a man so detached from the views and manners of the Virginia gentry that this behavior is one more facet of a startling otherness which Lacy finds irresistibly fascinating. He recalls earlier occasions on which Posey has breached the code of behavior which composes his father's way of ordering his life. As Lacy later puts it: "Our domestic manners and satisfactions were as impersonal as the United States Navy, and the belief widely held today, that men may live apart from the political order, that indeed the only humane and honorable satisfactions must be gained in spite of the public order, would have astonished most men of that time as a remote fantasy, impossible of realization." The familiar theme of an individualism which imposes a wider view than the given society countenances is brought forward here: Posey abolishes the distinction between public and private worlds by treating the Virginia gentry's conception of itself as wholly irrelevant to the most extensive power he knows, that of money.

Tate undertakes nothing less than an account of the genesis of a new breed, persons to whom fathers mean little and who, because they take everything personally, regard their world impersonally, chiefly as a set of conditions affecting themselves. Major Buchan, who is identified by descent and the place of his residence and who upholds principles and standards of honor which if breached by another will be maintained by a challenge to a duel, is encysted by tradition and finds Posey almost inconceivable.

In offering us a view of the outlook of this father, Major

Buchan, Tate presents us with an instance of the sort of character which conceives the meaning of life in public terms; Buchan leads a life which recalls that of the Virginia gentlemen who had contributed to the making and the definition of a new nation. He, like a number of these predecessors, sees slavery as an evil which distorts the holders of slaves as well as the slaves themselves. The reader learns that Buchan's grant of certificates of manumission to a family of slaves has not been carried out; Posey has sold them and used the money to pay off part of a bank loan, presumably secured by Pleasant Hill, the plantation which he had been entrusted with managing for the Buchan family. This conflict of purposes is only one instance of Posey's utter disregard of the settled expectations of those around him, who, as men of family, tradition, loyalty to Virginia in the approaching crisis, and blindness to economic forces, inspire his contempt.

Tate's triumph in imagining Posey extends to a convincing sense of his emotional makeup. He is, so to speak, an account of market man by a writer who sees us as fatally social creatures. Because Posey lacks a social shell, has no "father"—his own father is a dim and questionable memory—he lives exposed to the exigencies of the moment. He cannot face the death of Lacy's mother because he is in terror of his own extinction; he blushes at the scene in which the bull mounts the cow as if it were a demonstration of his own vulnerability, a confession of a need which overthrows the self-sufficiency without which he cannot exist. He is confident and competent with the impersonal, chiefly with the abstractions of money and profit.

This is Tate's nightmare version of Emerson's self-reliance. Posey's exposed condition makes him dangerous; his behavior is studded with instances of a violent response to any threat to his self, a self unsupported by trust in others.

Tate is at pains to suggest that Posey is not greedy. Money is his chosen means because it best expresses his sense that he is surrounded by impersonal conditions. He is a case that Georg Simmel might have described, a man whose sense of reality is enclosed by the humdrum metaphysic of money; money is the common term with the widest set of applications, and to see the world as he does ties you to nobody.[6] It is at the same time the closest thing to a universal defense against others.

Tate leaves it to us to infer that a multiplication of George Poseys—of this man who sheds the Confederate uniform he has briefly worn for the broadcloth of trade—has thereafter studded America with people who are no longer of a certain place, family, and tradition but are labeled, in keeping with their commercial callings, "steel men," brokers, and so forth. Tate's novel suggests the possibility that our ties to one another are being steadily reduced to monetary ties.

Faulkner's response to the threat of such an erosion takes more than one form. One of the most familiar, and most fruitful in melodramatic oppositions, is the Snopes tribe. If George Posey is roughly describable as a man deprived of a superego, we may say the same thing of the whole of this remarkable family. But they cannot all be described as governed by the ruling passion of Flem Snopes, for whom the pursuit of money cancels all else.[7] A Snopes, generically described, is a creature without any inhibitions, and thus is more closely akin to George Posey than might appear. Only a Snopes, we might say, can imagine what another Snopes might do. Falling in love with a cow or selling pornography or burning barns are among the realized possibilities. What is striking about Flem Snopes, when we juxtapose him with the account of our nature and our situation in a fragmented culture offered by Emerson, Whitman, and Thoreau, is the fact that he invades the scene from without; the money world washes into a town which had formerly been at least partially governed by analogues of Tate's more formal and elegant restraints imposed by an aristocracy. Both Tate and Faulkner cling to a sense that individuals once lived in an interdependent community.

If there is indeed a detectable American "difference" stemming from the enforced generality and impersonality of the money network, a difference which sets us off from other western cultures, it appears that those Americans who have felt and expressed their sense of it fall into two camps: those who, like Hawthorne, Faulkner, and Tate, see the human world as a set of relationships between persons which is fatally distorted by the intrusion of those with monetary motives, and those who, like Emerson, Thoreau, and Whitman, experience the intrusion within and say that it can be supplanted by a more inclusive vision of things which subdues our existing social selves in the name of a vision to come which all may share.

In order to view the money world in the first mode, as an intrusion on antecedent relationships, one must give it human avatars such as Faulkner's Jason Compson in *The Sound and the Fury* or Flem Snopes, who, in one of Faulkner's parables, defeats the devil himself because he is beyond good and evil. In order to contend with the world of those who, in Emerson's phrase, "dwell in a relation" to others and *ipso facto* in a world based on exchange, one must take the risky step of fighting a generality with a generality; that is, claiming for oneself a more inclusive view of things than the world of relationships and money affords.

By scanting the particular way in which Americans were isolated from each other to begin with, before they could assent to or find open or covert (transcendental) means of contending with the money network, our critics of literature, sociologists, and such Marxist commentators as Herbert Marcuse and Jurgen Habermas have neglected what is essential: the persistence of American individualism.

The effort to achieve a satisfying identity distinguished from the preoccupations of the money network leads the Emersonian individual to make claims so excessive as to put him at a distance from his fellows. These claims to possession of a supervening reality are analogous to those of the acquisitive individual who, likewise distanced from his fellows by acceptance of the impersonal nature of the money network, sees the world as imaginatively defined by money, possessions, and future monetary claims. It must, I think, be confessed that construing money values as intrusions from without, as Faulkner and Tate do, yields comforting fables but misses or scants the fact that they are felt *within* by all of us.

Considered in its effect on the view one takes of the nature and importance of our associated life, transcendentalism must be thought of as a covert attempt to blanket the money world by offering a fresh view of individual powers, a view sufficiently generalized to bring about a transformation of the individual's view of the world. With respect to opposition to the imaginative domination of money, it must be thought of as covert since it simply denies the power of the world of possessions without attempting to affect it or asserting total immunity from its effect on us. The open and explicit opposition speaks in the name of the welfare of community; the covert opposition speaks in the name of a transformation of individuals and remains open to the charge that it is simply touting a *superior possession*—the individual's inclusive vision—while the open attacks seem nostalgic sentimentality or golden age fantasies.

The contrast between the open and the covert modes of contending with the money universe is nonetheless useful in explaining the consequences of assuming either stance. No one can nowadays muster the faith in the limitless spiritual resources of each individual which Emerson called on us to realize. We have long been, and for the most part remain, Emersonians, in the sense that individuals call on inclusive conceptions of the world to anchor their identities and that the excessive inclusiveness of these ideas sets, as does money, a barrier between each and all. To put it plainly, we are playing god when we adopt speciously inclusive views of the world. As I shall attempt to show in the next chapter, these inclusive ideas are ostensibly social and public, but they are chiefly employed to shore up individual identities rather than to further the development of a fuller sense of the possibilities of associated or communal life. This restrictive judgment applies to those who treat language as a primary category, detached from the community in which it is employed. Brilliant and informative such critics may be, yet they fail to connect us with the human plight at large, and their tacit claim to a sufficient category leaves the rest of us in the dark about the place of poetry in our world.

CHAPTER 6

Public Worlds as Private Possessions

The impulse to wholesale rejection which animates the individualism of those Americans who deprecate our commercial culture makes for a telling difference from Europe, where connections between artists, schools of thought, and political parties arise as a matter of course.[1] When such ties are rare the work of cultural historians tends to lose its historical character, becomes paradigmatic, and those involved in historical events are seen as driven by abstractions. Those who contrive such ahistorical engines of theory actually gain the personal power they deny to those they write about, and they vie with each other in playing ever more inclusive intellectual games. Instead of reading publicly articulated needs and values into the past, as Whig historians have been accused of doing, they construct theses which make the distinction between past and present harder to discern.

It is not difficult to show that attempts to understand our cultural past have lately been dominated by the sort of wholesale theory dictated by the species of individualism which gives rise to an inclusive vision or ideology. In the two volumes of *The New England Mind*, published in 1939 and 1953, Perry Miller, a passionate historical dramatist, gave an almost Thucydidean account of origin and decline. His work was superseded by the ascendancy of the work of Sacvan Bercovitch, who posited an unvarying bourgeois apologetics as composing the central strand in the history of our culture without specifying any climax which was to attend it.[2] Such ahistorical theses about our culture now abound. All share the characteristic that may be called unanswerability; they preempt the possibility of contravening views. The historian's awareness that he is functioning as interpreter in a field which is open to other readings gives way to a governing universal whose sufficient character is assumed; the eternizing impulse wins out, and the acknowledgment of one's status as an interpreter is replaced by a tacit claim to an inclusive authority.

In many cases the ostensibly public view which is drawn from Marxism or a similarly all-embracing scheme serves the same function as the inclusive view earlier entertained by individuals who claimed to find it internally validated. In such contexts the American scene becomes an object envisioned by the solitary self. The concomitant effect is that the country is judged in the lump. All such views obscure the possibility of significant change in the future. No matter how many people adopt them, such static views keep their adherents equally cut off from a perception of the moving world about them. Their isolation is perpetuated. What purports to be public remains solitary, since it is removed not simply from the awareness of change over time but from the arena of critical investigation in which voice answers voice.

Such echoes of Emersonian detachment from awareness of our conditioned state—one grows up, after all, in a particular time—were far less noticeable during what I have called the interregnum, from the close of the Civil War to the 1950s, a period in which one might speak of a much higher degree of national self-confidence than we now show. The quasi-religious faith in the individual's inner resources diminished. Although the need it had satisfied persisted, expressing itself in somewhat diffuse forms among the women and the preachers whom Ann Douglas treats in *The Feminization of American Culture*, their disaffection was but a murmur as against the widespread glorification of the titans of industry. Social and collective expressions of protest from organizations of laborers and farmers came to the fore—and proved almost equally ineffective in the face of the overwhelming growth of industrial power. The extraordinary confluence of immigrants was believed to testify that we were an unparalleled success and served to lessen the possibilities of massive homegrown conflict. Never before had so many gained so much in so short a span. The chance that the means we employed might land us in personal isolation and anomie was hard to envisage, and few imagined any such outcome.

Much of what is thought of as making up American history falls into the period I am here treating as an interregnum. I call it that because it appeared that an immense and sudden material success had created bonds among us which would endure. In fact national cohesion, realized most fully in wartime, was relatively fragile. We did, however, profit as a collectivity from the existence of political parties which, corrupt though they often were, generated personal loyalties which palliated the desiccating impersonality of economic relationships—as did many other forms of local association I neglect here.

Toward the end of this span, the economic turmoil of the 1930s inspired strong impulses to reform or to transform the economic structure, and some Americans, largely middle class, were attracted to the communism of the Soviet Union as a solution. Although the appeal of this nostrum was that it complemented an impulse to find wholesale answers, it was nevertheless subscribed to in the name of a social cause. It was later, in the 1950s and 1960s, that the faith that we could go forward as a social collectivity visibly ebbed once more. Individuals once more claimed the power to stand outside the culture and make inclusive judgments of it. Emerson's successors appeared in the form of earnest seceders, such as Henry Miller, Norman O. Brown, and the Beats.

I first attempted a description of this Emersonian stance and its persistence in this country in *The Imperial Self* (1971). This was an initial exploration of the efforts of individual Americans to ground their beliefs and responsibilities in resources they held to be native to the self. The book emphasized what I took to be an interesting and significant anomaly in a democracy: that a handful of nineteenth-century American writers, regarded as representative of their culture, had devoted their imaginative energies to seeing themselves—and urging others to see themselves—in the perspectives of humanity rather than those their society afforded. They had written as if individuals could define themselves by achieving their own relation to nature—or even to being in general. In an earlier book (*The American Henry James*, 1957) I had called this presumption "the bootstraps myth," since it implied that one was in no way shaped by history, relations to others, or one's immediate cultural circumstances.

The Imperial Self was based on the presumption that the society might best be understood through the quality and character of the relationships among its members—relationships which were dimmed or erased by individualism. The reception of *The Imperial Self* made it clear that this presumption did not reflect a current preoccupation. Most people were directing their attention not to the civic order of a democracy but rather to the ways in which money was allocated, gained, and lost. The money world screened us from each other in a larger measure than I had realized. What I had somewhat naively thought of as a common concern with how our lives were lived with others was a second-order question; the community was actually being seen as through snow glasses: the slit was the "bottom line," and what absorbed most attention from most people, whether they were conservatives, radicals, or in between, was getting and spending and the institutions that controlled these activities. A number of commentators of various stripes, including Christopher Lasch, had written about what I came to see as our resulting estrangement from each other as an emerging narcissism, but its connection with the radical individualism which had appeared before the Civil War was ignored.[3]

If "society" didn't hold the place in our imaginative economy I had attributed to it, what had earlier been called American "individualism" had meanings I hadn't seen explored. I undertook to develop the thesis of the present book: American culture exhibits an individualism socially produced by the ascendancy of the money-saturated scene. Emerson, Thoreau, and Whitman had been alike in the respect that they had set out to escape this mind-set by becoming in effect one man cultures, built upon a hope that the self might attain a universal grasp of things. Such a claim forged no bonds, was in effect the proclamation of a glorious personal possession which others might try to realize for themselves. Lacking the residuum of Christian faith which their predecessors had found in the powers of the self, their successors borrowed universals and put them to Emersonian uses. *Individualism does not, however, escape possessiveness by claiming an exclusive grasp on reality*. The presumed escape hatch simply reinforced the passivity and isolation arising from the impersonality of monetary exchange.

In undertaking this book, in which personal agency, and the encounter with others it entails, is put forward as a value threatened by the form of individualism I have described, I was forced to acknowledge that I was battling a strong countercurrent in the intellectual world of the 1970s and 1980s. The denial that the human subject as envisioned in the past had ever existed was becoming more insistent. If individual identity was of so little consequence, the attempt to make a case for our fuller acknowledgment of each other was simply old hat. If particular human subjects had only a marginal significance, if there were no distinguishable interpreters of the world, if we were chips borne on the cultural tide, individualism was hardly an issue. Yet influence and power were all the while accruing to those who maintained the effectual nullity of the human subject and saw us all as the bond slaves of culture.

Does not Sacvan Bercovitch's denial of the possibility of antinomianism in its secular sense, that is, the possibility of individual agents who succeed in opposing or criticizing the culture, end with such wholesale proclamations as I have suggested? Has not Wai-chee Dimock pushed this position to its logical consummation when she says of her book on Melville that it "is an implicit argument against the idea of originality"?[4] All Melville's works, once thought valuable and discriminable from each other, are reduced to evidence of his imprisonment in Dimock's context, in which identities as well as goods are bought and sold. One has but to choose a sufficiently generalizable context to become emperor or empress over whatever artifacts one has in hand.

The assumption of an authority so complete is detached

from the conditions of human intercourse. Since it is simply one instance of a rather widespread set of intellectual behaviors, it must be acknowledged as a fascinating development in our response to the conditions in which we now live. It may be paraphrased in various ways; for example, does it not amount to a declaration that we are *all* outsiders, that the system, whatever it may be, gives us no access to a satisfying sense of things and no means of joining one another, even in opposition? What part does the performance of such exercises in disaffiliation play in the daily lives of those who undertake them? Will those who conduct such races toward the cultural exit tire of these games, or do they serve as indices of approaching forms of a more inclusive disintegration which will invade us all? What is of importance here is the fact that these proponents of inclusive schemes are one more instance of the persistence of an isolated individualism which shares the generic loneliness of celebrity. It seems clear that when celebrity fills the space once occupied by public issues, in which all were assumed to have a stake, the very notion of public concerns shrinks drastically.

In many quarters the exercise of individual judgment by liberals has been attacked. How can a "private" view of public questions serve to further the welfare of the community? Is it not clear that the human world is governed by inclusive systems in which particular personal views or dialogue among those who hold such views can have no effect? A conference held in Australia in 1979 led to the publication of its proceedings under the title *The Public and the Private in Social Life*. The editors provide a clue to the bad odor a distinction between these spheres had in 1979: "If, as all the authors acknowledge, a concern to differentiate public and private spheres is a distinctively liberal concern, the very centrality of this topic to liberalism may be taken as founding a fundamental critique of liberalism whether in Hegelian or Marxist terms." The aspiration to an undivided consciousness, in which public and private are merged, is plain here. It appears that liberalism, and with it respect for individual judgment on social questions, has become suspect. The very notion of the public realm has nearly vanished. What Richard Sennett's *The Fall of Public Man* (1977) sought to record seems to have been fully realized. The effect of the effort to cancel the significance of personal agency in society has seldom been noted by others.

What was at stake in the Australian conference does not seem to have been absorbed by most of those who took part. Can lawyers easily give up the assignment of personal responsibility? Consider the situation of the teacher of freshman English, laboring to get students to find a voice in prose, who is told by his or her own instructors in graduate school that we are all condemned to speak and write in the compelling codes of a dominant culture. To question individual agency and responsibility is to gut the presumed basis of the order in which we live and to make the hope for a democracy idiotic.

One instance of the erosion of the conception of personal agency emerges when we consider the contention over "consensus" history a generation ago. One of our greatest historians, Richard Hofstadter, was able to document areas of agreement among many figures in our history who had been thought of as showing crucial oppositions of view and practice.[5] This was widely taken to mean that those conceived as the standard bearers of social change, particularly those who singled out class struggle as primary, were being assimilated to an ongoing conservative outlook. In fact Hofstadter was reminding us that personal agency was important and that it was exercised in a public world in which much was shared by those who composed it. He was of course attacked by the partisans of schemes dependent on irresistible forces and factors.

The contention that we had proved unable to imagine and bring about major social changes, the thesis of Louis Hartz's *The American Liberal Tradition*, was not so much evidence of a consensus, a common satisfaction with our social state, as of an inability to conceive of any opposition to the going social order save the visionary capitalism of individualism. I would put it that "consensus" was actually the expression of an incapacity to react adversely, except in a fashion so total as to be unworkable. Hofstadter's discovery of likenesses among those who had been thought of as totally opposed could hardly be contested, but it did not betoken a conscious agreement to accept things as they were. John Higham, one of the critics of consensus history, had simply not seen that he was fighting a straw man.[6] The impersonal conditions of the money-saturated world had in fact lessened our power to imagine changes in the social order.

Two relatively recent books exhibit our difficulty in coming to grips with the individualism which hobbles our efforts to conceive of practical ways of altering our social state. Robert A. Ferguson's *Law and Letters in American Culture* (1984) undertakes to examine the period between the Revolution and the Civil War in which gifted lawyers and writers assumed the responsibilities of statesmen and wrote and spoke on the questions raised by the creation of a new state with proclaimed principles. They sought to act in behalf of the interests of the republic. The book has been justly praised, yet its scanty references to those who universalized the individual's claim on reality suggest plainly enough that Ferguson is unable to see that they represent a far more influential strain in our history than do those who sought to give our institutions a meaningful existence when the country was young. For Ferguson it is possible to recognize the literary achievement of these loners without a glimmer of suspicion that they are representative figures not simply because they wrote well but because they wrote close to the American grain.

The second book which is in point here is David Simpson's *The Politics of American English, 1776–1850* (1986). Simpson devotes a chapter to "The Transcendentalist Alternative," whose proponents "write of language . . . as a universal medium shared by all and enabling all to achieve the same access to God and to nature. In a system of doctrines that is, as Transcendentalism is, so completely mediated through the exemplary self and its utterances, the existence of languages as functioning to connect or divide *different* selves becomes so irrelevant as to seem impertinent." This is well observed; it recalls John Dewey's blindness to the limitations of communication. But Simpson's use of the word "doctrines" and his final disposition of transcendentalism as a "consoling mythology" make it clear that the individualism I have been following is beyond his ken. Ferguson and Simpson, from right and left respectively, both suggest that society is an all-enclosing context. When the notion of society is so much to the fore, the isolated individualism which has played so important a part in our history becomes invisible.

The fundamental role of our individualism has also been obscured by our treatment of the relation of our writers to literary modernism. We make the unjustified presumption that we encountered modernism as Europeans did, but rather later in time. What for most of our early American modernists was a continuing individual struggle was for European modernists an imaginative encounter with climactic historical change. What now appears to have been the essential aspect of that change—that western civilization was more and more dominated by the search for profits—was, and for American writers had long been, a settled aspect of their condition. In this sense, we were postmodern before modernism arose—not, of course, in the bulk of our literary production but in those writers who so arrested D. H. Lawrence in *Studies in Classic American Literature* and F. O. Matthiessen in *American Renaissance*.

Modernism was of course many things; but one thing that it certainly was for Europe it certainly was not for the United States, that is, an inclusive and various attempt, beginning toward the end of the nineteenth century, to cope with the burden imposed by the western past. I am now referring to the encounters with that past on the part of Proust or Joyce or Conrad or Thomas Mann or Rilke. That burden had first been fully shouldered by Nietzsche, who is held to be modernism's precursor. But we keep forgetting that it was Nietzsche who read Emerson, not the other way around.

The refusal of Emerson, Thoreau, Whitman, and Henry James to acknowledge the past cuts deeper than we have been able to admit; it was through them and the American attitudes they represent that we bypassed modernism. Their need to deny the shaping character of the past was fundamental. When Whitman writes, "I am the man, I suffer'd, I was there," he is incorporating the past as an aspect of the fullness of his present. That present must reach to the horizon and catch up past, present, and future in order to blot out a social landscape in which visions any less extensive regularly become articles of commerce. When Emerson says that he wished to convey to others a sense of their self union and freedom, he is also saying that both history and the behavior of the social beings around him are clouds that have to be dispelled if we are to discover what he calls our "common nature," that largely unrealized capacity for a total vision of things that is common to us all.[7] In Emerson it is society, the actual community, that drives us apart, confining us to single functions and estranging us from what ideally unites the self, a full awareness of our power to see the world as a whole, as an object. James engages us in a more active way by offering us participation in a widening circle of awareness within his fictions. He dramatizes an epistemological mismatch between the impulse to acquisition and the impulse to creative love we find in ourselves and in each other. This division between opposed desires that employ distinct ways of designating reality is more important to him than the boundary between the self and the society.

Henry James, then, was also postmodernist before modernism appeared in Europe. He had no need to encounter a society in being because society had no imaginative dominion over him; he was too much absorbed in his own version of Emerson's community of nature. The encounter of acquisitiveness and creative love was primary for him. The social scene he so brilliantly observed furnished him with a point of departure for a deliberate subversion of his readers' expectations as to what his characters ought to want and ought to be moved by, as well as of his readers' assumptions about the world in which they were "immersed or engaged."[8]

Yet the emotional returns yielded by James's works, the kind of pleasure they afford, are clearly those that satisfy the appetite of Emersonian individualism. Each reader is offered what at first appears to be a conventionally novelistic experience; each reader is at the same time offered the status of a licensed lord over all appearance, shares in a widening consciousness, and triumphs not only over the greed of others but also over the burden of guilt that the culture so often imposes on those who are ensnared in the money network.

A number of works prized highly at the moment epitomize the basic movement of those fictions of James in which individual consciousness comes to prevail: These are "The Beast in the Jungle," "The Jolly Corner," *The Wings of the Dove*, and *The Golden Bowl*. In each of these the selfish self is cast out and a loving self in the form of a woman stands ready to replace it. Too late, admittedly, for John Marcher of "The Beast in the Jungle"; just in time for Spencer Brydon of "The Jolly Corner"; posthumously in the case of Merton Densher of *The Wings of the Dove*, who is subdued to Milly Theale after her death; and with apocalyptic finality for Prince Amerigo in *The Golden Bowl*, who, when he learns to see, sees the whole world only in Maggie's inclusive vision of it. This vision, as I believe Laurence Holland was the first to point out, is just barely distinguishable from that of James, who thus permits himself an Emersonian moment.

In keeping with my illustration of the character and effects of the individualism exhibited in the case of Henry James, I turn to further illustrations of the use of public worlds as private possessions in some of those who are spoken of as the first of our literary "modernists," to show that what they felt and wrote has a cultural significance which extends beyond the realm of art. They blank out historical change and render the American world as an immediately presented object of an essentially invariant character.

European modernism is a record of various kinds of encounters with—and denials that one was constrained by—the past. What has been called American modernism as represented in James, T. S. Eliot, and Ezra Pound is the work of writers busy coping with what looked like an enduring present. What Whitman had met had in their eyes simply deepened and intensified. For Pound, American history had come to a disastrous conclusion in the epoch of Jackson and

Van Buren; what followed rang with a single note: the United States was lost to civilization.

Henry James's contemporary, Henry Adams, offers a useful contrast. Adams, a scion of ambassadors and presidents, wrote an excellent narrative history of the early American republic.[9] He had, perhaps inevitably, associated his identity and the significance of his work with the development of the republic his family had served. Overtaken by domestic misfortune and by what he regarded as the irretrievable decline in public integrity that accompanied a rising industrialism, he wrote the two books by which he is now best known, *Mont-Saint-Michel and Chartres* (1904) and *The Education of Henry Adams* (1907). In the first of these two books a magnificent concretion of distinctively human energies focused on the Virgin results in the building of Chartres; in the second Adams is confronted by a society that is undergoing a rapid dehumanization, symbolized by the impersonal force of the dynamo. Within this antithesis, however, is a more immediately felt personal predicament: the disappearance of public life as a basis for a distinctive identity. Adams's response to this loss is only the most familiar of a number of such efforts to invoke a preferable cultural scene in other societies or in other times—that of Dante, for example—as more humanly fulfilling models of society. For such seekers no extrasocial sanctions for selfhood were imaginable.[10]

Those Americans we call modernists are much more closely akin to Emerson, Thoreau, and Whitman. Their kinship shows in their common assumption, so different from that of Adams, that they were not caught up in their culture, which they tended to view ahistorically and *en bloc.* What separated them from it was their determination not to be defined by its commercial character. When, late in Henry James's career, such representative American modernists as

Ezra Pound, Gertrude Stein, and T. S. Eliot appeared, the American writer who meant most to them was James, who also held an inclusive view of the country's overmastering dedication to commerce. The effort at alchemical transformation of wealth into the fruits of consciousness is undertaken by Adam Verver in James's novel *The Golden Bowl.* Verver's museum in American City is a seriocomic rendering of the Emersonian effort to bring about an epistemological overturn in all Americans.

An extraordinary seriousness and a high degree of dedication were brought to the craft of writing by Ezra Pound, T. S. Eliot, Gertrude Stein, Robert Frost, and others—notably two who were close to Pound before he settled abroad, William Carlos Williams and Hilda Doolittle—the poet known as "H.D." The example of Henry James was important for this group, but knowledge of French poets and critics was perhaps more important. Some credit ought surely to be given to the institution Pound was so fond of denouncing, the university; all six of those named had for varying periods of time gone either to the University of Pennsylvania or to Harvard. They shared the conviction that art mattered profoundly, but, unlike Henry James, they did not begin their work with any inclusive assurance about the set of values art served, and their American origins made it inevitable that finding such an assurance was not, as it was for European artists, defining a place within—or against—one's own historical epoch. Nor was it to begin where Emerson had, as a member of the first generation to offer an inclusive denial of the values of the commercial republic. Yet their relation to the country was just as much a problem, since the United States had not so much changed its character as intensified that aspect that Emerson had rejected two generations before.

The solutions Williams, Pound, and Eliot found to the question of their identity and the significance art had in the world were in each case distinct, yet they shared a common root. What did it mean to be a writer in, or from, the United States if you lived abroad? You saw yourself as set apart from a nation predominantly concerned with business. A Frenchman, an Italian, or an Englishman might well have found it difficult to make such a wholesale judgment, but the commercial republic was in fact a less complicated spectacle. A sense of their detachment was at any rate the response of these three writers, who might well have agreed with Henry James's remark that in turn-of-the-century America the office of the language was chiefly that of facilitating commercial transactions.[11]

William Carlos Williams, the most self-consciously American of these three poets, wrote one of the books that most fully expose the stressed state of those who sought to be both Americans and poets in his time. *In the American Grain*, a prose work of 1925, ranks with D. H. Lawrence's *Studies in Classic American Literature* (1922) and Constance Rourke's *American Humor* (1931) as an early effort to describe a nation in which individuals had observably been forced to do more of the work of self-definition for themselves than was the case in Europe. The writers of these three books were arrested by a sense of the isolate quality of the American's personal existence. Williams's book attempts to overcome that isolation; it eroticizes the very landscape. Figures capable of touching and making love take on a heroic stature in contrast with the hard impermeable shells that surround individuals whom Williams thought of as repressed "Puritans"—a derogatory label current in the 1920s. His countrymen are seen as incapable of living in accord with the glorious spectacle of generative life that the continent had once offered them, and might still do so if they would stop befouling it with the sludge of money-making.

In the American Grain is an attempt to close the gap that

separates us from each other, an almost frantic burrowing into the past for instances in which heroic figures had achieved an imaginative grasp of the continent and its original inhabitants and for men and women whose union might serve as an example of form-creating energy—the kind of union Williams suggests in his account of the meeting of Aaron Burr and Jacataqua, leader of her Indian tribe.[12] He associates the defeat of sexual energy with a blockage of the imagination; he is especially vehement about the denial and distortion of the capacities of women. He writes in his exclamatory vein: "But a true woman in flower, never. Emily Dickinson, starving of passion in her father's garden, is the very nearest we have ever been—starving. Never a woman: never a poet. That's an axiom."[13]

We feel less assured now than Williams did in 1925 that the release of sexual and imaginative energy will create a culture that will erase the gap between us. But we recognize what has widened the gap and hardened the shells that enclose us when he writes, two paragraphs further on:

> Our life drives us apart and forces us upon science and invention—away from touch. Or if we do touch, our breed knows no better than the coarse fiber of football. Though Bill Bird [a publisher he had met in Paris] says that Americans are the greatest business men in the world: the only ones who understand the passion of making money: absorbed, enthralled in it. It's a game. To me it is because we fear to wake up that we play so well. Imagine stopping money making. Our whole conception of reality would have to be altered.[14]

A conception of reality rooted in "money making" had permeated the language; Williams undertook to scrub off these accretions so that people and things could once more be seen clearly, called forth by a use of words as bright, hard, and shining as pebbles in the bed of a brook.

Williams's exemplary uses of words have the effect of clogging his effort to convey the flow of life and the transformations of human energy in his long poem, *Paterson*, published in sections (1946–58). From Whitman's viewpoint it would be judged a failure because its pages are strewn with verbal artifacts, made things detached from the omnipresent maker who presides in Whitman's work. We cannot imagine Whitman sharing our pleasure in the wonderfully grainy and evocative flashes with which things and people present themselves in Williams from the 1920s on. But Whitman would have been in fundamental accord with Williams's search for an American "measure," a verse form to supplant those to which, as Williams thought, T. S. Eliot remained tied. This is a signal likeness to Whitman because it carries a crucial implication; this vast object, the United States, is in the process of formation as a whole, a thing to be apprehended by an equally comprehensive human subject. If a contemporary European had voiced such an ambition he would have appeared ridiculous, but Williams persists in the search for a national measure, for a voice that complements the whole shebang. This is not definitive of his accomplishment as a poet; rather it points to the effect of a limitation: seeing one's country as an object, one has to invent a maker sufficient to cope with that totality. Williams is both freed and constrained by this demand, which is also apparent in two modernists who did not stay in this country but were likewise affected by it, Ezra Pound and T. S. Eliot.

That both carried such an individualistic limitation abroad with them, and were on that account "postmodern" when they met European modernism, is a fact Lyndall Gordon and others have established in the case of Eliot, though the issue remains largely unexplored in the case of Pound, whose admirers often seem to feel that Pound's American origins count for little. The prime fact about the cultural situation in Europe when Pound arrived there in 1909 and Eliot in 1914 had already been shaping individual American lives for at least two generations. It was nothing less than a cultural horizon almost ringed by questions of money.

The youthful Ezra Pound, our first self-conscious "modernist," was equipped with a remarkably keen ear for the qualities of verse. He had ransacked the western past for voices he judged alive and was a tireless advocate of the talents of contemporaries he found worthy. His own considerable merits as a poet are less in point here than his faith in language as a medium of exchange and the relation of that faith to his American birth and upbringing. Long sections of his major work, *The Cantos* (1925–59), are devoted to American figures, Thomas Jefferson, John Adams, and Martin Van Buren among them. But Pound's admirers have been too much interested in his achievements as a poet to bring his relation to American culture into focus, in particular his conviction that the struggle with the National Bank conducted by Jackson and Van Buren was the crucial event in nineteenth-century American history. For Pound language was like money in that both were means of exchange and both could be debased; our humanity depended on the transmission of meaning or significance, that is, on exchange, whether of words, goods, or money.

Pound's view of what language does for us may be called naive in the extreme, not because it is wholly wrong but because it asks more of language than language can ever give. One may put it simply: neither works of art nor other ways of transmitting significance, like dollars and computers, can ever adequately define us because we are as a species still busy changing ourselves and our world. Yet in *The Cantos* our humanity depends wholly on a currency of meanings sufficiently stable to hold our world together, meanings that make up a realized or fulfilled humanity. Pound did not feel that such a structure of awareness was wholly inclusive; it might be but a shining platform in the surrounding darkness, but there was no other standpoint, our endowment was fixed. Emerson had asked us to transform ourselves in order to possess the world in vision; Pound's attention falls not so much on the potentialities of individuals as on our employment of the social means that bind us together. Both writers make an inclusive demand on us; they are equally exorbitant in claiming that our sense of reality must be reshaped and equally ready to gut history for timeless examples that accord with their views. But, unlike Emerson, Pound finds himself enclosed by a society in which, as he sees it, a false monetary currency contends with genuine exchange and broken and distorted verbal meanings must be replaced by full and precise meanings. He has no quarrel with the use of a medium of exchange that represents actual goods that fulfill human needs. His most scathing denunciations of the power of money are directed at those who create values out of thin air, as bankers do by lending more than they have.

Pound's tacit claims to power, the extent to which he appropriated both past and present for his imaginative use, seem no less inclusive than Whitman's and quite as representative of American individualism. Whitman, however, insisted that we emulate him, while Pound contended with social practice. Convinced that nothing less than the absolute power of a Chinese emperor could enforce the stability of meanings required to preserve and enhance our humanity, Pound moved steadily toward fascism. Even in this impulse we recognize something American; we have long been inclined to make disproportionate claims on reality precisely because of our fear of being saturated by economic motivations.

T. S. Eliot's relation to his American origins, masked by his deliberate assumption of English traits, is less easy to discern, although he is actually closer to Emerson than to Pound, in whose imagination the quality of our immediate social surroundings had a much more important place. Both men had an indubitable influence in the history of English modernism; both served as catalysts, provoking change, first Pound, who had been busy for five years when Eliot arrived in London, and then—with an effect that endured longer—Eliot. Before they appeared in London they had, in their separate ways, been profoundly affected by recent French poetry and criticism. Their discovery of fresh possibilities in the use of language and of critical opinions that cut through the fog of encumbering poetic practices proved immensely enlivening to them. Having carried to Europe the sense of detachment or distance from history that the relatively undifferentiated spectacle of their own culture had inspired in them, they found the European past a wonderful warehouse, a resource open to exemplary uses by a poet seeking an identity. Like Emerson, both Pound and Eliot tended to see history as meaningful primarily as a parable of their own "being and becoming."[15]

The part Eliot played in the modernist ferment of his time turns out in retrospect to have been misleading to many people on both sides of the Atlantic. When *The Waste Land* appeared in 1922 it was felt to be not simply a great poem but a testimony to a cultural despair that marked, as did the work of European modernists, the recognition of a profound social change, the end of a historical epoch. As recent studies have shown, however, Eliot's life exhibits a continuing struggle for religious assurance. This preoccupation with the manifestations of the eternal in the western past consorts with his American individualism and reminds us of the youthful Emerson's efforts to assure himself of the sufficiency of Christianity. Eliot was not so much testifying to a sense that an epoch was ending when he wrote *The Waste Land* as illustrating the fact that when a poet of genius sets about showing that the world is vicious and empty without God any age will offer abundant evidence.

In Eliot's plays as well as in his poems we encounter characters who claim nothing less than a total view of the human condition. Eliot's emphasis, like Emerson's, is always on an individual's inward transformation. Emerson, Thoreau, and Whitman had limited themselves to the exemplary mode, largely forgoing the effort to act directly on others, primarily because their claim to a wider sense of things than was available within society meant that it was meaningless to contend with society at all. They were passive in relation to public issues, a tendency in which they anticipate both Eliot and his uniquely illumined central characters.

Yet there is an important difference between Eliot and these earlier Americans. Eliot had taken refuge in England, hoping that Christian aspiration would continue to be given public recognition there. When this hope proved delusive Eliot's exacerbated sense of the need to preserve an authority that might foster belief led him to proclaim himself "classicist in literature, royalist in politics, and Anglo-Catholic in religion." This set of labels both acknowledges tradition and—because it is strikingly out of accord with the times—distances Eliot from his historical moment. It makes a claim on reality that rivals the extravagance of Emerson's assertion of total self-reliance. Despite Eliot's assumed Englishness, what remains clearly visible is his persisting American need to make a self removed from the aspect of the western world that the United States had first come to embody, in which, as Eliot put it, "the acquisitive, rather than the creative and spiritual instincts, are encouraged."[16]

Modernism is a term open to attack in an age that questions the prevailing literary canon as too narrow and exclusive. Few writers are called modernists, and those few have been given the status of an elite. This chapter offers evidence that the gap between individual Americans lamented by William Carlos Williams had been present in Emerson's time and that it was bound to widen in a commercial republic with no strong opposing tendencies. The visionary who claimed a grasp of the whole did not close that gap. He simply proclaimed that his vision was the source of an authentic identity that could not be gained from seeking possessions. The mid-nineteenth-century writers, and those modernists who share their world-possessing position, do not, in this light, appear an arbitrarily chosen elite but rather representatives of a recurrent response to an underlying cultural condition: to oppose the mere piling up of bits of the world and mortgages on its future, they asserted imaginative possession of the whole.

No such imaginative leap had been taken in Europe. The power of commerce was growing fast, yet it remained a discriminable aspect of the culture in Europe. It loomed over all others in the United States and became so pervasive that neither Christianity nor the republican ideal could withstand it. Americans were, as we have seen, more alone with money than were Europeans. They had a much greater measure of personal freedom, but its exercise was increasingly limited to the marketplace. Nineteenth-century European literature is of course shot through with brilliantly realized studies of the effects of commerce and industrialism on society and the individuals who composed it. Yet these works, and those of the European modernists who succeeded them, were launched *within* a social milieu and directed to it, whether their aim was a wide assessment of the past, an assault on outmoded conventions or social injustice, or an attempt at wholesale cultural destruction.

The Americans whose response to their culture was to deny that family, society, and history were the compelling sources of their awareness of the world had, from the European point of view, discarded all there was to think or write about. Europeans could hardly have guessed how massive and undifferentiated a few percipient Americans found the spectacle of their culture. Yet it is difficult to see how those few could have responded to what they saw with anything less than a massive blanketing assertion of their own. A self sufficiently commanding could create a picture of things in which possessions were insignificant. History might then appear, as Emerson had put it, an account of "one's own being and becoming."

Except for certain writers whose representation of life springs from a social soil, our early modernists were limited as well as freed by their efforts to stand outside our culture. William Carlos Williams saw this sixty-odd years ago. In *In the American Grain* he insists that only those who are in touch with each other and the past can hope to deal with the dominance that possessions have assumed in the imaginations of Americans.

CHAPTER 7

The Possibility of Individuation

Those selves which take the world for their object are claiming a hold on reality which is actually unavailable to them. Yet they are responding to an emotional need which the character of their culture often enforces. Both those absorbed in the fragmented world of possessions and those who try to escape it by making wholesale claims for the self lessen their capacity to grant that the conditions of our existence are social. Since we were from the outset a "made" society, created by our own fiat and notably less cohesive, less enclosed by a plurality of instituted habits, practices, and long-standing precedents than other societies, it may seem unfair to censure individuals for attempting an apocalyptic transformation of the money-saturated world. Yet the consequent isolation of those who make the attempt is grievously harmful to our future prospects. Talent which might have served the ends of the community is wasted in ineffectual opposition. We may hope that the harm is avoidable, since we live in imaginative constructions of the world that we can and do alter in the course of time. In keeping with my choice of particular individual instances—the only sort of evidence I have to offer—I return to Whitman as a case of the possibility of reverting to the complexity of an actual scene.

The Whitman who, approaching forty, abandoned his claim to imaginative possession of the whole shining globe for a lover plumped down into the plural world of those who choose and discriminate, love and lose. The poems in the "Calamus" section of the 1860 edition of *Leaves of Grass* and the wonderful although disguised torch song, "Out of the Cradle Endlessly Rocking," are those of a great poet. Yet both Whitman and his friends were aware that the pinnacle of his achievement was to be found not in these new poems of 1860, in which the lover first appeared, but in the poems of the world possessor in the editions of 1855 and 1856. The greatest poet is not necessarily the most admirable citizen.[1]

The poet who emerged in the 1860 edition of his book could write magnificently about loss and death, could write about a tie to another person, write about the deaths of young men, and of Lincoln in "When Lilacs Last in the Dooryard Bloom'd"—making in each case a reference to others or another. The world of his poems was no longer his alone, a representative or exemplary world; it was irrevocably peopled by others. The hollowness of late attempts to invoke the world in which he had been enclosed earlier is apparent in the late poem "Passage to India."

The Whitman who entered the plural world was likewise the citizen, whose anxious care for the nation was to result in *Democratic Vistas.* He no longer wrote in the exemplary mode, no longer professed an undivided consciousness or went in for wholesale appropriations of the scene of being. His critics and biographers have been far more comfortable with the citizen, who resumed his citizenship by singling out another man and thus dividing his world, as most of us do, by asserting a tie to a lover, although many have been loath to admit that he took up his membership for a reason that breached the conventions of his day.

To abandon the exemplary mode was to part rather decisively from Emerson, who never evinced the depth of concern about the future of the country that Whitman showed in *Democratic Vistas.* Harold Bloom rightly emphasizes the change in Whitman's sense of the world that follows on the poem called "As I Ebb'd with the Ocean of Life" in the 1860 edition of *Leaves of Grass.* The Whitman who had caught the past up into his own moment, who deplored philosophy because it purported to give laws to what welled out of the self alone and deplored love affairs because they blinded you to the unity of the spectacle of being, had of course been wholly incapable of seeing his own history or that of the nation as constitutive of the character of the present, incapable of acknowledging the process of growth I call "individuation," which can go forward only within society.

The opposed mode of achieving identity, which Thoreau called "building up a life,"[2] is first visible in Emerson. Pushing to their logical limit Emerson's repeatedly emphasized figures of speech which relate us to the whole of things—such as his assertion of the necessity of receiving "rays" from every quarter so that the soul may attain "her due sphericity"—we are faced with an apparent anomaly.[3] Our consciousness is not simply the receiver of all that surrounds us; it must be conceived as emitting all that it receives as well; consciousness is treated as both receiver and creator. This is what his use of the term "individualism" comes to when rigorously construed. The world about us is at once matter for our handling and, ideally, constitutive of our existence, for in receiving it we make it ours, *make it* in this double sense ourselves. Such moments of experience as this may be rare, yet they are held to be definitive: events outside of time which bleach out such immediacies as sexual longing, fear of death, dramatic encounter—in brief, the matter of stories—to pallid insignificance. This is the cost of the ever-present temptation, provoked by a desiccating culture, *to make it alone*. The melding of vision with creation is in fact an effort to make selves without reference to the social medium in which selves actually develop.

This chapter is focused on the possibility of acknowledging immersion in a social world and on instances of personal growth or individuation. No absolute division between such lives and those marked by the wholesale demands of individualism is possible, but examples provide suggestive contrasts and even help to differentiate phases in a single life, as does the case of Whitman, who surrendered an imperium of selfhood for the sake of love and acknowledged his place in the history of his time. He had of course always done so as a matter of daily practice; the man who wrote editorials was this very man. But the poems of the world possessor, those to which Americans respond most passionately, had canceled the limitations he later accepted as a poet.

How does the contrast between an emphasis on the daily drama in which others count and an emphasis on the exemplary, with its accompanying focus on solitary imaginative possession, affect one's view of future possibility? Both for those absorbed in the pursuit of money and for those with visionary claims for the self, the term "future" refers to acquisition—more profit or broader visionary claims. In the case of those who experience their lives as lived in the presence of family and community, the future is to a much greater degree a question of desires, hopes, and actions directed and qualified by interaction with others. Insofar as people are isolated from one another by the pursuit of money or disproportionate claims on reality they are blind to their own growth and to historical changes in the society. The more absorbed they are in their own possessions, real or imagined, the less capable they are of taking in the events which are significant for the community at large.

The latter part of the nineteenth century was, it is often said, pervaded by a sense of the enlivening possibilities of the future. But aside from the fact that the number of those who stood to realize those expectations was limited, the character of those possibilities might, we now see, have been described as progressively narrowing the variety of the chances for intercourse among individuals. Broadening, yes, with respect to profit, but, with respect to what may be called events of significance for humanity, growing less diverse and more specialized in accord with technological advances which marched arm in arm with profit. We cannot think of the period as heartening to those whose hopes centered on the quality of their relations with others.

What was happening was rather a leveling of distinctions between a variety of skills, interests, and passions, substituting the market's "futures" for the invocation of possibility which animates life with others. Each of the chances for profit came to be carefully examined and analyzed as an entrepreneurial opportunity, a development culminating in our own century, in which, for example, businessmen batten on our distinguishable pursuits by founding magazines for fishermen, ceramicists, coin collectors, and breeders of cocker spaniels. Discussion of such dismaying modes of dissolving interests into money has bred a scholarly industry on the subject of consumption which tells us a great deal about attempts to constrain us to buy and very little about what buyers are like, that is, about the sort of ties to each other that, while in bed, at breakfast, and abroad in the town, we are able to create and sustain.

Historians have offered very full accounts of the institutions and social conditions of this industrialized capitalist nation, but the way in which these have conditioned the existence of American selfhood is less often a central concern of their work. Why, for example, did this country respond to psychoanalysis, which had met such a grudging reception in England and Italy and had to be transformed to win its way in France? This receptiveness stems from our individualism. Why have we been so insistent that social class isn't primary among us? Why do attempts to dower us with an American mythos or national consciousness simply slide off the land they are supposed to describe? There are many studies which characterize contemporary Americans as lonely, isolated from each other, but the historical dimension of that separateness, that individual habit of viewing our world in the aggregate as a colossal other to be opposed or embraced, is best understood when we address the question of the conditions of achieving identity within the culture discussed in the preceding chapters.

As in the case of John Dewey's early writing on ethics, the characteristic focus is on the inward state of the self, not its relation to other selves. Dewey holds that if we are in an ethically desirable state, each of us a monad reflecting an appropriate view of the world and our obligations to others, we will feel *complete*, that is, will be universal possessors, who are nonetheless members of a democratic community. Note that the source of assurance is our own emotional state, just as in the instance of Captain Delano in Melville's "Benito Cereno," whom I have described as a human lighthouse, comprehending no more than what he himself illumines. We are once more facing one of the implications of "pragmatism": we see that *starting over* is undertaken from within the redoubt of a self unhampered by its own history or by feelings and experiences issuing from encounters with others—in short, by a person resembling Whitman's "new man," who is described as in total accord with what he experiences and needs no collaborators, past or present. It is such an American approach from inwardness to outwardness that I have called "imperial." If we juxtapose this stance with what is implied by such expressions as "the rights of man and the citizen," we are struck by its remoteness from the concept of citizenship and by its emphasis on the status of a person endowed with the power and the ability to authenticate whatever universal he has chosen.

The chief of these capacities is of course that of construing all that happens to you solely in your own terms. This is again reminiscent of the early Whitman's war on discriminations, comparative judgments, estimations of relative worth, and ties that bind us together: all are to be free, and no one is to be beholden to anyone else. Neil Coughlan quotes Randolph Bourne's conclusion that Dewey's instrumentalism "had no place for the inexorable"—which recalls Melville's assault on readers who seek to escape the realization of mortality. Coughlan is led to call Dewey a representative figure; he is "the philosopher par excellence of American liberalism; he shared with it the root conviction that we can have both self-defined self-fulfillment and social justice for all."

By insisting that money has worked to build walls around us and that within these walls we tend to grow fantasies which claim a wider grasp on reality than isolated people can humanly or logically maintain unless they call on a company of recognized others to consider them, I raise the question: how are we to learn to recognize others more fully? Doing so is clearly a condition of freeing ourselves from a culturally produced isolation. The contemporary philosopher Richard Rorty has urged that Dewey is to be highly valued, that he furthers the chances for a profitable intellectual commerce among us. Yet if there is plausible doubt that Dewey has himself managed to preserve what he thought he had done, that is, articulate the bonds between the individual and his community, he has left us in the dark, as Coughlan suggests Dewey did—has once more landed us in the contradiction between our own personally defined fulfillment and fruitful membership in the society.

The issue is addressed by Giles Gunn when he puts the following question in a discussion of the work of Richard Rorty, asking, "Would the historical record bear him out, for instance, in his contention that the vocabulary of self-creation is always and inevitably private, the vocabulary of justice always and necessarily public?"[4] The answer I have emphasized throughout is that history would not bear out the view he attributes to Rorty. But I have only the fact that our species has not and will not escape from history to justify my hopes. We are still, as a species, busy making ourselves. If a complex of notions as broad and practically powerful as Marxism can melt away, we are free to suppose that the imaginative sufficiency of what we call the "market" may lose its present dominance.

The historical fact appears to be that American intellectuals show a reluctance or inability to admit that any limitation of the goal of "self-fulfillment" is implied by membership in our community. In Emerson, Thoreau, and Whitman this was the ground of a rooted suspicion of fiction, which confines its characters to roles defined by the presence of others. In the course of the late nineteenth and early twentieth centuries this threat to imperial claims came to seem less apparent as art was freed of its obligation to mirror the national purpose and values and was granted an independent realm.[5] Active participation in politics continued to be seen as dangerously confining by our intellectuals. Until the end of the 1920s it was often felt to be the affair of Mencken's "booboisie" by those who thought themselves abreast of advanced thought and the latest movements in the arts.

What followed was an epoch in which a society ordered by monetary exchange was threatened with collapse, that of the Great Depression which began in 1929. The period in which the society was viewed from a distance—seen as given over to crass pursuits unworthy of the attention of intellectuals—came to an abrupt end. Many of those whom the depression had led to despair of capitalism or to find it the root of all social ills were attracted by the millennial pretensions of the Soviet Union. Even though there was no apparent hope of finding and mobilizing an oppressed proletariat in this country, the wholesale doctrine of communism proved intellectually appealing to a significant number of Americans, many of whom had earlier lived at a remove from political ideas. Unlike their contemporaries in France, for example, they had not been prepared for Marxist politics by earlier experience of politics based on class divisions. They thought of their subscription as an independent choice.

Exceptions were of course discernible among the hard-nosed members of the American Communist Party, acknowledged and unacknowledged. Their convictions had to do with actual revolutionary hopes and the shifting priorities dictated by Moscow; their presence and influence were indeed political. But the majority of sympathizers and fellow travelers were serving their own emotional and intellectual needs. Many had been deeply affected by the Great Depression but had no life-and-death stake in a cause. Emerson, confronted by a society he saw as fragmented by its focus on exchange, had found a glorious recourse in claims for individuals. In this later period what had at the outset counted for Americans entranced by Stalinism was a similar complement to their personal needs rather than an engagement with a proletariat destined for triumph. *This apparently public idea had a private use for persons whose outlook was that of individualism.*

When events in Russia led to disillusionment a growing number became actively anti-communist. They continued to cherish hopes for beneficent social change but came to see the American Communist Party as the agent of a monstrous betrayal of such hopes. It followed that in rejecting Stalinism one rejected the inclusive dreams that attended individualism. Others who had been attracted by what was often called "the great experiment" in the Soviet Union refused to believe in the horrors it exhibited. They were inclined to shy away from the activities of the Communist Party but remained obstinately attached to the notion that the USSR was a shining example to mankind. This very obstinacy is the clearest indication of the emotional function of Stalinism for middle-class Americans. True to their Emersonian inheritance, they conceived of social issues in an apocalyptic mode, saw them as requiring a thoroughgoing transformation of individual belief rather than a shared class consciousness. For this latter group the depression intensified and focused the need for an inclusive view of the world which those who despised the atmosphere of their commercial culture desperately wanted.

We owe to Henry James one of the most telling illustrations of the nature of their need. When his Princess Casamassima, who deeply resents being sold into marriage with a wealthy nobleman as a crime representative of a loathed culture, on learning of the anarchist plot, inquires, "Then it *is* real, it *is* solid?" she is voicing an all-inclusive desire to pull the social structure down.[6] The demand is hardly political in any sense; it is rather an invocation of apocalypse. What the fellow travelers of the 1930s and after were indeed demanding was a world transformed, a satisfyingly complete other or antithesis to the United States as they saw it. The insularity of such adherents made them awkward to handle; they were not ready-made conspirators. Moreover their demand was rather a cherished fantasy than a willingness to undertake a revolution. A displaced Emersonian hope is not a politics. People who found it pleasing and exciting to follow the "correct" party line (an echo of the term is heard in the call for the "politically correct" in the 1990s) might be relied on for contributions, but they had no interests at stake that moved them to take real risks. They had a stick to beat their own society with; they could be scornful of its institutions; but for the most part they knew very little either of Marxism or of what went on in the Soviet Union. To repeat, it was the conception of a countering ideal that they cherished, often at the cost of blanking out disillusioning information and the firsthand accounts of visitors to Moscow.

The individualism of fellow travelers showed, and still shows in the 1990s, as sympathy for Americans who were blacklisted or summoned before a congressional committee, a sympathy extended without regard to the distinction between dedicated Party members and more or less well-meaning fellow travelers. The most familiar examples may be found among the Hollywood Ten, notable for their contempt for our institutions and our democracy and skillful at playing on the emotions of their gulls.[7] These latter were being true to their individualism; they failed to consider the fact that they were encountering members of a group organized to overthrow the very conditions in which sympathy for individual expressions of opinion had an institutional sanction. References to American Stalinism are often met with blank incomprehension in the 1990s. Why fret about what was never an actual threat to the United States? The answer is clear: for the greater number our "Stalinism" was simply a variety of our imperial impulse to see our world in a lump and reject it in the name of a transforming universal; it was complemented among conservatives by an equally mindless impulse to exact an unthinking loyalty to things as they were.

Once more we meet the American presumption that individual rights are not something bestowed within the polity but are aboriginal, as in Emerson, who looked to each of us to claim an inner kingdom enjoying sovereignty. This familiar kind of personal assertion is passive in the very degree that it is extensive; if all those around me would have to undergo alteration to fulfill my social program, it becomes quite clear that nothing will happen in response to my sentiments. Many ostensibly social causes are tacit demands on the part of isolated people for wholesale conversions. Such demands bypass the existing powers and organizations in behalf of what remains an abstraction. Our present mode of selecting presidential candidates reinforces this impulse: we make causemongers of the candidates; fitness to govern has little to do with the process. The number of those who might have the imagination and aptitude to think and act within the community and society is lessened; actual political power slips increasingly into the hands of those who can in one way or another purchase or enforce the compliance of the officials presumed to be in the service of the public.

The "Stalinism" I refer to is just one instance of the impulse to find a universal which answers one's emotional needs. I take an example of the persistence of these needs from *The New Yorker* of the middle 1980s. After a discussion of the bumbling President Reagan's visit to a military cemetery at Bitburg in Germany and the confusion he displayed about Hitler's legacy and the Soviet role in Hitler's defeat, the editors introduce one of the interlocutors they customarily employ in "The Talk of the Town." His letter reports that he finds himself "extremely disoriented" by the suggestion that the Soviet Union, our ally in combating Hitler, is now being treated as somehow equally blameworthy.

> I had always thought we were simply mentioning to ourselves, as a sort of footnote, that we—the anti-Nazis—were somewhat anti-Communist as well. Now, Hitler, of course, was an anti-Communist. You could even say he was the most determined anti-Communist who has ever lived. And Hitler could never understand why certain Western countries, like England, refused to join with him in a crusade against the Soviet Union. England simply wanted no alliance with Hitler, and neither did we. Instead, we fought side by side with the Russians to destroy Hitler's regime. And so I had thought that it was a shared but unspoken assumption, unchanged since that time, that with Communist regimes we might sometimes find, somehow, some common ground, but that we simply could not find common ground with Hitler. And why was this? To put the matter very, very simply, the writings of Marx, which are the basis of Communism, contain many ominous undercurrents and have been used to justify many horrors, but I had thought that we all at least granted that Marx wrote what he did out of compassion for humanity, and that therefore those who followed him could not automatically be assumed to be inhumane. Hitler's ideology, in contrast, was *grounded* in inhumanity—was

> fundamentally based on hatred, on a merciless, demented racist theory, of which the assembly-line slaughter of innocents was the perfectly logical expression. And so I had thought that we were all united in this understanding, and that if the Second World War were happening today we would not hesitate for a moment to join once again with the Soviet Union to fight against Hitler, with whom we never made peace and never could make peace.
>
> But some of the things I've been hearing recently have made me doubt whether this is so; and if it isn't so, then I guess I'm living in an entirely different country from the one I always thought I was living in. I'm amazed to discover what pride I took in that country—how I accepted its faults, how, as I walked its streets, I quietly admired all the unknown citizens who walked beside me, how I pulled my own personal vigor and enthusiasm from that country's well. Deprived of that country, I feel old and weak. I don't know how to live among strangers.[8]

In this instance an undivided consciousness, eager to grasp the world on its inclusive terms, tries to preserve a long-cherished impression of the central importance of the fact that the United States and the Soviet Union had fought Hitler as allies. The ostensible witness explains that, although Marx's works exhibited "ominous undercurrents" and that "horrors" had been associated with Marxism, he had remained hopeful that since Marx had *meant well* "those who followed him could not automatically be assumed to be inhumane." Hitler could, since his regime was "*grounded* in inhumanity." The extraordinary assertion that Marx's *intentions* could blank out the millions of deaths which followed the collectivization of agriculture, the Moscow show trials, the Nazi-Soviet pact, the camps, and all else that had happened in the Soviet Union and to its satellites in the decades following the end of the war makes it plain that the writer is unable to distinguish his demands on the world from a supervening historical reality. Others have found it possible to differ with him, and he feels lost and alone. Individualism of this order makes its demand on reality a kind of absolute, which in this case boils down to a distinction between Marx's good intentions and Hitler's utter inhumanity. Stalinism, American style, was a commitment to an abstraction which stubbornly resisted evidence of the brutal terror which ruled Soviet Russia because it served the needs of an individualism which demanded the transformation of the United States into an ideal Other. This fantasy long outlived the period in which the Communist Party had played an active political role in this country and served as a substitute for an actual politics among many writers and intellectuals. It was less visible than the indiscriminate assaults on our liberties by the Red-baiters and their blacklists, yet it did a great deal of harm; intellectuals who were stoutly anti-communist were often lumped with reactionaries and condemned, a strikingly anomalous occurrence in a country presumably committed to democracy.

An individualism based, as Emerson's had been, on a claim to inner personal resources emerged once more in the late 1950s, after an interval of a century or so. (Henry Miller had played a John the Baptist role some years earlier.) The coming of the Beats in the 1950s amounted to a paler imperial claim; like Emerson, Thoreau, and Whitman, they proclaimed inner resources which were native to them. One of Allen Ginsberg's most telling remarks in the 1960s was that all separate identities were bankrupt; that is, *social* roles had become hollow; only those who stood outside could claim an integral selfhood. The sort of selfhood Ginsberg asserted was not, one may put it, that of a character, for character is felt to be fatally tied to established social roles.

The concept of character as distinctive has been as resolutely discarded by a good many contemporary commentators on our culture as it was by Emerson, who chose to view humanity as possessed of a single nature whose leading traits are epitomized in those who appear in his *Representative Men.* Leo Bersani's *A Future for Astyanax: Character and Desire in Literature* aims at dissolving the conception of character in literature in behalf of the enactments of desire. This is a logical extension of Foucault's effort to demonstrate that western social institutions constitute an array of modes of domination. The conception of character is seen as a fatally constricting armature issuing from institutional domination, which extends into the self and stifles the expression of personal desire.

The consequence for the conception of character and the possibility of individual agency is illustrated in an essay on Theodore Dreiser's *Sister Carrie* by Walter Benn Michaels.[9] Dreiser (who subsequently made a total flip-flop and became a Communist) is shown to have adopted in his first novel a conception of individual existence as wholly given over to an unbounded expression of desire. Michaels juxtaposes William Dean Howells's novel *The Rise of Silas Lapham* with Dreiser's to exhibit the distinction between fictional characters endowed with personal autonomy as against those of the early Dreiser, who perish of inanition when they stop pursuing an open-ended search for more money, fame, and power. Autonomy in Howells is assumed to rest on moral convictions. Unbounded appetite rules in Dreiser's book. Communism, construed as the totally opposed universal, was, it appears, the logical choice for the later Dreiser. We are more accustomed to instances of movement from communism to a rigid conservatism, equally doctrinaire and all-inclusive, but movements from one inclusive context to another are alike in their inflexibility and impracticality, since both cancel the middle ground of action and personal agency.

Many commentators on our culture adopt such doctrinaire starting points for their analysis, choosing initial premises which similarly erase the possibility of personal autonomy and see character as the product of forces—usually those proposed by Marx. Myra Jehlen, not the least able among them, tells us in *American Incarnation* that American fiction exhibits "a tragic vision inspired precisely by the fulfillment of the ideology of liberal individualism."[10] She assimilates Emerson's individualism to capitalism, and in so doing she denies his opposition to a world in fragments and ignores what is most important about it: the fact that it is too inclusive an opposition to capitalism to be effective. In other words, she is herself using a principle so inclusive that it cannot work as an effectual judgment and incitement to change in any actual state of human affairs.

Yet such analyses touch on a truth and dance away from it: Emerson was indeed a visionary capitalist; he, like the William James who so admired him, could not conceive of the self except in terms of possession, of ownership, whether of visions or of bank stock. But this is not a ground for denying his opposition to our immersion in acquisition; it is ground for asserting our need, as persons who live with others, to break out of the isolation money enforces. C. B. MacPherson is right in saying that individualism, as I describe it, is possessive, but it is of course wrong to suggest that there is any possibility of an apocalyptic solution to its insularity.[11] *Actions and events do not issue from structures but from characters, from human agency.* Once the conception of effective personal agency has been canceled by the scholar, there is no effectual limit to the play of such theoretical constructions as are employed by contemporary "Americanists."

A writer who was equally clear about the contradiction between personally defined self-fulfillment and democracy that Bourne found in Dewey, was Richard Hofstadter, who, in *The American Political Tradition*, sought to reinstitute the importance of human agents in our history at a time when historians dealt chiefly in impersonal forces and factors. For such historians the culture rolls on, massive and irresistible, propelled by forces with which individual agency has nothing to do, because each person is wholly subdued to them. Hofstadter documented the effect of such oversized ideas in history in *The Progressive Historians*, who notably fail to make any effectual connection between individual agency and social events, a failure perpetuated in the residual Marxism of American departments of literature in the 1990s.

We may be confident that the international deflation of Marxist power and conviction will have its effects in this country, but it may not much lessen the threat to our national capacity for political awareness posed by those who make a hidden claim to power in the name of impersonal or even apocalyptic modes of thought. These schemes will not disappear because Marxism no longer appears to be what William James called a "live option."

James is himself an instance of our long-standing vulnerability to a species of individualism which makes light of our actual interdependence. Delightfully distinctive and hospitable to others as he appears, he nonetheless is leashed to the notion of ownership as lying at the heart of selfhood. Profoundly convinced that each of us is distinguishable and inwardly incommunicado, he clung to Emerson's conviction that we were not qualified by the particular history of our relations with human others. This left him with property rights as the only available terminology to describe selfhood.

An important recent essay by Ross Posnock details the struggles that went into James's self-making and emphasizes his failure to specify any social—I would add any familial—conditions of its genesis and growth.[12] It is not surprising that James's work, *The Varieties of Religious Experience*, leaves one in the dark as to how a *community* of believers could ever have existed.

I employ the term "individualism" to suggest both the heroism it sometimes exhibits in contending with the desiccating money culture and the harm it can do to our sense of each other, to our common needs and the kind of hopes we may sensibly entertain. In recent years most of the instances of the use of this term that I have seen pay lip service to the notion that individualism is opposed to social good. On occasion it is hypostasized as an *essential* American trait. We find a reviewer of Walter Dean Burnham's *The Current Crisis in American Politics* commenting that the legitimacy of a government which is based chiefly on the middle-class vote shouldn't be questioned as the fruit of capitalism, since "the real enemy of a genuinely left wing politics is the individualist cultural ethos of America, as Burnham well knows. But are they alienated from this cultural ethos? I doubt it." As the reviewer sees it, "it amounts to the national character."[13] I would of course contend that leaving out what is here called "capitalism," that is, the pervasive pressure of the money-saturated scene, would make our individualism unintelligible.

It was in the 1930s that a significant number of American intellectuals, chiefly New Yorkers, who had discarded Communism but had no sympathy with the conscienceless purveyors of a Red scare showed a capacity for independent thought and openness to discourse with others. Although they often clung to the hope for a democratic socialism, they were led to suspect wholesale solutions for social ills; these burnt children of the experience of a universal mode of thought appeared to have freed themselves from its American variety, an Emersonian individualism. The unmistakable novelty of their position was their readiness to acknowledge that they had a place in history. This awareness opened their eyes to a wider context than that envisioned by any previous group of cultivated Americans. A few entered politics in the period of Roosevelt's New Deal, but most had a residual suspicion of efforts to save capitalism; the plural world they were willing to enter was international and chiefly literary, was peopled by thinkers and artists hitherto largely neglected among Americans.

What I wish to do here is to characterize this singular epoch in American culture during which these possibilities of individuation were at least marginally realized. It extended from the late 1930s into the early 1960s, a period during which some notable Americans came together to constitute an intellectual and artistic scene of an unparalleled diversity and capacity to recognize and assess each other's powers and those of the great modernists abroad. The period was a partial realization of the hope for a "middle ground" between idealism and practical affairs that Van Wyck Brooks had entertained.[14] No earlier generation had been bold enough, sure enough of its own powers, to face up to contemporary European accomplishments. This was in large part a question of catching up, of acknowledging figures from Gogol to Kafka, Kierkegaard to Rilke, whose American readers had hitherto been few. The general effect was an unprecedented expansion of the cultural horizon for a significant number of Americans.

The term now applied to those involved, "New York intellectuals," is both suggestive and, as is inevitable in all such labels, a bit misleading. New York is not Paris, a city in which politics, literature, journals, cafés, educational institutions for a chosen elite, and the pursuit of all the arts interpenetrate, a city in which movements in the arts and politics are intertwined. Yet if we compare what came about in American intellectual life in this period with earlier periods the difference is striking. In the generation of the "modernists" of the 1920s, Gertrude Stein, Ezra Pound, and T. S. Eliot, the image of America as a featureless chaffering nation had prevailed; all three had emigrated, leaving William Carlos Williams behind to follow his own course and be rewarded with a keener sense of this country than the other three achieved.

In the 1930s, to reject Stalinism was to enter a pluralist world. It was for some people a fruitful cause of a conscious individuation. It may verge on comic exaggeration to say so, but it almost seems that a few Americans had suddenly been provided with a past, a place in history. This is precisely what individualism cannot afford, since it assumes the capacity to make a fresh start of a pragmatic kind. If one had one's own peculiar history, had been shaped by one's very own past, then there might be, indeed must be, a scene embracing both writers and readers on which individual accomplishments were assessed and recognized.

To open one's eyes on that world was, it turned out, to become more aware of what Europe had been up to and of what Americans had painted and written, thought and said. This does not mean that all those who may be called intellectuals altogether ceased to assimilate the public sphere to their private or Emersonian needs or that Stalin's emissaries no longer had any success among them. The remnant that mattered, however, had entered, at least for the time, an international scene, and Americans in their turn began to obtain a recognition there which they had not enjoyed earlier.

I am here writing large what others have writ small; it is not a familiar contention that American intellectual life reached a pitch and displayed a variety during the 1940s, 1950s, and early 1960s from which it has since receded. When we take into account the heritage of individualism and the strong pressure to adopt this Emersonian stance exerted by the money-saturated culture, the distinctiveness of the achievement of the period we are considering stands out more dramatically. New York had somehow acquired the panache to consider itself a center of art and thought. Letters from Paris and Rome which appeared in our little magazines testified to a sense that New York not only counted as recipient of reports of the cultural life of these cities but was itself a center. Those with high aspirations in literature and the arts no longer thought it necessary to flee abroad. In this regard the Second World War favored us, since it led many distinguished refugees to settle here.

More than one American tradition has worked to lessen our sense of the importance of what happened at the midcentury. It has always been easy and reassuring to many Americans, defending, as they imagine, the democratic ideal, to attack the play of mind. Emerson, reflecting in his later years on the Brook Farm community and the propensity of its members to dispatch notes to each other about their utopian aims, called it "an Age of Reason in a patty-pan,"[15] and Harold Rosenberg, one of the most prominent among this later generation, was similarly amused, if not as dismissive, when he called New York's intellectuals "a herd of independent minds."

Accounts of this period have focused largely on the *Partisan Review* circle in New York. The magazine had been founded in 1934 by editors close to the Communist Party;

their disillusionment made for a very different periodical when it resumed publication in 1937. Still socialist, but no longer associated with a political party or faction, it became rather fiercely independent and steadily opposed to Stalin and all his works. It called on contributors from this country and abroad who were recognized as particular persons rather than as proponents of one or another political nostrum. The shift to literary concerns did not erase the impulse to extensive comment, often acerbic, on current political affairs and cultural issues. *Partisan Review* quickly became the bellwether of an American avant-garde.

Among these anti-communists a fresh sense of the chances for a mature intellectual scene arose, one on which artistic and intellectual achievements were pursued and assessed with an assurance unknown to preceding generations. Earlier, such achievements as those of Bourne, the younger Van Wyck Brooks, and Edmund Wilson had been those of single voices and were appreciated by a few but were denied the sense of a part in a shared endeavor. *Partisan Review* must not be thought of as having a merely local influence. Small though its circulation was, it reached little cultural enclaves all across the country and penetrated university communities, in which criticism of contemporary literature and culture was beginning to make head against the remnants of the genteel tradition and the devotion to philological study. At the same time the new criticism, most prominently represented by the *Kenyon Review*, was offering "revaluations" which involved starting up afresh with established writers. A wide spectrum of little magazines reinforced the conviction that Americans were not simply abreast of high culture but had been (as F. O. Matthiessen's *American Renaissance*, published in 1941, sought to show) substantial contributors to it in the past.

The office of the critic in the 1940s and 1950s was that of

a person who aspired to a distinctive voice; Leslie Fiedler in far-off Montana contended with the easterners, but in the act of doing so he contributed another voice. Admittedly, nothing like the intricately interlaced intellectual scene of London or Paris ever emerged here; these were locales in which the quantum of taken-for-granted cultural awareness was far greater, and less dependent on its diffusion in print because so much of its discourse was indeed conversational. But it cannot be denied that the emergence of individuals who had their being in each other's presence, if only in print and responses to print, marked a striking change. The individualism I have deprecated hardly disappeared, but it was a very different thing to speak to and be recognized by those you acknowledged as peers than to speak from an embattled conviction that money was all for most of your fellows, an isolating conviction which had led some to flee.

Subsequent cultural shifts have led to the devaluation of what was accomplished in that period; the last thing anybody seems to want in the 1990s is a distinctive critical voice addressing an explicitly recognized audience. One way of describing what was characteristic of the best work of the mid-century cultural commentators is to note their assumption that there was a public, a recognized audience, and that one addressed that audience as a particular person rather than as the representative of a group or the proponent of a method claiming impersonal authority. Such a claim for impersonal mastery offers a striking contrast with the mid-century epoch. A list of those who were prominent in that period nails down the contention that particular voices, not systems, were what was prized.

Leafing through the issues of *Partisan Review* from the late 1930s into the 1950s, one encounters Albert Camus, Jean-Paul Sartre, André Malraux, Paul Valéry, Jean Gênet, Ignazio

Silone, George Orwell, Nicola Chiaromonte, Maurice Merleau-Ponty, W. H. Auden, T. S. Eliot, and such resident talents as John Crowe Ransom, Leslie Fiedler, Isaac Rosenfeld, Sidney Hook, James Burnham, Arthur M. Schlesinger, Jr., Delmore Schwartz, Richard Chase, Robert Warshow, R. W. Flint, Wylie Sypher, Eric Bentley, C. Wright Mills, William Barrett, Robert Penn Warren, Arthur Koestler, I. A. Richards, Diana Trilling, Lionel Trilling, Harold Rosenberg, James Agee, Meyer Schapiro, Elizabeth Hardwick, Mary McCarthy, Frederick Dupee, Steven Marcus, and the editors, Philip Rahv and William Phillips. This is only a partial list of an array of distinctive talents which gave the readers of the magazine a sense of an international intellectual scene.

One of the clearest ways of demonstrating the central importance of this period in our cultural history was touched on earlier in connection with the discrimination of our nineteenth-century trio of Emerson, Thoreau, and Whitman from the English romantics. The romantics saw themselves over against society; for them it was an inescapable presence. But these nineteenth-century Americans bypassed society in behalf of a big idea. The imagined cancellation of the whole American social order among the Stalinists is once more an instance of American individualism of the kind so brilliantly represented by the earlier trio, who abandoned society and substituted "nature" or a picture of the order of being in general. Without an awareness of the part individualism has long played among cultivated Americans, their engagement with Stalinism, so remote in most cases from their own material interests or involvement in a posited class struggle, is hardly explicable. This contrast underscores the importance of what the *Partisan Review* circle accomplished.

Despite the publication in the 1980s of a number of books on the period in which this variety of voices was heard, the unprecedented degree of their break with American individualism of the Emersonian strain has not yet been recognized. It was relatively brief and narrowly based, but it is to be cherished as an indication that we may hope for the recurrence of a time in which a company of able minds proves capable of mutual recognition and overcomes the temptations of impersonal systems which seek to dissolve the very conception of personal agency.

In its palmy years this group, including of course those who wrote from abroad, constituted a forum that wielded a kind of authority absent in the professions and the institutions of learning with which many of those who took part were affiliated. The disputes among its members had a resonance felt beyond the modest circulation of *Partisan Review*, and the questions posed in its printed symposia and meetings for discussion were tempests in a larger teapot than the United States had boasted earlier. This is not to say that the result was a notable accretion of political sagacity, but rather that it was a period that afforded a hitherto unequaled opportunity for the public display of talent and its recognition by its peers.

Unhappily the significance of this intellectual blossoming is highlighted by its relative brevity; it stands out clearly because it tailed off and vanished so quickly. What succeeded it that bears on the themes of this essay is a saturnalia of individual assertion which canceled or obliterated the conditions of discourse and once again actively sought to endow individuals with universal claims, often disguised as impersonal methods which masked their personal agency. Cultural discourse involving recognition of the views of distinctive others diminished once more. In the 1970s literary criticism began to draw on theories of language from abroad and on continental philosophic movements which British and American philosophy had largely ignored. The employment of ideas derived from these movements by writers who had an insufficient awareness of their genesis in the history of European thought often reminds one of Constance Rourke's observation that when ideas crossed the Atlantic, shorn of the context in which they had arisen, they resounded like voices in an empty room. In this later period individualism seized on such arguments as Derrida's against the belief that authority could be lodged in language or Foucault's assertion of the omnipresence of the impulse to domination in cultural constructions of reality as initial premises so inclusive that all chances to state the disproving case were ruled out. But I am anticipating a later phase in the development of individualism in this country in the 1970s and 1980s.

It was in the late 1950s, coincidental with the waning of the intellectuals' faith in the possibilities of discourse, that claims based on an Emersonian self-reliance reappeared. We may hazard a guess that this was a reaction to the Eisenhower years during which a sense of a terrible sameness spread across the land—a feeling that the country had been Howard Johnsonized, flattened out to a dreadful bareness in which nothing but creature comforts, domesticity, and washing machines mattered. It was in this period that undisguised assertions of self-sufficiency, unsupported by such borrowed universals as Marxism, got a fresh hearing.

They were made by the erudite and impassioned Norman O. Brown, author of *Love Against Death*, and by the Beats, Allen Ginsberg, Jack Kerouac, Gregory Corso, and such collaborators as Neal Cassady, the somewhat older William Burroughs, and the poet Lawrence Ferlinghetti. Park Honan finds a continuity between what the Beats said and wrote and the work of Emerson and Thoreau. I quote from Honan's introduction to an anthology of Beat poetry and prose.

> Though beat writing is usually religious and mystical it is freed from any religious or mystical certainty in doctrine. It is Transcendental exactly in the New England sense of Emerson and Thoreau, since illuminations are to come from looking at the here and now, in this case, at the streets and geography of America.[16]

As Honan has it, "They tried to get *outside* America while living and observing *in* it."[17] Since almost all their observation was of the state of their own minds, not much of America got observed. But what is of importance here is the fact that when these young men were first heard from Whitman and the other two were their acknowledged predecessors, men who had succeeded in being outsiders.

The invocation of Whitman, Thoreau, and, less frequently, Emerson in the late 1950s and the 1960s by those who sought a position from which they could attack the whole business-ridden culture as an object to be condemned must not be confused with the more recent work of Harold Bloom, Richard Poirier, and the philosopher Stanley Cavell in the 1980s. These three are not concerned with the assertive and even extravagant early Emerson who preached self-union in a commercial culture. Among the cultural radicals of the late 1950s and the 1960s, Emerson, Thoreau, and Whitman were valued as opponents of the culture they were attacking.

When Ginsberg, Kerouac, Corso, and Orlovsky caught the attention of the press in the late 1950s it was not this tie with an earlier individualism which conferred an instant fame; it was their success in outraging the public—Ginsberg's poem "Howl" was originally condemned as obscene—and their behavior on public occasions which titillated and provoked people.

Not long after a particularly riotous and deliberately

shocking appearance of the Beats at Hunter College in New York, a Beat poetry reading was held at Columbia, which both Ginsberg and Kerouac had attended as undergraduates. The occasion turned out to be especially revealing, a kind of crux in literary and cultural history. Diana Trilling, a literary critic and commentator on cultural affairs whose notable essays published in *Partisan Review* included one on Alger Hiss's trial for perjury and another in which she maintained that Robert Oppenheimer had been improperly denied a security clearance, attended this reading.

Her essay on the event, "The Other Night at Columbia: A Report from the Academy," appeared in *Partisan Review* in 1958.[18] It was published before Allen Ginsberg had become a presence in the culture, both as poet and as a striking performer of a variety of public roles.

The essay is written, is voiced, rather, in a mode which grants the reader the privilege of a friendly intimacy; the writer recounts, muses, recalls, compares, catches herself up, and revises, as if carrying on an uninterrupted chat with a hearer. The essay merits further examination because it so clearly contravenes the impulse of American intellectuals to assert that we can live and write as *outsiders*; that the self develops and achieves its integrity without being enveloped in social circumstances. It is clearly this position that led to an almost universal condemnation of what Diana Trilling had written about this occasion.

The persona put forward as present, observing and commenting, speaks from an established social vantage point. She is one of three faculty wives who, disregarding the doubts and the scorn others have expressed for the Beats, determine to go together to hear them. The size of the crowd and the presence of the police suggest the possibility of a repetition of the disorder which had accompanied previous occasions.

Thanks to Professor Frederick Dupee, who presides, and to Ginsberg himself—Kerouac does not appear—the evening is decorous throughout. The writer had known of Ginsberg for more than a dozen years as a student who had repeatedly gotten into trouble and been rescued by her husband, Lionel Trilling, and by Mark Van Doren and others. She describes her own feelings about this troublesome student who nonetheless had talent and literary preoccupations, a youngster, in short, whose behavior had so often raised the question: how much must be forgiven to aspiring poets? She has a distressing awareness that Ginsberg makes extortionate emotional demands on others for an obvious reason: he had early lost his mother to madness and sought compensation for a deep psychic wound.

In the discussion following the poetry reading Ginsberg challenges the English department in which he had studied; it exhibits, he claims, no awareness of the possibility of English verse which escapes the pentameter. Diana Trilling sees in this a reassuring sign of a workmanlike concern with poetics which transcends the exhibitionism of previous Beat performances and finds herself affected by the reading of a poem Ginsberg addresses to her husband, "Lion in the Room." When she returns home a professional meeting is going on, and she is somewhat embarrassed by her need to convey that she had been moved by the occasion. She is gently scolded by W. H. Auden, as she had been earlier in the day by Dwight McDonald, who was inclined to dismiss these brash youngsters.

This twenty-page essay embraces a wide range of observations and judgments. There is her account of what she had known of Ginsberg's behavior and relations with his teachers; there is the episode in which the bewildered dean asks Lionel Trilling's view of his student's having written "Fuck the

Jews" on a dusty windowpane and Trilling is unable to explain to the dean what he finds understandable but impossible to translate into terms that official can grasp. A reflection on the contrast between the character of the 1930s and that of the late 1950s may serve to suggest the conversational immediacy of the essay.

> Intellectuals talk now about how, in the thirties, there was an "idea" in life, not the emptiness we live in. Actually, it was a time of generally weak intellection—or so it seems to me now—but of very strong feeling. Everyone judged everyone else; it was a time of incessant cruel moral judgment; today's friend was tomorrow's enemy; whoever disagreed with oneself had sold out, God knows to or for what; there was little of the generosity which nowadays dictates the automatic "Gee, that's great" at any news of someone else's good fortune. But it was surely a time of quicker, truer feeling than is now conjured up with marijuana or the infantile camaraderie of Kerouac's *On the Road*. . . . As they used to say on Fourteenth Street, it is no accident, comrades, it is decidedly no accident that today in the fifties our single overt manifestation of protest takes the wholly nonpolitical form of a group of panic-stricken kids in blue jeans, many of them publicly homosexual, talking about or taking drugs, assuring us that they are out of their minds, not responsible, while the liberal intellectual is convinced that he has no power to control the political future, the future of the free world, and that therefore he must submit to what he defines as political necessity.[19]

The essay proved remarkably perceptive; the impulse shown by the youthful Ginsberg to join the academy has been resoundingly validated: he is now a well-placed and respected professor. Her judgment about the importance of his mother's madness has been confirmed by his biographers. But her essay touched a cultural nerve and provoked attacks of a kind easily recognizable as the reactions of Americans who accord Ginsberg the status of an imperial outsider which they demand for themselves.

G. S. Fraser, a British writer chosen by the editors of *Partisan Review* to review *Claremont Essays*, the volume in which the essay was reprinted in 1964, fastened on this piece to characterize the writer's work.[20] His adverse description is based on what he somewhat incoherently construes as the writer's "Puritan," "Jewish," and "Freudian" bias, and he characterizes what she has done as exhibiting "pride," "uncharity," "ruthlessness," and, to cap it all, "brutality." What provoked Fraser to such ill-judged extravagance is an interesting question, but it is subsidiary here. What is significant is that six years after the event Trilling was still being attacked.

When Norman Mailer refers to the essay ten years after its original publication in 1958, he does not concern himself with Fraser's scurrilous review, but he does suggest a reason for the denunciation of the essay. In the course of writing about Norman Podhoretz's *Making It* (1967), in which Podhoretz chronicles his success in entering the intellectual circle we are discussing (Podhoretz called it "the Family"), Mailer suggests that Podhoretz had offended by "exposing himself."

> Indeed Establishment writers displease the Family only when they fail to present themselves as critical, intelligent, superior, and *in their cool*. The only piece remotely comparable in its innocent assault on the total temper of the Family was Diana Trilling's account of going to

> hear Allen Ginsberg read his poetry at Columbia. That is writing with such simplicity of affect and directness of response that it may live longer in literature than anything else by the lady—it has the tone of enduring literature—yet it was loathed in its time, loathed one may suspect for the defenselessness of its approach since Diana presented herself not as a distinguished critic (which had hitherto been implicit in her style) but as a bewildered faculty wife: the Establishment reacted as if they were being thereby sucked down into a mucker's muck.[21]

The writer is not in the least "bewildered," nor does the experience she recounts as a member of the so-called "Establishment" have any relation to Podhoretz's account of his effort to enter it, but the essay clearly merits Mailer's suggestion that it has the quality of "enduring literature." Although the writer's presence in the essay is quite distinct from Mailer's, it merits comparison with what Mailer accomplished in the best passages of "On the Steps of the Pentagon,"[22] especially in its generosity, the openness of its acknowledgment of others who are seated in their awareness of themselves and each other down to the very way they dress. The essay is, however, clearly apart from Mailer's book in its avoidance of Mailer's play with his own self-regard. The writer is not uneasy about where she comes from or where she stands in this social nexus. If she had been she would hardly have braved attendance at the reading, a somewhat subversive act which questions the opinions of such people as W. H. Auden and Dwight McDonald about these obstreperous youngsters and the audience which feels drawn to them.

But what Mailer recognizes as a characteristic of the "Establishment" is accurate and has a wider application than he suggests. He has uncovered the impulse to make one's world an object. Those who wish to appear "critical, intelligent, superior and *in their cool*" are the very Americans who have not succeeded in escaping the imperial stance; who implicitly deny that they are the growth of a given social soil and do not acknowledge membership in a social class or confess that they are affected by a discernible cultural atmosphere. Only fiction is permitted to use such materials. It was an overweening self-reliance which provoked those who so disliked the essay. Fraser was being more American than he may have realized when he coupled his savage denunciation of "The Other Night at Columbia" with this startling remark: "If the essay had been a short story, I would have hailed it as one of the great contemporary American short stories."

It is clear that fiction, along with the other arts, enjoyed an exempt status won since Emerson's time. An artist could do or say anything he pleased, but self-begotten breathing persons must not be represented as fatally embroiled with each other—or discriminated and valued over against a social background rather than against some outsize context like Emerson's "nature."

To pull identifiable people down into their daily human environment, into what Mailer, with a somewhat forced inelegance, calls "a mucker's muck," is to assault the cherished citadel of the world-possessing self; to show that there is indeed an inescapable social world. Many readers reacted as if they and Ginsberg himself, viewed as they wished to be viewed, as presences who stood outside the conditions of their genesis, were being deprived of their American independence. It is no wonder that writing biographies of Emerson, Whitman, and Thoreau has proved difficult. They devoted much of their energy to showing that they were beholders of a world which, fully grasped, would fit them like a glove. They did not wish to see their lives as stories in which others figured.

The violence of some of the reactions to this essay attests to the fact that a cultural nerve had been touched; it suggests an offense comparable to that which might follow the claim that Joseph had after all been the father of the infant Jesus. What had gotten under the critics' skins? It is clear that such judgments as those made by Diana Trilling assume the existence of a society in which certain standards of behavior obtain and are generally observed. It would appear that such judgments of actual people, unless embodied in a fiction, are taken to be an assault on their native dignity. We hear them saying: how dare you circumscribe the infinite potential of another person? You have hurt a fellow being and added to the number of those harmed by society. You have no right to try to include people in the cage of your judgments; they are not to be seen as members of the community in *your* conception of it! We all know, one hears them murmuring, that anybody who talks about how our fellows behave fails to see that society itself is an instrument of oppression. To depict Ginsberg as a character with a personal history caught up in a moment of cultural time is felt to be a transgression. As the objectors have it, Ginsberg is essentially what we now know him to have been all along, a cultural icon, a recognizable and triumphant outsider.

The fate of Trilling's essay testifies to the vulnerability of the scene of discourse which *Partisan Review* had fostered among intellectuals. Their hard-won sense of the heavy cost of wholesale judgments of society and of the value of the free circulation of a variety of opinions, as well as of the recognition of many diverse talents, proved hard to maintain. The hope for our society at large, as Richard Hofstadter observed, lay in the possibilities fostered by our appreciation of its diversity, which finds expression in those who, assuming the existence of a civic order worth preserving, try to understand its character and further what they judge best in it.

In the ensuing decades those institutions which have been presumed most useful in holding our culture together, universities, publishing houses, the national government, have exhibited a distressing incapacity to preserve the sense of a scene on which intelligence is welcomed. Those interests which proclaim themselves publicly responsible nowadays are often founded on abstractions such as race, class, and gender, all appealing before a forum which they themselves do not believe exists, that is, the civic order itself. When those we have elected are not trusted to act in behalf of the public welfare, we cry out before a forum we have declared empty. Instead of valuing those who seek to foster a civic order and are willing to try to consider the resolution of conflict within and between group interests, we often turn, in accord with our imperial conception of individual existence, to celebrities, people who appear to have achieved the sort of self-begetting we desire.

Nothing is more definitive as an indication of the diffusion of our attention to the scene through which we move. We cannot, it appears, bring our common interests into focus. *People*, a magazine which celebrates a terminal effect—that of being well known, of living in the aura of mass attention—proposes nothing to its readers. They are lookers on, spectators, nonparticipants in the work which leads to celebrity. Celebrities take no apprentices: it is not the work they do which has engaged us; nothing comes of celebrity for those who seek immersion in the atmosphere it creates except the expectation of its increase or the registration of the fact that it has lessened. There is a frightening degree of passivity in this consumption of images of the well known, a drizzling conviction that nothing larger than a regnant individualism exists where there was once a public world in which all played parts, large or small.

From the 1890s to the end of the 1920s there was an earnest effort to represent business success and moneymaking at large as heroic effort, deserving of admiration and emulation. The depression qualified all such efforts to equate wealth with heroic achievement but did not lessen the fascinated attention it received.

I have proposed that the conception of individual agency entertained by cultivated Americans has exhibited a division: on the one hand we have cherished representative literary figures who have played outsider roles; on the other we have recognized capitalists as exerting massive power both economically and politically, and these men have been admired as well as denounced. Collis Huntington, Andrew Carnegie, John D. Rockefeller, Henry Ford, Samuel Insull, J. P. Morgan, and such lesser phenomena of more recent times as Donald Trump and Michael Milken are figures robbed of almost everything but money, too bleached by its presence to figure in narrative as distinctive human characters. Their use of inclusive contexts, such as the corporation or a network of holding companies, has led to suggestions that there is a likeness between these fields of arcane manipulation and the wide territory claimed by visionary figures.[23] But for most Americans what the very rich do is almost as remote from comprehension as the domain of particle physics.

An essay such as this book, dependent on descriptions of particular written responses to the humdrum metaphysic of money, can hardly do more than refer to such figures; they are like irruptions from below which appear and dive into the deeps without leaving an intelligible trace in a continuing story. My book must be thought of as an indirect plea for the individuation which free intelligence requires, an expressed trust in the possibilities which the species still offers.

In stressing the centrality of the conception of human agency I have offered the frail skein of western history, thought, and literature as indispensable evidence of the powers and constraints within which our species exists. Our recently developed skill in dissecting those sources of assurance on which we have hitherto relied has not, after all, succeeded in abolishing our sense that what we must rely on, develop, or attack is the very strands which compose that skein. The universe at large is neither friend nor enemy; for all the purposes that matter to us, our world, the construction of our imaginations, built out into the space we have created, comprises our humanity. Our continued existence is not guaranteed; we may be destroyed by forces we cannot control; we have the power to so act as to destroy ourselves; but whatever comes about within the civilizations we have developed must be thought of in relation to what we have done, built, thought, and felt; we cannot even think about what we are doing except in its relation to what has earlier been done and said.

What is coming to seem the central strand in the western construction of the world is the realm of thought and figuration we call money, credit, debt, and the whole array of mensurations it includes, which is referred to here as the humdrum metaphysic of money: the containing framework of our culture. The work of Marc Shell, Kurt Heinzelman, and others has demonstrated the interdependence of money, language, and thought, to employ the terms which serve Marc Shell as a title.[24] As Kurt Heinzelman has shown, money and poetry are constructions of our world which interpenetrate each other in demonstrable ways.[25]

It was the fate of the United States to exhibit the power of money to win more imaginative ground than it had as yet acquired in other western nations and to demonstrate the difficulty of preserving other human interests in the face of its spreading influence. As Marc Shell observes, the whole western past has shown that money tends to level all things to an equality based on the possibility of exchange.

It is my premise that the world-possessing or imperial self is the shadow cast by money, a dangerously inclusive claim on reality, the *specious other* of acquisition, which generates an individualism that apes the impersonality of what it opposes and attenuates our ties to human others. The unhappy result is a visionary or ideological capitalism or a still more crippling intellectual development, a dedication to various kinds of thought which assert that human agency has been wholly abolished by one or more of the imaginative constructions we ourselves have built into human existence.

Most contemporary systems of cultural analysis, passive, exemplary, atemporal, reductive of awareness of other people, would vanish if we found a way to reinstitute our belief in the importance of the human subject. We cannot carry on a discussion with a system or acknowledge other people while maintaining that we are shut up to a constraining context. Such contexts are cocoons made by individuals who have lost their power to conceive of others and are unable to think of themselves as trying for common ends. The intellectuals who are in this wholesale business are all singing swan songs for humanity.

But not simply the intellectuals. We have all been somehow reduced, driven back on our own concerns to an increasing degree. How to be a particular person, alive in the present, has become a topic for discussion among intellectuals, but more widespread effects of the money-saturated world are apparent in other ways, our attention to celebrities, for example, or the wasting away of our sense of public concerns suggested in this quotation from a review by Alan Wolfe of James D. Hunter's *Culture Wars: The Struggle to Define America.*

> Americans have reversed the usual understanding of public and private. The great political and economic forces that are usually understood to shape public policy are viewed as clashes between private interests. At the same time matters of religious belief, aesthetic taste, and cultural preference—once thought to be private and individualistic—assume center stage in the large public dramas enacted in the media. We shine light on the shadowy regions of the soul even as we darken the theater in which our common destiny is enacted.
>
> Because they practice politics in cultural terms, Americans cannot be understood with the tool kits developed by political scientists. . . . It is not because Americans are politically sophisticated that they constantly frustrate those who would understand them, but because they are politically innocent. Unable to abolish war, they have abolished politics; the state has not withered away, but the amount of attention paid to its affairs has withered badly.[26]

The "regions of the soul" are not so "shadowy" as the writer appears to believe; no matter how many varieties of character we present, the degree of self-absorption, of individualism each of us shows, remains perceptible. The virtual disappearance of what is thought to be of public concern has shrunk in concert with our capacity to value and esteem other people. To lose the capacity to appreciate the otherness of others is to reduce them to mere objects, feeding or threatening our little empire of selfhood.

An essay such as this, which makes a plea for the recognition that universalizing the human plight is the most dangerous of our uses of our intelligence, may seem peripheral in an age when our civic order appears to be in desperate shape. We are at the moment led by those who foster internal divisiveness, and the opposition party seems largely composed of professional officeholders. But the choice of an apocalyptic view of this or any other time is a clog, or, better, a blindfold, over our awareness of the possibilities of change. The instant moment is not an absolute, but a prelude.

The plea I have made here to search out every possible means of dissolving the isolation money enforces is made in behalf of the possibility of acting in concert to foster our national and global welfare. The realization of this hope must begin with a revived sense of the crucial importance of the conception of human agency. No effectual action on the part of such ends is feasible for those who see each other through money-glazed eyes or in the terms of any other impersonal scheme. All such means were invented by humanity, and if we are to survive we must so use them as not to deny each other.

If we wish to know why works of art have ceased to be discriminable and valued save as instances of underlying cultural forces, or why the conception of personal agency has been denied in favor of recipes for the making of selves which draw on analyses of cultural forces, or why, generally speaking, particular objects and choosing and judging persons have been swallowed up in the maw of systems—why, in short, our sense of the world is so ridden by the systems in which we imprison ourselves that we cannot find each other or conceive of history as an actual scene of change which affects real people—the term which is coming to loom over all answers is "the market." It is the atmosphere generated by money (science is merely accessory) which has saturated human concerns and made us system mongers.

The market won't help us to what we most desperately need, a modicum of free intelligence which grants reality to others—something which few Americans seem able to provide. When we make detached analyses of an atemporal, ahistorical order, we are denying the presence of urgent current problems. As Emerson once said: "Let us treat the men and women well; treat them as if they were real; perhaps they are."[27] I ask that we remove the qualification.

Notes

Chapter 1: Builders of Their Own Worlds

1. Alexis de Tocqueville, *Democracy in America*, ed. Phillips Bradley, 2 vols. (New York: Random House, Vintage Books, 1945), vol. 2, Second Book, chap. 13; Third Book, chap. 19.

2. Henry Nash Smith, "Emerson's Problem of Vocation," *New England Quarterly* (March 1939), 12:52–67.

3. *In Re Walt Whitman, Edited by His Literary Executors*, ed. Horace L. Traubel, Richard Maurice Bucke, and Thomas B. Harned (Philadelphia: David McKay, 1893), pp. 5, 311–12, 316, 387.

4. John Burroughs, *Notes on Walt Whitman as Poet and Person* (New York: American News Company, 1867), p. 32. For the use of "interior republic" and "new man," see the essay "Whitman's New Man" by Quentin Anderson in *Walt Whitman: Walt Whitman's Autograph Revision of the Analysis of Leaves of Grass (For Dr. R. M. Bucke's Walt Whitman)* (New York: New York University Press, 1974), pp. 11–52. An earlier discussion of Whitman appears in Quentin Anderson, *The Imperial Self: An Essay in American Literary and Cultural History* (New York: Knopf, 1971), chaps. 3, 4.

5. *The Complete Works of Ralph Waldo Emerson*, ed. Edward Waldo Emerson, 12 vols. (Boston and New York: Houghton Mifflin, 1903–04), vol. 10, *Lectures and Biographical Sketches*, "Character," p. 95. I note that the "moral sense" was an endowment of each of us, rather more plainly secular than "conscience." Subsequent ref-

erences to Emerson's published works drawn from this edition are hereafter cited as *Works*, followed by volume number and title.

6. *Works*, vol. 2, *Essays First Series*, "The Over-Soul," p. 267: "There is a difference between one and another hour of life in their authority and subsequent effect. Our faith comes in moments; our vice is habitual. Yet there is a depth in those brief moments which constrains us to ascribe more reality to them than to all other experiences."

7. *Christian Examiner* (Sept. 1836–Jan. 1837), 21:374–75.

8. *Works*, vol. 3, *Essays Second Series*, "Experience," p. 81. See *The Journals and Miscellaneous Notebooks of Ralph Waldo Emerson*, ed. William H. Gilman et al., 14 vols. (Cambridge, Mass.: Harvard University Press, 1960—), vol. 8, p. xi: "Union is only perfect when all the uniters are absolutely isolated." Subsequent references to this edition are designated as *JMN*.

9. *Works*, vol. 3, *Essays Second Series*, "The Poet," p. 42.

10. Richard Hofstadter, *Anti-intellectualism in American Life* (New York: Knopf, 1963), p. 48.

11. *Nature* (1836), in *The Collected Works of Ralph Waldo Emerson*, vol. 1, *Nature, Addresses, and Lectures*, ed. Robert E. Spiller and Alfred R. Ferguson (Cambridge, Mass.: Harvard University Press, 1971), p. 10.

12. *Christian Examiner* (March 1829), 6:5.

13. *The Works of William Ellery Channing*, 3 vols. (Boston: 1848), vol. 1, pp. 89 ff.

14. Michael Walzer, Introduction to *Regicide and Revolution: Speeches at the Trial of Louis XVI* (London: Cambridge University Press, 1974), pp. 1–89.

15. Yehoshua Arieli, *Individualism and Nationalism in American Ideology* (Cambridge, Mass.: Harvard University Press, 1964).

16. Conor Cruise O'Brien, *God Land: Reflections on Religion and Nationalism* (Cambridge, Mass.: Harvard University Press, 1988).

17. *Leaves of Grass*, Comprehensive Readers Edition, ed. Harold W. Blodgett and Sculley Bradley (New York: Norton, 1965), "Song of Myself," sec. 38, line 970. All following references to *Leaves of Grass* are drawn from this edition, except as noted.

18. *The Early Lectures of Ralph Waldo Emerson*, vol. 3, 1838–42, ed. Robert E. Spiller and Wallace E. Williams (Cambridge, Mass.: Harvard University Press, 1972), p. 381.

19. *The Journal of Henry D. Thoreau*, ed. Bradford Torrey and Francis H. Allen (originally published in 1906, reprinted in 14 vols. bound as 2; New York: Dover Publications, 1962), vol. 4, p. 433, Dec. 28, 1852. Future references to *Journal* are to this publication unless otherwise specified.

20. John A. Thompson, "American Dreamers," a review of *Eccentric Design* by Marius Bewley, *Hudson Review* (Autumn 1959), 440–45.

Chapter 2: Nature's Brothers

1. Orestes Brownson, "Mr. Emerson's *Address,*" *Boston Quarterly Review* (1838), 1:512.

2. *Works*, vol. 2, *Essays First Series*, "Friendship," p. 214.

3. *Works*, vol. 12, *Natural History of Intellect*, "Thoughts on Modern Literature," p. 316.

4. *JMN*, vol. 5, p. 254.

5. *JMN*, vol. 5, p. 410: "In conversing with a lady it sometimes seems a bitterness & unnecessary wound to insist as I incline to, on this self sufficiency of man."

6. *Collected Works*, vol. 1, "Divinity School Address," p. 80.

7. *Works*, vol. 10, *Lectures and Biographical Sketches*, "Historic Notes of Life and Letters in New England," p. 326.

8. *Works*, vol. 2, *Essays First Series*, "History," pp. 26–27. See Thoreau, *Journal*, vol. 4, p. 290, Aug. 8, 1852. Referring to Sadi, he writes: "By the identity of his thoughts with mine he still exists."

9. Richard Poirier, *A World Elsewhere* (New York: Oxford University Press, 1966).

10. Among Emerson's numerous references to the disabling effect of the pursuit of money and possessions, this sentence from "Self-Reliance" is one of the best instances: "And so the reliance on Property, including the reliance on governments which protect it, is the want of self-reliance." He goes on to say of those who are so hobbled: "They measure their esteem of each other by what each has, and not by what each is." *Works*, vol. 2, *Essays First Series*, "Self-Reliance," p. 87.

11. *Works*, vol. 10, *Lectures and Biographical Sketches*, "Aristocracy," p. 33.

12. *Leaves of Grass*, "Song of Myself," sec. 19, line 388.

13. *Leaves of Grass* ([Published by Whitman himself] Brooklyn, N.Y.: 1855), p. 63.

14. Ibid., p. 64.

15. Ibid., p. 57.

16. John Burroughs, *Birds and Poets* (Boston and New York: Houghton Mifflin, 1877, 1895), chap. 10, "The Flight of the Eagle," p. 209.

17. *Democracy in America*, vol. 2, Fourth Book, chap. 3, p. 311.

18. *Leaves of Grass*, 1855 Preface, pp. 717–18. "Did you suppose there could be only one Supreme? We affirm there can be unnumbered Supremes, and that one does not countervail another any more than one eyesight countervails another. . . ."

19. *JMN*, vol. 13, p. 51.

20. *Norton Anthology of American Literature*, ed. Ronald Gottesman et al., 2 vols. (New York and London: Norton, 1979), vol. 1, pp. 862–63, Nov. 10, 1838.

21. *Birds and Poets*, p. 210.

22. *The Writings of Henry D. Thoreau*, gen. ed. John C. Broderick, *Journal*, 1: 1837–44, ed. Elizabeth Hall Wetherell, William L. Howarth, Robert Sattelmeyer, and Thomas Blanding (Princeton, N.J.: Princeton University Press, 1981), p. 69.

23. *Journal*, vol. 2, p. 470, Sept. 7, 1851: "Do I not impregnate and intermix the flowers, produce rare and finer varieties by transferring my eyes from one to another?"

24. *JMN*, vol. 13, p. 51.

25. *JMN*, vol. 9, p. 242.

26. *JMN*, vol. 13, p. 187.

27. *Leaves of Grass*, "Song of Myself," sec. 29, line 647.

28. Ibid., sec. 25, lines 560–63.

29. See *Works*, vol. 3, *Essays Second Series*, "Experience," p. 71.

30. John Burroughs, "Walt Whitman and His 'Drum Taps,' " *Galaxy* (Dec. 1, 1866), 2:605–15.

31. Walter Harding and Carl Bode, eds., *The Correspondence of Henry David Thoreau* (New York: New York University Press, 1958), p. 45.

32. *Journal*, vol. 4, p. 150, June 26, 1852.

33. See note 42 below.

34. *Journal*, vol. 1, p. 284, Sept. 5, 1841.

35. *Leaves of Grass*, "Crossing Brooklyn Ferry," sec. 8, lines 96, 97.

36. Ibid., sec. 9, lines 126, 127.

37. Ibid., sec. 3, lines 30, 31.

38. Hugh Blair (1718–1800), *Lectures on Rhetoric* (1783), and Henry Home, Lord Kames (1696–1782), *Elements of Criticism* (1762).

39. *JMN*, vol. 3, p. 199. The editors use angle brackets to indicate words Emerson canceled.

40. Jacques Derrida, *Of Grammatology*, trans. Gayatri Chakravorty Spivak (Baltimore and London: The Johns Hopkins University Press, 1974).

41. C. Carrol Hollis, *Language and Style in Leaves of Grass* (Baton Rouge: Louisiana State University Press, 1983). Tenney Nathanson's recently published *Whitman's Presence: Body, Voice and Writing in Leaves of Grass* furnishes an ampler treatment of the topic of "presence."

42. See Stephen Railton, "Thoreau's 'Resurrection of Virtue!' " *American Quarterly* (May 1972), 24:210–27; Michael West, "Scatology and Eschatology: The Heroic Dimensions of Thoreau's Wordplay," *PMLA* (Oct. 1974), 89:1043–64; Michael West, "Charles Kraitsir's Influence upon Thoreau's Theory of Language," *Emerson Society Quarterly* (4th Quarter 1973), 19:262–74; Michael West, "Walden's Dirty Language: Thoreau and Walter Whiter's Geocentric Etymological Theories," *Harvard Library Bulletin* (2 April 1974), 22:117–28.

43. *The Writings of Henry D. Thoreau, Journal*, 1:1837–44, p. 52.

44. *The Early Lectures of Ralph Waldo Emerson*, vol. 2, 1836–38, "Being and Seeming," p. 296.

45. *Works*, vol. 3, *Essays Second Series*, "Experience," p. 70.

46. *Works*, vol. 1, *Nature*, p. 46.

47. *Leaves of Grass*, "Crossing Brooklyn Ferry," sec. 8, lines 95–100.

48. Henry James, Sr., *The Secret of Swedenborg, Society: The Redeemed Form of Man*, and other works.

49. John Bayley, reviewing two books on Whitman in the *Times Literary Supplement* (11 March 1977, 258), says of Whitman's verse that "[D. H.] Lawrence, who much admired Whitman but could not resist trying to cut him down to size, as he did with all manifestos but his own, replied to his expansive query, 'What is impossible or baseless or vague? . . . all things enter with electric swiftness softly and duly without confusion or jostling or jam' with 'if that is so, one must be a pipe open at both ends, so everything runs through.' This metaphor is indeed perfect for Whitman, and higher praise than Lawrence presumably realized. It expresses the physical relief and freshness ('the bowels sweet and clean') he gets into poetry, and suggests, too, the lapses into vacancy when we are not concentrating on it. It leaves little or no mark on the memory or mental consciousness, and is then renewed when we go back to it again and plunge in."

50. *Works*, vol. 3, *Essays Second Series*, "Experience," p. 77.

51. See chap. 1, note 3.

52. See note 11 above.

53. *Works*, vol. 3, *Essays Second Series*, "Character," pp. 90–91.

54. *Works*, vol. 7, *Society and Solitude*, "Books," pp. 216–17.

55. *JMN*, vol. 7, p. 418.

56. *Works*, vol. 12, *Natural History of Intellect*, "Europe and European Books," p. 377.

57. *Works*, vol. 12, *Natural History of Intellect*, "Thoughts on Modern Literature," pp. 316–17.

Chapter 3: Selfhood Beset

1. Mark Twain, *Life on the Mississippi*, chap. 18, "I Take a Few Lessons."

2. *Moby Dick*, ed. Harrison Hayford et al. (Evanston, Ill.: Northwestern–Newberry, 1988), chap. 96, "The Try-Works."

3. *Moby Dick*, chap. 111, "The Pacific."

4. *Moby Dick*, chap. 27, "Knights and Squires–Continued."

5. *Moby Dick*, chap. 47, "The Mat-Maker."

6. This passage is from a review of *Typee* in *Graham's Magazine* (May 1846), quoted in Jay Leyda, *The Melville Log, A Documented Life of Herman Melville, 1819–1891*, 2 vols. (New York: Gordian Press, 1969), vol. 1, p. 216.

7. As Burke employs the term in *A Grammar of Motives* (Englewood Cliffs, N.J.: Prentice-Hall, 1945).

8. Diana Trilling, *Claremont Essays* (New York: Harcourt, Brace & World, 1964), pp. vii–ix.

9. Pseudonym of Donald Grant Mitchell, author of *Reveries of a Bachelor* (1850) and *Dreamlife* (1851).

10. Allan Silver, "The Lawyer and the Scrivener," *Partisan Review* (1981), 3:409–24.

11. *Moby Dick*, chap. 45, "The Affidavit."

12. Herman Melville, "Hawthorne and His Mosses," *The Piazza Tales and Other Prose Pieces, 1839–1860*, ed. Harrison Hayford et al. (Evanston, Ill.: Northwestern–Newberry, 1987).

13. Quoted in Warner Berthoff, *The Example of Melville* (Princeton, N.J.: Princeton University Press, 1962), p. 24. This book offers a

good account of the character and quality of Melville's achievement as a writer.

14. From a manuscript journal kept jointly by Nathaniel and Sophia Hawthorne, 1842–54, now in the Morgan Library.

15. *The Works of Nathaniel Hawthorne*, Centenary Edition, ed. William Charvat et al. (Columbus: Ohio State University Press, 1963–85), vol. 3, *The Blithedale Romance*, chap. 12, "Coverdale's Hermitage," p. 103.

16. *Mardi and a Voyage Thither*, ed. Harrison Hayford et al. (Evanston, Ill.: Northwestern–Newberry, 1970), chap. 161, "They Hearken Unto a Voice from the Gods."

Chapter 4: Wholesale Appropriations: John Dewey and Henry James

1. *John Dewey: The Early Works, 1882–1898*, ed. Jo Ann Boydston, 5 vols. (Carbondale: Southern Illinois University Press, 1969–72). Future references are to this edition unless otherwise specified.

2. John Dewey, *Characters and Events, Popular Essays in Social and Political Philosophy*, ed. Joseph Ratner, 2 vols. (New York: Henry Holt, 1929), vol. 1, pp. 69–77. Originally published under the title *Emerson—The Philosopher of Democracy* (1903).

3. John Dewey, *Democracy and Education, An Introduction to the Philosophy of Education* (New York: Macmillan, 1916), p. 47.

4. *JMN*, vol. 3, p. 199.

5. *Early Works*, vol. 1, p. 175.

6. *Early Works*, vol. 1, *Leibniz's New Essays Concerning the Human Understanding*, p. 295. See chap. 3, note 16, for Melville's "sovereign kings."

7. Hodgson's article, "Illusory Psychology," is reprinted in *Early Works*, vol. 1, 1882–88, as an appendix, pp. xxv–xli. The quoted phrase is on p. xxx.

8. See chap. 2, note 1, for Brownson's charge.

9. Neil Coughlan, *Young John Dewey* (Chicago: University of Chicago Press, 1975), p. 109.

10. *Early Works*, vol. 5, p. 23.

11. *Early Works*, vol. 4, p. 147.

12. *Early Works*, vol. 5, pp. 4–24.

13. *Early Works*, vol. 1, p. 160.

14. John Dewey, "From Absolutism to Experimentalism," in *The Golden Age of American Philosophy*, ed. Charles Frankel (New York: Braziller, 1960), pp. 385–95.

15. *John Dewey: The Middle Works, 1899–1924*, gen. ed. Jo Ann Boydston, 37 vols. (Carbondale: Southern Illinois University Press, 1976), vol. 1: 1899–1901, "Psychology and Social Practice," pp. 127–28.

16. *Early Works*, vol. 4, p. 244.

17. *Early Works*, vol. 4, p. 244.

18. *Early Works*, vol. 4, p. 244.

19. Morton G. White, *The Origins of Dewey's Instrumentalism* (New York: Octagon Press, 1943), pp. 100–02.

20. John Dewey, *The School and Society* (Chicago: University of Chicago Press, 1899, rev. 1915, 1956 ed.), pp. 61–62.

21. John Dewey, *Democracy and Education* (New York: Macmillan, 1916), pp. 203–04.

22. *Leaves of Grass*, 1855 Preface, p. 718.

23. William Faulkner, *The Sound and the Fury* (1929).

24. Horace M. Kallen, "Individuality, Individualism and John Dewey," *Antioch Review* (Fall 1959), 19:299–314.

25. Richard Rorty, *Philosophy and the Mirror of Nature* (Princeton, N.J.: Princeton University Press, 1979).

26. F. W. Dupee, *The Question of Henry James* (New York: Henry Holt, 1945).

27. *Works*, vol. 10, *Lectures and Biographical Sketches*, "Education," p. 136.

28. Quentin Anderson, Introduction to *Henry James: Selected Short Stories* (New York: Rinehart, 1957), pp. xvii–xviii.

29. Ian Watt, "The First Paragraph of *The Ambassadors:* An Explication," in *The Ambassadors*, ed. S. P. Rosenbaum (New York: Norton, 1964), pp. 465–84.

30. Henry James, *The Wings of the Dove*, 2 vols. bound as 1 (New York: Scribner, 1945), vol. 1, chap. 16.

31. Laurence B. Holland, *The Expense of Vision: Essays on the Craft of Henry James* (Princeton, N.J.: Princeton University Press, 1964).

32. William James, *The Varieties of Religious Experience*, introd. Reinhold Niebuhr (New York: Collier Books, 1961), p. 389.

33. Henry James, *Autobiography, The Middle Years*, ed. F. W. Dupee (New York: Criterion Books, 1956), p. 563.

34. Henry James, *The Tragic Muse*, 2 vols. New York Edition of the Novels and Tales of Henry James, vol. 7 (New York: Scribner, 1908), vol. 1, p. 148.

35. These characters appear in the following novels: Julia Dallow in *The Tragic Muse*, Kate Croy in *The Wings of the Dove*, Madame

Merle in *The Portrait of a Lady*, and Charlotte Stant in *The Golden Bowl*.

36. Jacques Barzun, "Henry James, Melodramatist," in Dupee, *The Question*, pp. 254–66.

37. William Troy, "The Altar of Henry James," in Dupee, *The Question*, pp. 267–72.

38. Alfred Habegger, *Gender Fantasy and Realism in American Literature* (New York: Columbia University Press, 1972), preface, p. xi: "James's American novels appear to endorse some grave misapprehensions about American life. The most influential of these is that a country consisting of many races, immigrant groups, social castes, and codes of manners was in some way blank, uniform, devoid of interest."

Chapter 5: Detached Critics and Engaged Novelists

1. Harold Bloom, "Emerson: The American Religion," in *Ralph Waldo Emerson, Modern Critical Views*, ed. Harold Bloom (New York: Chelsea House, 1985), pp. 97–122.

2. Richard Poirier, *The Renewal of Literature* (New York: Random House, 1987).

3. Edward Everett Hale's story (1863) of a man condemned to live in permanent exile for cursing his country.

4. Hugh Henry Brackenridge, author of the novel *Modern Chivalry* (1792–1815), which is suffused with social commentary.

5. Allen Tate was a critic, poet, and novelist. *The Fathers* was published in 1938.

6. Georg Simmel, *The Philosophy of Money* (1900).

7. Flem Snopes is the central character in William Faulkner's trilogy, *The Hamlet* (1940), *The Town* (1957), and *The Mansion* (1960).

Chapter 6: Public Worlds as Private Possessions

1. Barry D. Karl and Stanley N. Katz, "Foundations and Ruling Class Elites," *Daedalus* (Winter 1987), 1–40. See passage on 31–32. Commenting that foundations "appear to fulfill certain aspects of the Gramscian program," the authors continue, "Beneath all such issues, however, is the fundamental problem that ultimately limits the degree to which any of the elite theories of European political analysis can be profitably applied to the United States. While such theories may reveal significant aspects of the relationship between foundations and the American polity, they cannot ignore the fact that European theorists regarded political parties as the essential link between politics and intellectuals. . . . Whether the objective was to gain power or to maintain the *status quo* made less difference to them than the correct understanding of the realities of political party organization, and its inevitable relation to social class. Acknowledging the existence of an elite was not a problem for Europeans."

2. His views are first developed in the following works: *Typology and Early American Literature* (1972), *The American Puritan Imagination: Essays on Revaluation* (1974), and *The American Jeremiad* (1974). See Giles Gunn, "Beyond Transcendence or Beyond Ideology: The New Problematics of Cultural Criticism in America," *American Literary History* (Spring 1990), 2:1–18.

3. Christopher Lasch, *The Culture of Narcissism* (New York: Norton, 1978).

4. Wai-chee Dimock, *Empire for Liberty: Melville and the Poetics of Individualism* (Princeton, N.J.: Princeton University Press, 1989), p. ix.

5. Richard Hofstadter, *The American Political Tradition* (New York: Knopf, 1948).

6. John Higham, *Writing American History: Essays on Modern Scholarship* (Bloomington: Indiana University Press, 1970). For "consensus" history see pp. 73–74 and *passim*.

7. *Works*, vol. 2, *Essays First Series*, "The Over-Soul," p. 277.

8. Henry James, *Autobiography, The Middle Years*, ed. Dupee, p. 563.

9. Henry Adams, *History of the United States During the Administrations of Thomas Jefferson and James Madison*, 9 vols. (1889–91).

10. T. J. Jackson Lears, *No Place of Grace: Antimodernism and the Transformation of American Culture 1880–1920* (New York: Pantheon Books, 1981).

11. Henry James, *The Speech and Manners of American Women* (Lancaster, Pa.: Lancaster House Press, 1973), pp. 71–72.

12. William Carlos Williams, *In the American Grain* (New York: New Directions, 1925), pp. 186–87.

13. Ibid., p. 179.

14. Ibid., p. 179.

15. *Works*, vol. 2, *Essays First Series*, "Self-Reliance," p. 66. Lyndall Gordon quotes this passage with reference to T. S. Eliot in her *Eliot's Early Years* (see following note).

16. Lyndall Gordon, *Eliot's Early Years* (Oxford, London, New York: Oxford University Press, 1977), p. 139.

Chapter 7: The Possibility of Individuation

1. See Quentin Anderson, "Whitman's New Man," pp. 37 ff., cited in chap. 1, note 4.

2. *Journal*, vol. 6, p. 45, Jan. 1, 1854.

3. *Works*, vol. 3, *Essays Second Series*, "Experience," p. 80.

4. Giles Gunn, *"Rorty's* Novum Organum," *Raritan* (Summer 1990), 101.

5. See Henry Nash Smith, *Democracy and the Novel* (New York: Oxford University Press, 1978), chaps. 7, 8, for this shift in the way Henry James's work was viewed by critics.

6. *The Princess Casamassima* (London and New York: MacMillan, 1886), p. 308.

7. See Martin Peretz, "Cambridge Diarist," *The New Republic*, 15 April 1991, p. 42, where he cites Victor Navasky, *Naming Names*, p. 85, as saying that they were all "deeply involved in Communist affairs."

8. *The New Yorker*, 27 May 1985, p. 29.

9. Walter Benn Michaels, *"Sister Carrie's* Popular Economy," *Critical Inquiry* (Winter 1980), 7: 373–90.

10. Myra Jehlen, *American Incarnation: The Individual, the Nation, and the Continent* (Cambridge, Mass.: Harvard University Press, 1986), p. 17.

11. C. B. MacPherson, *The Political Theory of Possessive Individualism: Hobbes to Locke* (Oxford: Clarendon Press, 1962).

12. Ross Posnock, "William and Henry James," *Raritan* (Winter 1989), 1–26. See also Posnock's *The Trial of Curiosity: Henry James, William James, and the Challenge of Modernity* (New York: Oxford University Press, 1991).

13. Jack Beatty's review of Walter Dean Burnham, *The Current Crisis in American Politics*, in *The New Republic*, 21 March 1983.

14. Quentin Anderson, "Practical and Visionary Americans," *The American Scholar* (Summer 1976), 45: 405–18.

15. *Works*, vol. 10, *Lectures and Biographical Sketches*, "Historic Notes of Life and Letters in New England," p. 364.

16. Park Honan, Introduction to *The Beats: An Anthology of "Beat" Writing* (London: J. M. Dent, 1987), p. xviii.

17. Ibid., p. xvii.

18. Reprinted in Diana Trilling, *Claremont Essays* (New York: Harcourt, Brace & World, 1964), pp. 153–73.

19. Ibid., pp. 160–61. This we must recall is the time in which some were answering the threat of atomic war by proclaiming "better Red than dead." A round-table discussion of the moral and political questions surrounding the possibility of a nuclear war was sponsored by *Commentary* in May 1961. The transcript furnishes striking instances of the views of the proponents of unilateral disarmament in this period, who were ably opposed by the philosopher Sidney Hook. See "Western Values and Total War," *Commentary*, Oct. 1961, pp. 277–304.

20. G. S. Fraser, "Impolite Essays," *Partisan Review* (Winter 1965), 1:127–33.

21. Norman Mailer, "Up the Family Tree," *Partisan Review* (Spring 1968), 2:248.

22. In *Armies of the Night* (New York: New American Library, 1968).

23. Howard E. Horwitz, "The Standard Oil Trust as Emersonian Hero," *Raritan* (Spring 1987), 97–119.

24. Marc Shell, *Money, Language, and Thought* (Berkeley: University of California Press, 1982).

25. Kurt Heinzelman, *The Economics of the Imagination* (Amherst: University of Massachusetts Press, 1980).

26. *The New Republic*, 11 Nov. 1981, pp. 39–40.

27. *Works*, vol. 3, *Essays Second Series*, "Experience," p. 60.

Index